Praise for
Monopolies Suck

"A provocative call to restore economic competition by dismantling the ruling plutocracy."

—*Kirkus Reviews*

"Hubbard's cogent, accessible analysis makes a persuasive case that unchecked monopolies have rigged the system against ordinary Americans. Policymakers and voters will want to take note."

—*Publishers Weekly*

"In this important book, Sally Hubbard explains with winning clarity, concision, and humor the many ways monopolies hurt us all—and what citizens can do to combat the hydra-headed menace of concentrated corporate power."

—Nancy MacLean, author of *Democracy in Chains: The Deep History of the Radical Right's Stealth Plan for America*

"With expertise and an engaging writing style, Sally Hubbard's *Monopolies Suck* is a must-read for anyone wanting to understand how monopolies endanger our pocketbooks and our democracy. The book will leave you enraged at the role monopolies play in every facet of our daily lives, but encouraged that we can, in fact, beat them."

—Denise Hearn, coauthor of *The Myth of Capitalism: Monopolies and the Death of Competition*

"Sally Hubbard is a rare combination: a former antitrust enforcer who knows the law deeply and a sharp, pull-no-punches writer. In this light, accessible guide, Hubbard shows how today's corporate giants are breaking the laws intended to protect you—and what you can do about it."

"In my twenty-plus years in the tech industry, I have never witnessed the scale of monopolization that exists today with dominant internet platforms. They flagrantly steal ideas, suppress innovation, and limit consumer choice. We need meaningful change—before it's too late. Sally Hubbard's book spells out these pressing threats in lucid prose that reminds us how urgently we need to act."

"The creative community is paying a steep price in monopolized America, with millions of artists struggling to make a living under rules that prioritize Big Tech profits. Sally Hubbard lays out the case for how we fight back—and why we must."

"Antitrust law is a tool that belongs to the people, and Sally Hubbard breaks it down in a way that everyone can understand. Hubbard lucidly explains how monopolies threaten democracy, worsen inequality, and imperil the American Dream—and why it's more important than ever to take action."

"Hubbard has done the important work of relating monopolism to your daily life—the ways in which you, personally, are made worse off, every day, by unchecked corporate concentration and power. . . . An outstanding and important read."

MONOPOLIES

SUCK

7 Ways Big Corporations Rule Your Life
and How to Take Back Control

SALLY HUBBARD

SIMON & SCHUSTER PAPERBACKS

NEW YORK   LONDON   TORONTO   SYDNEY   NEW DELHI

Simon & Schuster Paperbacks
An Imprint of Simon & Schuster, Inc.
1230 Avenue of the Americas
New York, NY 10020

First Simon & Schuster trade paperback edition September 2021

SIMON & SCHUSTER PAPERBACKS and colophon are registered trademarks of Simon & Schuster, Inc.

For information about special discounts for bulk purchases, please contact Simon & Schuster Special Sales at 1-866-506-1949 or business@simonandschuster.com.

The Simon & Schuster Speakers Bureau can bring authors to your live event. For more information or to book an event, contact the Simon & Schuster Speakers Bureau at 1-866-248-3049 or visit our website at www.simonspeakers.com.

Interior design by Ruth Lee-Mui

Manufactured in the United States of America

1   3   5   7   9   10   8   6   4   2

The Library of Congress has cataloged the hardcover edition as follows:

Names: Hubbard, Sally (Antitrust expert), author.
Title: Monopolies suck : 7 ways big corporations rule your life and how to take back control / Sally Hubbard.
Description: First Simon & Schuster hardcover edition. | New York, NY : Simon & Schuster, [2020] | Includes bibliographical references and index.
Identifiers: LCCN 2020032883 (print) | LCCN 2020032884 (ebook) | ISBN 9781982149703 (hardcover) | ISBN 9781982149727 (ebook)
Subjects: LCSH: Monopolies—United States. | Corporate power—United States.| Corporations—Moral and ethical aspects—United States.
Classification: LCC HD2757.2 .H83 2020 (print) | LCC HD2757.2 (ebook) | DDC 338.8/20973—dc23
LC record available at https://lccn.loc.gov/2020032883
LC ebook record available at https://lccn.loc.gov/2020032884

ISBN 978-1-9821-4970-3
ISBN 978-1-9821-4971-0 (pbk)
ISBN 978-1-9821-4972-7 (ebook)

To my children. May you learn to speak up,
take action and trust that possibility is infinite.

CONTENTS

Introduction   1

7 WAYS MONOPOLIES RULE YOUR LIFE

1. Monopolies Take Your Money   17
2. Monopolies Gouge You When You're Sick   34
3. Monopolies Lower Your Pay and
   Crush the American Dream   64
4. Monopolies Spy on and Manipulate You   105
5. Monopolies Threaten Democracy and
   Your Freedom   134
6. Monopolies Destroy Our Planet and
   Control Your Food   153
7. Monopolies Ramp Up Inequality   174

HOW TO STOP MONOPOLIES

8. How to Take Back Control   197

Acknowledgments   227
Notes   231
Index   295

INTRODUCTION

America isn't alright. Our economy is working for a select few. Even before the coronavirus pandemic wreaked its devastation, most Americans could see that our country—the Land of Opportunity—wasn't how it was supposed to be. But COVID-19 spelled it out for us in neon lights.

When the world as we knew it came crashing down, some of the lowest-paid Americans were revealed to be our most essential workers, risking deadly exposure to keep their jobs while supporting everyone else. Communities of color were among the hardest hit by the virus, laying bare the compounding effects of systemic racism. As of this writing, small businesses are fighting to survive, and unemployed Americans face hunger and homelessness, while some of the wealthiest profiteer.

The clear coronavirus victors are monopolies, and we now depend on them even more. But in a winner-take-all economy, their strength has come at the expense of all others, leaving the rest of us to battle the pandemic from a point of weakness. Monopolies will make it out of the crisis just fine, but will we?

Decades of rampant health-care mergers made us sitting ducks for COVID-19, with only a few big companies left to produce critical supplies. Masks, ventilators, gowns, reagents—we couldn't get enough because so few suppliers remain, and they have stopped making things in America. Ever since the 1980s, politicians, antitrust law enforcers, and judges have bought into the myth that bigger is better, which has allowed monopolies to take over with barely any resistance. They sacrificed our resiliency and made America fragile.

The policy choices our government has made amid the COVID-19 crisis will shape power and wealth for years to come, and the most dominant companies have used their political influence to grow even more so. Most of us just have wanted our lives to go back to normal. But normal isn't good enough.

In normal times, if you're like many Americans, no matter how hard you work, you feel like you can't get ahead. You race through your days, but you can't possibly get everything done. You keep trying because you don't know what would happen if you eased up. Maybe you're burnt out, but you don't see a path out of the grind. Nothing feels certain or stable.

Overcoming your daily struggles is up to you—or so you're told. You just need to get better at "self-care" and setting boundaries at work. And if only you meditated every morning, decluttered your home, and stopped eating gluten, you'd have the energy and presence of mind to manage an avalanche of stressors headed your way.

But perhaps you have a nagging sense that your everyday problems go beyond you.

You're living in the New Gilded Age after all, a time of excess wealth reminiscent of the late 1800s, when industrialist tycoons accumulated riches off of workers' backs. Inequality today is stark, like in San Francisco, where 75 billionaires coexist with thousands of homeless people. The American government has failed to ensure its citizens have access to the basics of humanity, from affordable health care to a habitable planet to safe food and water. You may ask yourself: why do taxes keep going up—for everyone except the ultrarich—when government doesn't do the bare minimum its job requires?

People all across America feel the ground is constantly shifting underneath them. Inequality and hopelessness are making some people so angry they have to find others to blame, like immigrants, people of color, LGBTQ+ individuals, and/or women. But those with historically less power in our society are not the source of America's problems.

Beneath all of this pain lies a hidden culprit: pure, unbridled monopoly power. No matter your race, gender, age, sexual orientation or identity, religion, class, or political party, we're all getting screwed on a systemic level by the same menace of monopoly. The most vulnerable among us get hit the hardest.

Monopolies pervade our everyday lives in ways we don't realize. When your expenses keep going up but your income does not, when you're price-gouged buying an EpiPen for your child's life-threatening allergy, when you struggle to parent a child who is addicted to social media, and when you can't find common ground with millions of your fellow Americans, monopoly power is playing a key, destructive role. But you can help stop it. In this book, I will show you how monopoly power rules your life and what must be done to put an end to it.

Monopolists of the past who controlled entire industries like railroads and oil were aptly called robber barons because they built their business models on exploitation. I'll explain how today's global monopolies are no different. They're robbing us of money by charging high prices, skirting taxes, and reducing our pay and economic opportunities. This theft is only the beginning. They're also robbing us of innovation, choice, the ability to take care of our sick, a healthy food supply, a habitable planet, our privacy, fair elections, a robust press, and, ultimately, the American dream.

While Amazon promises low prices, and Facebook and Google offer services for "free," in truth, tech giants' prices are exorbitant, but you have no way of knowing how much you are paying. This book will expose the true costs.

But America's monopoly crisis is not just about Big Tech. It's big health care, big agriculture, Big Pharma, big . . . pick an industry, any industry. Big *everything*. Our economy is ruled by behemoths because, decades ago, our government chose to dismantle anti-monopoly laws and policies.

We blame the economy for our financial struggles, but the economy—apart from the COVID-19 catastrophe—has been doing just fine. The problem is that the ultrarich are hoarding its spoils. What changed from the 1980s to today that made the economy stop working for the middle class? A big piece of that puzzle is monopoly. When Boomers were raising their families, few industries were highly concentrated in the hands of giant companies. Now, few are not. This concentration of power allows corporations to adopt business models that are extractive rather than generative, or more simply, they're focused on *taking* rather than *making*.

If we don't act immediately, corporate giants will control more and more of our lives, and their economic power will buy ever-increasing political power as they spend their monopoly money on lobbying. It's now, or possibly never, as our democracy continues to slip away before our eyes. The will of the people is losing out to the will of the monopolists.

In this book, I'll show you seven ways giant corporations are making your life harder every day by breaking the laws that were designed to protect you. I'll share a positive vision of life without monopoly, an escape route from being stressed out, overworked, underpaid, and underrepresented. A better future can be yours—ours—and I'll show you what must be done to get back the power and control that rightly belong to you.

Defeating monopoly is not a silver bullet that will automatically solve every one of our problems, but *we won't be able to cure America's ills if we don't first weaken corporate giants' power*. Like constructing a house on a faulty foundation, building a better world upon the flawed structure of monopoly is doomed from the outset. If we don't fix the systemic problem of concentrated power, our efforts to gain control of our lives will be like trying to empty an ocean with a slotted spoon.

The first step to loosen monopolies' grip on our lives is to become informed citizens. Active citizenship is even more important than trying to change your consumer habits—your power as a citizen is greater than your power as a consumer.

The onus isn't on the consumer to stop using monopolies when monopolies have become essential infrastructure for our economy; often, you simply have little or no choice but to depend on a monopolist. The onus is on the government to make companies obey the law, to protect consumers from their harms, and to promote an open and competitive marketplace. Pressuring government to do its job is the best way we can make a difference.

In that sense, the onus *is* on us, as citizens, to fight for shared prosperity and power. America has always been "about what can be achieved by us, together, through the hard and slow, and sometimes frustrating, but ultimately enduring work of self-government," said former U.S. president Barack Obama in his 2016 Democratic National Convention speech. And as abolitionist leader Frederick Douglass famously said in 1857: "Power concedes nothing without a demand. It never did and it never will." The Black Lives Matter movement shows this still holds true today.

We must demand our government work for the people instead of big corporations. You *need* to know about monopoly rule because that's how we fight back—learning about it, getting pissed off about it, and not being willing to take it anymore. With the world in upheaval and transition in the wake of COVID-19, this is the time to demand the change we need.

Now for the good news: we've already overcome this exact challenge in our nation's past. We have dismantled monopoly power before! We already have the tools, we just need to use them again. Just as we defeated the original robber barons of yore, we can weaken the power of today's monopolies and take back what they've stolen from us.

It was the outrage of citizens that took down the most notorious monopoly in American history, Standard Oil. Investigative journalist Ida Tarbell exposed the market power abuses and political corruption of the Standard Oil Company in a series of articles for *McClure's Magazine*, which were compiled into a 1904 book, *The History of the Standard Oil Company*. Tarbell sparked a citizen outcry that spurred the government to break up Standard Oil and pass important antitrust reforms.

Your awareness is critical for change to occur. In our battered democracy, where our elected officials are beholden to powerful monopolies and their lobbyists, we the people must still have the final say.

Why I Became an Octopus Hunter

I became a trust-buster, an anti-monopolist, or as Teddy Roosevelt was called, an octopus hunter, partly by accident and partly by fate.

I long aspired to fight for women's equity as a career, and somehow convinced myself that law school was the best way to do it. After trying unsuccessfully to get an unpaid internship at any women's advocacy organization, despite being at one of the best law schools in the nation, I decided to take a job at a big law firm upon graduation to pay down my student loan debt. I remember confessing to my grandpa Andy, who believed in enjoying life and doing what you love, that I was going to work at a big law firm even though I knew I would hate it, assuring him that I only planned to do the job for one year. He shook his head and grumbled disapprovingly, "It's gonna be a long damn year."

Like Google in its early days, I set out to not "be evil" in my new role. But on my first day, a partner assigned me research for the defense of a corporate executive in the Enron scandal, one of the biggest corporate accounting frauds in American history. I saved my pennies, sold my possessions, paid off as much of my student loan debt as I could, and quit after one year and one day.

I went to work at the D.C. Circuit Court of Appeals, where now-chief justice John Roberts was a judge. He was personable and pleasant, the kind of guy who's hard not to like. But I disagreed with most of his decisions. In one case, I was alarmed at what I considered a vote to violate a person's constitutional rights. In another, I was troubled by what, to me, was a vote for the outcome that aligned with Roberts's conservative political views instead of the outcome the law supported. So when Roberts was nominated to the U.S. Supreme Court, I didn't sleep a wink that night, worrying about how his lifetime appointment could impact equity and justice for decades to come. Little did I know that the court would skew so far to the right that Roberts would become viewed as a comparatively moderate swing vote.

After leaving the D.C. Circuit job, I struggled to find my place and was on the verge of giving up law entirely when I landed a job as an assistant attorney general in the Antitrust Bureau of the New York Attorney General's Office. Going into it I believed that I had long ago given up my dream of fighting for equity—but I couldn't have been more wrong. The moment I started fighting companies that were consolidating power, now fifteen years ago, I started fighting inequity. I simply expanded who I was fighting for. I was still fighting for women, but not only women—all Americans. The vast majority of us lose power, wealth, rights, and opportunities when dominant companies control our economy and influence our government. Women and people of color suffer some of the worst consequences, a topic we'll explore in chapter 7.

I've come to realize that the inequality monopolies wreak also threatens democracy. In 1933, Edward Keating, a congressman and confidant of the late Supreme Court justice Louis Brandeis, penned an editorial called "Stop the Concentration of Wealth." He wrote: "Justice Brandeis declared some years ago that America, before long, must make a choice. We can have democracy, or we can have a horde of multi-millionaires. We cannot have both."

Anti-monopoly is a cause that Americans can unite around because concentrated wealth and power hurts us all.

ANTITRUST IS NOT JUST FOR NERDS

If the word "antitrust" makes you yawn and want to shut this book, please don't yet! That's exactly what monopolists want you to do, for they don't want you to understand antitrust law. "It's complicated" is code for "do nothing," which is what those holding all the marbles want us to do—nothing.

When the main U.S. antitrust law, the Sherman Act, was passed way back in 1890, inequality was causing widespread discontent. It was the original Gilded Age, and powerful monopolies, like the oil and railroad trusts, dominated the U.S. economy. As he proposed the law, Senator John Sherman pronounced: "If we will not endure a king as a political power, we should not endure a king over the production, transportation, and sale of any of the necessities of life." One hundred and thirty years later, we are once again ruled by the types of kings Senator Sherman sought to prevent.

If you were king, would you want peasants to know *how* to overthrow you? Of course not! Today's monopolists don't want people to know how antitrust law can be used to weaken their power. But it can! And you can help. Let me break it down for you because it's actually not that complicated.

Senator Sherman's law has two main parts. Section 1 of the Sherman Act prohibits companies from agreeing to restrain trade. This means companies aren't allowed to agree with one another to not compete; for example, by conspiring to charge the same prices or div-vying up business among themselves. You may have seen the Sherman Act in action from recent Section 1 cases that have alleged chicken producers conspired to inflate chicken prices and drug manufacturers agreed to fix the prices of generic drugs. Not only do these kinds of illegal agreements cost a company greatly in fines and damages, but they also can land executives in jail.

The next part of the Sherman Act, Section 2, reads, "Every person who shall monopolize, or attempt to monopolize, or combine or conspire with any other person or persons, to monopolize . . . shall be deemed guilty of a felony." This tool allows us to go after big companies that use their muscle to squelch competition.

In 1914, Congress passed another important antitrust law, the Clayton Act, following the breakup of Standard Oil. Section 7 of the Clayton Act prohibits mergers and acquisitions where the effect "may be substantially to lessen competition, or to tend to create a monopoly."

If you think antitrust laws passed more than a century ago couldn't possibly address our problems in the digital age, you're mistaken. The laws were designed for exactly the same challenge we face today— concentrated power. And much like the U.S. Constitution, the anti-trust laws were written broadly enough to handle whatever the future might hold.

The Cops on the Beat

Our mighty antitrust enforcers at the federal level are the Federal Trade Commission and the Department of Justice. Or often less mighty than we'd hope. Here's how it should work: The agencies re-ceive notifications from corporations that they plan to merge, or the agencies get a complaint, tip, or news report about anticompetitive be-havior. After investigating corporations and finding they've violated the above antitrust laws, enforcers can't just declare that a corporation broke the law or that a merger is illegal. Unlike their counterparts in other parts of the world, America's antitrust enforcers must sue corporations in court (and the FTC can bring administrative charges). If they win, the judge will grant the remedy that enforcers seek, such as blocking a merger, punishing and stopping anticompetitive behavior, or, in the most severe of cases, breaking up corporations.

While sometimes antitrust enforcers lose in court, more often they settle their cases rather than taking the risk of losing and spending a ton of time and money bringing an antitrust case. Merger cases can be done quickly, but cases involving anticompetitive behavior can take years. Here's where one of our main problems shows itself: these government settlements can be too much of a compromise and often don't fix the issues that enforcers sued over in the first place. From airlines to pharmaceuticals, I'll show you how this happens all too often.

When the FTC and DOJ drop the ball or don't do their job, state attorneys general can step in and fill the void that federal agencies leave, without having to take direction from the feds. State AGs can bring their own antitrust cases, having state antitrust laws plus the power to enforce the federal ones. That's the beauty of federalism, with its built-in checks and balances.

Regular people and businesses also have the power to bring cases under the antitrust laws. Antitrust class action lawsuits brought by consumers used to be an effective way to keep monopoly power in check, but in recent decades conservative courts have made it difficult for class actions to see the inside of a courtroom. Corporate defendants in the 1990s and 2000s persuaded courts to erect obstacles to such lawsuits, so that an antitrust class action has to overcome lots of hurdles just to avoid getting dismissed.

Antitrust agencies in other parts of the world can enforce laws against global corporations that do business with their people. The European Commission has made headlines for multibillion-dollar antitrust fines against Google (fines that unfortunately amount to pocket change for the tech giant). Europe's antitrust laws have some differences from U.S. laws, but I'd argue that many of the European Commission's enforcement actions against Big Tech prosecuted behavior that is also illegal in America. What has been lacking until recently in the United States is enforcers' political will to take on America's superstar companies.

Antitrust Off the Rails

In spite of our broad antitrust statutes and the antitrust agencies empowered to enforce them, America faces a monopoly crisis. Between 1997 and 2014, corporate concentration increased in 80 percent of industries by an average of 90 percent, according to economists. The crisis pervades our economy: baby formula, where three companies control 80 percent of the market; washer and dryer manufacturing, where three companies control 100 percent of the market; dialysis centers, where two companies control more than 90 percent of the market; textbooks, where three publishers control 80 percent of the market, and so on. At the time of this writing, two of those textbook publishers are seeking antitrust clearance to merge, even though college textbook prices increased 88 percent between 2006 and 2016.

Our antitrust statutes were designed to protect us from kings of commerce, and yet a few kings dominate nearly every industry. What went wrong?

What's right are our main antitrust statutes—the Sherman Act and the Clayton Act, which prohibit monopolizing, restraints of trade, and mergers that may lessen competition. But the case law interpreting these statutes is broken and has made way for monopolies to take over. Violations of antitrust law are not open-and-shut like, say, exceeding the speed limit. When judges apply the law to the facts before them, they make case-by-case determinations about what's illegal anticompetitive behavior and what's legal aggressive competition. Two judges presented with the same set of facts can each come to a different conclusion on whether the antitrust laws have been violated. I argue throughout this book that big corporations are breaking the antitrust laws, but those companies of course would contend the opposite, and the outcome of any individual case can depend on the judge assigned to it. Judges' case-by-case decisions create a body of case law called legal precedent, which sets standards going forward. In recent decades, legal precedent has strayed far away from the legislative intent of our antitrust statutes.

We can thank a not-so-noble fellow for helping create our current monopoly crisis: Robert Bork, a legal scholar and judge who promoted an ideology called the Chicago School of Economics, originating at the University of Chicago. Bork, incidentally, served as solicitor general under President Nixon and fired the special prosecutor who was investigating the Watergate scandal, after the attorney general and deputy attorney general resigned rather than do so. With Bork's help, the Chicago School of Economics started to fundamentally change the interpretation of antitrust law in the early 1980s, convincing the courts that the laws' goal first and foremost is to promote corporate efficiency. What companies gain in efficiency they would pass on to consumers as lower prices, the ideology claimed, to the benefit of "consumer welfare."

But the Sherman Act says nothing about corporate efficiency! The law is about promoting competition and preventing concentrated power. The craziest part? The Chicago School takeover of antitrust law has actually led to higher prices for consumers by allowing monopolies to rule America, as you'll see in the next chapter, even as it promised the opposite result.

This obsession with corporate efficiency meant antitrust plaintiffs suing to stop big corporations from kicking out rivals could rarely win monopolization cases in court unless they could prove the anticompetitive behavior raised prices. And antitrust enforcers couldn't block mergers unless they could prove to a court that the merger would almost certainly cause prices to go up. Antitrust cases became duels between highly paid economists, with corporate defendants offering complex economic models to convince courts that eliminating competition is, perversely, good for consumers. Corporate efficiency became the excuse to let monopolies take over America.

Several decades of bad court decisions have made it harder for antitrust enforcers to win cases. Partly for this reason, Sherman Act Section 2 is long neglected, and in fact, it's so underenforced that most Americans think illegal monopolization is just the way business is done.

Because the Chicago School takeover of the courts made mergers harder to block, decades of merger mania and a massive consolidation of corporate power ensued. Since the 1980s, mergers and acquisitions have climbed, both in number and value. In 2018 alone, there were 19,757 mergers and acquisitions in the United States. This is a main reason we find ourselves living under the rule of monopoly kings. The Boomers, in contrast, raised their families in an economy that was far less monopolized, benefiting from decades of robust antitrust enforcement up until the early 1980s.

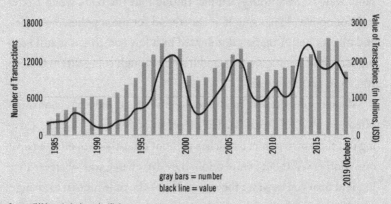

MERGERS & ACQUISITIONS UNITED STATES OF AMERICA

gray bars = number
black line = value

Source: IMAA analysis; imaa-institute.org

The current federal antitrust agencies include decision makers who believe the market will cure almost everything, which only compounds the problem of bad case law. The (wrongly named) "free market" ideology teaches that enforcement of antitrust laws will create more problems than it'll solve. But I disagree, and so do many lawyers working at the antitrust agencies who struggle to get approval from agency heads to bring cases. The way I see it is, the market can't fix problems if the market isn't working. When antitrust enforcers and lawmakers don't ensure that markets are indeed free and functioning, monopolies run amok. Allowing monopolies to rule is in fact the *opposite* of a "free market."

The short history of monopolies in our country is that money and power fought the people, and money and power won. Such is the eternal struggle of all humankind. Whenever the people get lulled into complacency and lose their vigilance, power consolidates.

When I Say Monopolies Suck, I'm Talking About Duopolies and Oligopolies Too

Many markets are ruled by just one king, and many others are ruled by two or three. Markets ruled by two companies are called *duopolies*, and markets ruled by a few are called *oligopolies*. Although more desirable than monopolies, duopolies and oligopolies operate in the same way. To keep things simple, throughout the book when I refer to "monopolies," I'm using it as shorthand for monopolies, duopolies, and oligopolies. A market dominated by a few companies is still *not* a properly functioning market, and it's not enough competition to keep you from getting screwed.

When only a few corporations dominate an industry, companies often just play "follow the leader" on prices or divide up business, carving out their own particular niches without robustly competing against one another. Without competition, they can charge you whatever they like and treat you however they want. Now's the time for that to change.

We must fight back.

7 WAYS MONOPOLIES RULE YOUR LIFE

MONOPOLIES TAKE YOUR MONEY

"All this extra legroom wasn't cheap, but maybe we should have upgraded to the pressurized cabin."

MONOPOLIES SQUEEZE YOU WITH HIGH PRICES

Wait, what? Your airfare didn't include a single suitcase? Not even a carry-on? Why on earth would you take a five-hour flight and not bring any clothes? You've got no choice but to fork over the extra fifty bucks. Next you'll waste money on overpriced food at the airport because your flight doesn't come with a meal, which used to be a given. You'll be lucky if the airline gives you a bag of pretzels without an extra charge!

Your monthly expenses practically swallow your paycheck whole.

Your broadband bill feels like a rip-off, but what are you going to do? You wouldn't be able to do your job without an internet connection. If you're lucky enough to have a choice of broadband providers, the price of the other option is pretty much the same. You pay up. Next comes your mortgage or rent, your wireless bill, and your food. You're just covering your overhead, and you're already running out of cash.

At least you get a whole bunch of stuff for free in the digital age, right? You can connect with friends, have a GPS in your pocket, and watch unlimited YouTube videos. Maybe there is such a thing as a free lunch! But wait, these tech giants are making billions off of our data (a topic we'll cover in detail in chapter 4). If the price for these "free" services is data, how come you don't know how much you're paying?

Lattes Don't Make You Broke, Monopolies Do

Get your spending under control. So the narrative goes—if only you were more frugal with your spending, you wouldn't feel so stretched. You just need to stop buying lattes! Curb your late-night online shopping! Get some self-discipline! Although we all could benefit from less consumerism in our lives, when we focus only on individual choices we become blind to systemic forces, like the monopolies (and oligopolies and duopolies) that are fleecing us with high prices left and right.

Let's start with airlines. If the Chicago School mentality is that mergers end up benefiting the consumer in the end with lower prices, let's check that theory with this one industry that probably has changed during your travel history. Merger upon merger took away your choices and allowed airlines to start robbing you with fees and abusing us all with terrible treatment, like squeezing in more seats that worsen already-cramped conditions. Airlines have divvied up routes so you have only a few choices on any particular journey. What allowed for this to happen is that the Department of Justice waived through nine large airline mergers starting in 2001.

Remember, Clayton Act Section 7 prohibits mergers and acquisitions that may substantially lessen competition or tend to create a monopoly. In 2013, with the benefit of hindsight, the DOJ started to get a clue that airline mergers were devastating competition. Finally the DOJ had had enough, and it sued to block one of these anticompetitive mergers: the combination of American Airlines and US Airways. Announcing the lawsuit, Bill Baer, the then-head of the DOJ's antitrust division, said, "Increases in the price of airline tickets, checked bags or flight change fees resulting from this merger would result in hundreds of millions of dollars of harm to American consumers." On a press call, Baer said that after investigating the deal for six months, the DOJ had concluded it was "pretty messed up," and "pretty bad for consumers." The airlines "don't want to compete," Baer concluded, adding that reducing the number of "legacy" airlines, those with extensive routes and fleets, from four to three would make it easier for the airlines to coordinate prices with each other.

The DOJ's complaint described how past mergers had allowed the major airlines to raise prices, impose new fees, and reduce service. It even quoted senior executives touting these merger-induced price increases as an achievement! US Airways then-president Scott Kirby said publicly, "Three successful fare increases—[we are] able to pass along to customers because of consolidation." Executives' private emails to their competitors exposed efforts to stick together on prices, and the DOJ presented evidence that airlines had matched each other's fee increases in the past. "By reducing the number of airlines, the merger will likely make it easier for the remaining carriers to coordinate fee increases, resulting in higher fees for consumers," the DOJ argued when announcing its suit to block the deal.

But then, seemingly out of nowhere, the DOJ let the deal go

through despite its harsh allegations in its complaint. It settled the case and accepted merger conditions that couldn't possibly fix the wide-ranging problems the DOJ had identified. The DOJ's settlement required the combined American Airlines/US Airways to sell off a number of airport gates and slots, which represent an airline's right to schedule a takeoff or landing during a certain time period at particular airports. Selling slots couldn't solve the main problem of the merger, that four legacy competitors would be reduced to three, making collusion easier and more likely. The only real solution to that problem would be a full block of the merger.

Some commentators suggested that politics played a role in the DOJ's decision to settle the case, as the airlines engaged in a major pro-deal lobbying effort with pressure from political leaders, advertising campaigns, and even Capitol Hill rallies. Baer denied this claim. We might never know what happened, but we sure know how it turned out for us. We all live with absurd fees on everything from baggage to flight changes. These fees are a form of *monopoly rents*—excess returns above what airlines could bring in if they faced competition. So next time you're packing a week's worth of clothing into a backpack and emptying your wallet for a snack on your flight, you can thank the DOJ for *not* having your back.

Your Disappearing Paycheck

You're not just being squeezed through travel. When it comes to your fixed monthly expenses, monopoly power has caused prices to rapidly rise and put pressure on stagnant wages. Let's look at a few of your expenses, the first being your home. A recent study shows how oligopolies have raised home prices. Economists studied 137 housing markets between New York and Washington, D.C., and found most were controlled by only a few home builders. The study concluded that between 2013 and 2017 the prices of homes increased at more than double the rate they would have gone up if the market hadn't become concentrated.

These housing markets became highly concentrated for two reasons. One, a series of mergers between large home builders between 2009 and 2017. Two, Congress passed a stimulus package in 2009, during the Great Recession, that gave billions of dollars in tax benefits to the largest home builders, while smaller home builders suffered bankruptcy. If the markets had remained competitive, the study estimated 150,000 more housing units would be built each year in these areas, with greater supply keeping prices in check. Stimulus bills shape markets for years to come, and congressional decisions amid the COVID-19 pandemic that favor big companies will similarly have long-lasting effects on competition.

As for internet access, fewer than 20 percent of U.S. census blocks have access to more than two high-speed broadband providers, meaning these companies can charge monopoly prices in most of America. A study by the *Wall Street Journal* found that Comcast offers 25 percent higher discounts in areas where people have at least one other high-speed option. People think broadband companies are "natural monopolies," meaning competition isn't really possible because of the high costs of building out broadband networks. But anticompetitive behavior is a major source of the problem. Consider this typical practice: An upstart network begins to challenge a monopoly broadband provider, and the monopoly lowers its prices just long enough to drive out the challenger. Once the challenger has been decimated, rates go right back up.

Another tactic broadband monopolists use is to lobby state politicians to pass laws prohibiting competition! One way to create broadband competition is through city-run networks, also called municipal broadband networks, but thanks to lobbying, nineteen states have laws discouraging such networks. In 2011, for example, North Carolina's state legislature passed HB 129, a law that prevents communities in the state from investing in broadband infrastructure, after the city of Wilson had decided to invest in its own broadband network. Telecom lobbyists drafted early versions of the bill and handed them off to lawmakers, and community broadband advocates were no match for industry influence over state politicians.

Turning to your wireless bill, only three companies compete for your business, forming yet another oligopoly. In 2019, the DOJ approved a merger between Sprint and T-Mobile, which narrowed your options from four down to three: AT&T, Verizon, and T-Mobile. Several state attorneys general sued to block the deal, in a bid to protect your pocketbook. The states' expert predicted the deal could lead to $8.7 billion in price increases in 2020 alone. Roger Solé, Sprint's former chief marketing officer, even said in a 2017 text message to Sprint's then-CEO that the deal could allow a five-dollar monthly increase in revenue per subscriber. Solé added that Verizon and AT&T would also gain from the deal, texting that this was "the benefit of a consolidated market."

At trial, the states produced evidence of the DOJ's Antitrust Division chief, Makan Delrahim, exchanging text messages with the then-CEO of T-Mobile. As the *New York Times* reported, "The text messages show that he played a crucial role in bringing together top executives of T-Mobile, Sprint and another company, Dish, for negotiations." Delrahim's job is to sue to block illegal mergers on behalf of the American people, but instead he seems to have acted more like a corporate deal lawyer on behalf of the merging companies. The DOJ even advocated for Sprint and T-Mobile in the states' case, filing a brief arguing that the deal should be cleared. The judge ruled in favor of Sprint and T-Mobile in a stunning decision that ignored even today's weak antitrust standards, under which a merger from four to only three competitors with projected price increases should easily be blocked. The judge bizarrely credited "the demeanor" of the T-Mobile execs at trial, whose charisma and hot pink shirts apparently convinced him, despite all evidence to the contrary, that the merged company would slash prices the way T-Mobile had done in the past.

The food industry, like the rest, is highly concentrated, a subject we'll explore in detail in chapter 6. A recent lawsuit alleges the big four poultry companies agreed to rig prices and screw you over for a decade, costing the average American family $330 more a year. And that's just chicken! Imagine how much less you'd pay for food if every food category were competitive. Your monthly overhead creeps higher and higher as competition goes lower and lower.

The Illusion of Choice

Even when you think you can choose among a range of companies competing for your business, such choice is often an illusion. You're looking for a deal on shoes online. Should you choose Amazon or 6pm.com or Zappos? Same company. Renting a car? Eleven rental car brands are really a mere three companies. Mega-corporations create the false appearance of choice, tricking you into believing you're in the driver's seat.

No wonder you can't find a deal! False choice means you don't really have the power to vote with your feet when companies treat you poorly or rip you off.

If Au Bon Pain raises its prices, you could go to Panera or Pret A Manger instead for lunch. But surprise! They're all owned by the same private equity firm, JAB Holding Company. So JAB can charge you more or give you crappier service without risk of losing your business. If you switch to a competitor, odds are high that JAB owns them, too. JAB also owns Keurig Green Mountain, Caribou Coffee, Krispy Kreme, Peet's, Einstein Bros., Stumptown—the list goes on.

Comparing prices between detergent brands Tide, Gain, Bounce, Era, Cheer, and Downy? They're all owned by Procter & Gamble. Even Burger King and Popeyes have the same owner! Thirsty for some beer and deciding between Pilsner Urquell, Blue Moon, and Miller Lite? They're all owned by Molson Coors, which owns 107 brands of beer, cider, and other beverages. AB InBev is even bigger, with over 500 brands and 42 percent of the beer industry as of 2017.

Perhaps you are wary of mega-corporations, and their tendencies to prioritize profits over quality of ingredients or fair trade. You support smaller brands like Burt's Bees, Tom's of Maine, and Ben & Jerry's ice cream. But you might not know that Burt's Bees is owned by Clorox, Tom's of Maine is owned by Colgate-Palmolive, and Ben & Jerry's is owned by Unilever. Even I was taken aback when touring the Ben & Jerry's factory on a family vacation in Vermont and the Wi-Fi network popped up on my phone as Unilever! Talk about killing the small-town Vermont charm. Even if these particular acquisitions of small brands may not individually run afoul of the antitrust laws, the illusion of choice creates the impression that our markets are more competitive than they really are and that you have more power as a consumer than you really do.

Monopolies Tax You Like Governments

More often than not, we as consumers don't even know we're paying inflated prices. Take iPhone apps. In the recent case *Apple v. Pepper*, the U.S. Supreme Court ruled that consumers have the right to sue Apple for charging them a 30 percent commission on every app sale. The plaintiffs are consumers who argued that Apple used its monopoly power to charge them more for their iPhone apps than they would have paid in a competitive market.

Like other tech giants, Apple extracts revenue on its own terms because it lacks competition. In 2019 alone, the 30 percent so-called Apple tax, which is embedded in the app prices users pay, brought in $15 billion of revenue for Apple. Why is Apple's cut called a tax? Just like the IRS, Apple sets the rate and iPhone users pay it. Taxpayers can't bargain with the IRS, nor can they choose a different IRS if they don't like the one they've got. iPhone users similarly don't have the choice to lawfully buy their apps elsewhere. When app prices increase, iPhone users are unlikely to respond by switching to an Android phone, so the Android app store doesn't meaningfully constrain the tax that Apple can charge.

When AT&T had a monopoly over phone networks, before its 1982 breakup, consumers were required to purchase AT&T phones to connect to its network. But the Federal Communications Commission ruled in 1968 that phones and devices made by other companies could connect to the AT&T network, allowing innovation and competition to flourish. Just because Apple makes the iPhone doesn't mean it should face no competition on every feature that connects to or could interoperate with the iPhone. Multiple app stores could compete for iPhone users' business by offering innovation and low prices. Apple can charge whatever it wants in its App Store because it lacks competition, but it doesn't have to be this way, nor should it be.

Data Is the New Monopoly Money

But hey, at least we get a lot of free stuff in the digital age, right? Wrong. What you don't pay for in dollars, you pay for in data. Even though it's not easy to assign a dollar amount to our data, we know it has tremendous value. Only by tracking us and targeting ads to us based on our data, a topic we'll cover in detail later, did Facebook make more than $70 billion in 2019. Brad Smith, the president of Microsoft, reinforced just how valuable our data is, saying in an NPR interview last year, "I worry that if all of the data on which the world relies is in the hands of a small number of tech companies, you're going to see a massive transfer of economic wealth."

Facebook and Google have long evaded antitrust enforcement

because they are purportedly "free." But not only are they not free, economists say the platforms should be paying you because your information is more valuable than the services you're getting. If digital markets were competitive, platforms could even compete against one another to offer you the best price for your data!

Tech companies should be paying us for how rich our data is *and* because we're basically already working for them. Yep, you are actually doing work for big tech companies, helping to train their algorithms. The concept is called "digital labor," and we're all doing it without compensation. As entrepreneur Joe Toscano explains in his TEDx Talk, "Want to Work for Google? You Already Do," Google Maps is only as good as it is because billions of us effectively work for Google, taking pictures of meals, adding ratings and reviews, and pinning locations. "Companies have turned billions of us into unpaid machine trainers," said Toscano, creating "a multi-trillion-dollar stream of unpaid untaxable labor."

HOW MONOPOLIES SUCK
AWAY TAX DOLLARS

A large piece of your paycheck disappears before it even hits your bank account, as the government takes its cut. Meanwhile you hear that some corporations manage to avoid income taxes altogether, despite high profits, and Congress keeps giving them more tax breaks. You're contributing more than your fair share, while big companies aren't paying their part.

If you're a parent, you receive endless requests from your child's school to volunteer at fund-raisers, even to pay for basic supplies like paper towels and pencils. What are your tax dollars paying for anyway?

Too Powerful to Pay Taxes

Ninety-one corporations paid zero federal income tax in 2018, according to a study by the Institute on Taxation and Economic Policy. Several companies paid a negative tax rate, meaning they actually received a check from the IRS. That list was full of companies with monopoly or oligopoly power, including Amazon, Molson Coors, Delta Air Lines, Whirlpool, and Halliburton. Amazon's federal income tax rate in 2018 was negative 1.2 percent, and its income taxes were negative $129 million.

"The tax breaks identified in this report are highly concentrated among a few very large corporations," the study reported, explaining that just "25 companies claimed $37.1 billion in tax breaks in 2018." That figure is about half of the $73.9 billion in tax breaks that all 379 companies in the study received.

Facebook is currently fighting a lawsuit from the IRS, which is seeking up to $9 billion in back taxes. Thank you, Mark Zuckerberg, for donating $25 million for therapeutics research during the COVID-19 pandemic, but $9 billion would help the country a lot more. Whenever you see acts of charity from monopolists, know that they give a little with one hand and take away a lot more with the other.

Monopolies use their political power to influence tax policy, get sweetheart tax breaks, and evade taxes without being held accountable. Of course, the problem of corporate power having undue influence on our government is not a new one; it existed before our economy became so consolidated, and it was exacerbated by the 2010 U.S. Supreme Court case *Citizens United*, which deemed corporate political spending to be protected speech. But a handful of companies having unprecedented wealth means that political power, just like economic power, is highly concentrated among the few. Monopolies and oligopolies are like corporate power on steroids.

Monopoly power and political power create a self-reinforcing feedback loop. As monopolies' economic power grows, they buy up increasing amounts of political power. That political power, in turn, strengthens their monopoly power as they use the government to pursue laws and policies that further tilt the playing field in their favor. And monopolies use their political power to stave off attempts to regulate against their interests or enforce antitrust laws against them.

Buying a Heli-Pad for the Richest Man in the World

New York City public schools commonly display a "Buy On Amazon" button prominently on their home page. When parents click on the link, they are taken to a website that explains Amazon will donate 0.5 percent of eligible purchases to the charity or school of your choice, under the heading, "You Shop. Amazon Gives." Parents feel like they're doing a good deed by shopping on Amazon, and Amazon gets credit for funding schools. Meanwhile, Amazon escapes blame for all that it takes away, the billions of dollars that it has depleted from state and local tax bases—the same tax coffers that fund many of our schools.

On top of not paying income taxes and getting paid by the IRS, Amazon avoided sales taxes altogether for years, amounting to billions of dollars drained from tax bases. Amazon got its start by being an internet company where you could buy books but not pay sales taxes, and a large part of its initial success was due to this discount. Amazon eventually capitulated and began paying taxes for products that it sells itself, the "sold-by-Amazon" products. But until recently Amazon still refused to ensure taxes were collected for products sold by third-party marketplace sellers.

When I was working as an investigative journalist, a source shared an extensive data set with me that showed that third-party sellers on Amazon's marketplace failed to pay an estimated $1.9 billion in state sales tax in 2016 alone. Nearly $2 billion in a single year would buy a lot of pencils, snacks, and books for schools and their students. Under political and legal pressure in 2018, Amazon began to collect taxes on third-party sellers in most but not all states that collect sales tax. Billions of dollars in back taxes still have not been collected.

As consumers, we loved buying stuff without sales tax, and we think we're getting a good deal on Amazon, but we just end up paying in other ways—by our schools not having basic necessities like paper towels, by decrepit public transportation making our commutes slow and miserable, or by higher income taxes to make up for budget shortfalls. After starving public institutions of the tax funds needed to succeed, big corporations then point to government failures and push for privatization, so that profit interests can further overtake the public interest.

When Amazon skirts taxes, small businesses still pay up, distorting the competitive playing field even further. The state of Virginia recently gave Amazon up to $550 million in cash incentives to open headquarters in Crystal City. This taxpayer-funded deal particularly rubbed salt into the wounds of local bookstore owners, who had always contributed to the tax base, while Amazon didn't pay taxes in Virginia until 2013, nearly two decades after it was founded. Kelly Justice, owner of an independent bookstore called Fountain Books, told the *Richmond Times-Dispatch*, "I actually voted for people who are using my tax dollars to put me out of business." Ward Tefft, owner of Chop Suey Books, told the paper, "It's like we're bowing down and kissing the hand of the king just to get some scraps."

Back in the day, Senator Sherman wanted to save us from the rule of kings for exactly this reason. We didn't vote for King Bezos. But Amazon can make the nation's local governments dance for it, in hopes of bringing a second Amazon headquarters to their communities. More than 200 cities submitted bids for HQ2, in major efforts that involved elaborate, detailed presentations and were paid for with taxpayer dollars. In hindsight, the HQ2 city tour seems more like an opportunity for Amazon to gather data about cities and their citizens to use for business intelligence than a legitimate search for a headquarters location.

When New Yorkers got wind of the sweet deal their governor and mayor had offered Amazon—$3 billion of incentives—they rose up and resisted. New York City's public infrastructure, from subways to schools, is greatly underfunded, so taxpayers were not pleased with the notion of funding a helipad for the richest man in the world. Nor were they happy that local residents likely would get priced out of their homes as Amazon employees moved in. After grassroots activists mobilized to defeat the incentive package, Amazon backed away. Months later, Amazon quietly announced it was coming to New York City regardless, without the taxpayer help that the company, valued at nearly a trillion dollars, never needed. New Yorkers revolted, showing the power of citizen outrage, but Amazon has reportedly received close to $3 billion in subsidies from local governments around the country.

A company is nearly four times more likely to receive an economic incentive package in a state where it gives money to state-level political candidates than in states where it doesn't, according to a recent study. The study also shows that incentive packages given to corporations that didn't give money to state politicians generate greater job and economic growth than incentives given to corporations that did. This study quantified what we already knew—corporate bribery is good for politicians but not their constituents. Monopoly money only exacerbates this problem because the concentration of wealth in the hands of fewer corporations translates to inordinate influence over policymakers.

On top of taxes, Amazon has used its political muscle to pass its utility costs on to regular people like you and me. In Virginia, citizens objected to a power line Amazon wanted to lay across a Civil

War battlefield to one of its data centers. The citizens' activism was victorious, or so they thought. Amazon agreed to bury the line underground, but the utility and state legislators simply passed the $172 million cost onto the people, tacking on a monthly fee to Virginians' utility bills. Virginia's House of Delegates did the bidding of the tech giant at a direct cost to voters. Amazon data centers don't even bring a large number of jobs, as data centers industry-wide tend to employ less than fifty people.

You Foot the Bill When Monopolies Exploit Their Workers

Amazon is not alone in converting its monopoly power to political power that extracts wealth from taxpayers. In 2017, Walmart had sixty-two lobbyists working to influence the government. Walmart has spent tens of millions of dollars lobbying against things like minimum wage laws, estate taxes, and corporate taxes and in favor of food stamp funding. Walmart pays its employees so little that they make up the single largest group of food stamp recipients in many states. You pay higher taxes so that Walmart employees can live.

In another sickening twist, Walmart earns about $13 billion in annual revenue from the food stamp program, as an estimated 18 percent of all food stamps are redeemed at Walmart. Amazon, too, is joining in on this double-extraction from taxpayers, participating in a pilot program that allows food stamp recipients to buy food online at the same time that many of Amazon's employees receive food stamps, including one-third of its employees in Arizona. But influencing policy that takes from taxpayers and gives to Walmart is only the beginning. Walmart has allegedly skimped on $2.6 billion tax dollars using a purportedly fake Chinese joint venture and has reportedly sheltered $76 billion in tax havens. To put that nearly $80 billion of unpaid taxes into context, the Centers for Disease Control's public health preparedness and response budget is only a fraction of that amount,

$850 million in fiscal year 2020. We are underprepared in a pandemic while monopolists line their pockets with taxpayer dollars.

Tax breaks for behemoths don't tend to result in those companies investing their gains in employees or innovation. In a monopolized economy, corporate profits are high because of extraction—from customers, employees, taxpayers, and suppliers. The Trump administration rolled out corporate tax cuts in 2017 that led to record levels of companies buying back their own stocks, which then led to inflated stock prices. Big corporations' incentives to invest in research and development vanished along with competition because, among other reasons, they can charge high prices and make a ton of money without improving their products and services, as long as consumers lack alternatives.

The same corporations that bought back their own stocks came begging for taxpayer dollars when COVID-19 hit. Major airlines spent 96 percent of their free cash flow buying back their own stocks in the last decade, more than $47 billion, but they still received a $58 billion bailout in the 2020 Coronavirus Aid, Relief, and Economic Security (CARES) Act. We can see the Senate cares . . . about oligopolies. The rest of us are expected to have saved our money for a rainy day, but the biggest corporations can tap into taxpayer funds like a cash machine.

Your Life, Better

It's time to dethrone America's monopoly kings and put the people in charge. We as citizens must demand campaign finance and tax reform, but our efforts will not succeed if we build them on the faulty foundation of monopoly markets. Reviving antitrust law and enforcement and restoring competitive markets will disperse giant corporations' economic and political power, creating the structural change needed for real reform.

If markets were open across the board and prices were at competitive levels, think of how much more wealth would be in your hands instead of the hands of airlines, private equity firms like JAB, Amazon, your wireless provider, and all of their CEOs, to start.

Your monthly overhead would be lower, with competition driving down prices for the must-haves in your life. If you weren't filling the gaping hole left by corporate giants that don't pay their due, your taxes and utility bills could be lower, too. You'd have a chunk of change that you don't have now. What would you do with it? Would you invest it for a nest egg for more financial security? Would you put it toward your child's college? Would you take your family on a much-needed vacation? Monopolies are standing in the way of you living a more financially abundant life.

We don't have to take it anymore.

TWO

MONOPOLIES GOUGE YOU WHEN YOU'RE SICK

"And these you'll need when
the insurance bill arrives."

MONOPOLIES ENDANGER
OUR HEALTH

We pay more for health care in America than citizens of any other country, but when COVID-19 hit, we didn't have enough ventilators, hospital beds, masks, gowns, swabs, or reagents. How could that be?

Our government let big corporations take over medicine and kick smaller companies out of the competition through mergers and monopolistic behavior, making our health care markets highly concentrated. Only two companies make the swabs used for coronavirus testing, for example. Prioritizing profits and efficiency, big medical corporations offshored manufacturing and moved to "just in time" production, a manufacturing model that focuses on keeping costs and inventory low and having the parts arrive at the plant just in time. Or in the case of COVID-19, not nearly in time.

The Chicago School's takeover of antitrust law, with its narrow-minded focus on efficiency, sacrificed our resiliency. Corporate concentration in health care put critical supply chains at risk of collapse in the event of a pandemic or other shock to the system. When antitrust went off the rails, it put lives at risk.

One of the reasons why our health care supply chains are so consolidated is the perverse incentives of group purchasing organizations (GPOs), which hospitals use to buy drugs, medical equipment, and medical supplies. These GPOs are supposed to work for hospitals to keep costs down, giving hospitals bargaining power to negotiate with big suppliers of drugs and equipment. But instead of getting paid by hospitals, GPOs are paid by the suppliers, who kick back to them a percentage of the hospital contracts they negotiate. In 1987, Congress created a legal safe harbor for these kickbacks, meaning GPOs couldn't be criminally prosecuted for them. The law was supposed to benefit hospitals, but it aligned GPOs' financial incentives with those of the biggest medical and drug suppliers.

The bigger the contract that a GPO secures, the bigger the kickback. GPOs designate the biggest corporations as "preferred" vendors for hospitals, and get them the lion's share of the business. Smaller companies don't get a real chance to compete for hospital contracts. The result is less competition, less innovation, drug and medical supply shortages, and a fragile supply chain. Research has shown that GPOs don't even get hospitals lower prices than they would get if they did their own negotiating!

The anticompetitive practices of GPOs have been the subject of scrutiny for decades, including antitrust investigation, multiple congressional hearings, and a months-long *New York Times* investigation in 2002, and yet nothing changes. Why? GPOs and the biggest drug and medical supply manufacturers spend huge sums to lobby Washington, but no such powerful lobby exists for America's patients. That's where our voices come in. We may not have the millions of dollars that lobbyists can spread around, but as voters we have the power to remove politicians who work for GPOs and medical monopolists instead of us.

On top of anticompetitive practices that exclude competitors, health care mergers have dangerously put all our eggs in a few baskets, crippling our medical response to the pandemic. When a company buys a competitor just to eliminate it, antitrust lawyers call it a "killer acquisition." An apparent killer acquisition—taking that term to a grotesque level—contributed to the U.S. ventilator shortage when COVID-19 arrived.

In 2010, the U.S. Department of Health and Human Services awarded a contract to a small company, Newport, to make affordable ventilators for the U.S. stockpile, paying it over $6 million to get started. But in 2012, before Newport finished making those ventilators, it was bought up by a larger company, named—you can't make these things up—Covidien. "Government officials and executives at rival ventilator companies said they suspected that Covidien had acquired Newport to prevent it from building a cheaper product that would undermine Covidien's profits from its existing ventilator business," reports the *New York Times*. The FTC cleared the merger quickly, without conducting a longer, in-depth investigation. Covidien had little interest in building the lower-cost ventilators for the government, and it managed to get out of Newport's contract in 2014. The health agency started over, agreeing in 2014 to pay Philips, a giant in medical equipment, to design ventilators for the stockpile. After FDA approval, the agency placed its ventilator order in September 2019, but the contract didn't require full delivery until 2022. Philips hadn't yet supplied a single ventilator when COVID-19 hit America's shores.

Part of a larger pattern, Newport was only one of 17 companies that Covidien bought between 2008 and 2014, before being bought itself by an even bigger company, Medtronic, in 2015. Medtronic has made almost seventy acquisitions in the last two decades, and the FTC let the Covidien deal go through, resolving its competitive concerns by merely requiring Medtronic to sell a single product line. Buying Covidien made Medtronic's stock value instantly jump, in large part because Medtronic structured the deal as a controversial "corporate inversion," where the acquiring company moves its headquarters to the country where the company it purchases is based. Medtronic switched its Minnesota headquarters to Ireland, where Covidien was based, taking tax dollars away from America.

Medical companies' relentless drive for corporate profits and efficiencies have made shareholders rich, robbed taxpayers and patients of money, and built a fragile system where only a few companies make the things Americans need in a pandemic. And the FTC, beholden to the Chicago School ideology that prioritizes efficiency above all else, let it happen.

Medical Monopoly Money

It's not just you—your health insurance costs more and covers less than just a decade ago.

And the prices Americans pay for medicine can be downright shocking. In a notorious example, millions of parents fill their children's EpiPen prescription diligently upon expiration, with a list price of $600. Allergies can be a life-and-death matter, so these parents have no choice but to pay whatever price is dictated to them. Worse, sometimes the pharmacist says supplies have run out. Parents get on a waiting list for when the shortage ends and hope their child doesn't encounter any life-threatening peanuts in the meantime. Even if you're lucky enough that you don't personally need any high-cost drugs, you're still paying a price for them through your insurance premiums and taxes.

The reasons used to explain these high costs is that insurance companies have gotten too greedy, and that Americans pay more than everyone else for health care because we consume more medical services than people in other countries. Plus, we have the best quality medical care, and you get what you pay for, including funding research, which costs a lot. Under this line of thinking, the solution to our problems is to stop corporations from being greedy and convince Americans to go to the doctor less.

But that's not going to work.

Corporations, under current interpretations of corporate law, are designed to be greedy and are focused on maximizing short-term profits for their shareholders. Lawmakers are the ones who are charged with protecting us from that greed, constraining corporations from pursuing profits in ways that hurt us and ensuring competitive markets that get us the best prices and service. They have failed us.

When your health insurance premiums, copays, and deductibles go up or you get an insane medical bill, you probably don't blame monopoly power. But you should. A lot of things are wrong with America's health care system, but monopoly is a huge root of the problem. Fixing monopoly problems alone would return billions of dollars to hardworking Americans—in 2018, the average cost of health care for a family of four in the United States with a preferred provider organization (PPO) plan through their employer was over $28,000. These families pay on average nearly $12,000 directly out of their pocket in premiums and copays. As for the roughly $16,000 covered by the company, it's considered part of an employee's compensation package, and employers ordinarily just allocate less money to the employee's pay and other benefits. With a median household income in 2018 of $63,179, even families who are lucky enough to have health insurance through an employer spend nearly 20 percent of their income on health care. How are those numbers supposed to work, let alone for families that don't get coverage through an employer?

When Boomers were raising families, it wasn't anything like this. Employees' insurance premiums rose by a whopping 242 percent between 1999 and 2016. On top of premiums, deductibles have increased eight times as fast as wages between 2008 and 2018.

Before assuming that health insurance companies are public enemy number one when it comes to high prices, focus your attention on hospitals. Hospital bills make up the biggest piece of our collective health care costs—a full one-third of total health care spending, to be precise. In a mere seven years, from 2007 to 2014, hospital inpatient prices grew 42 percent.

To explain the skyrocketing of hospital prices, look no further than hospital mergers. Hospitals are merging at a rate of more than 100 per year, becoming local monopolies in many areas. When hospitals merge, they often cut hospital beds, and these mergers are a big reason why America faced a shortage of beds to handle COVID-19. The number of hospital beds declined from 1.5 million in 1975 to approximately 900,000 in 2017.

The most recent hospital merger wave has been driven by private equity firms buying up hospitals. These firms borrow money in order to buy the hospitals but then turn around and saddle them with their debt, while often collecting fees and dividends from the hospitals to enrich the private equity owners. In 2017, for example, the private equity firm Cerberus bought the small rural hospital Easton in Pennsylvania. It loaded up the hospital with debt, making it pay inflated rent on the building it had owned for over 127 years. Cerberus then threatened to close Easton in the midst of the COVID-19 pandemic unless it received a taxpayer bailout. Cerberus received a commitment of millions of dollars in taxpayer funds through the CARES Act, even though Cerberus had financially weakened the hospital as part of its highly lucrative business model.

When hospitals merge to monopolies, prices go up. Insurance companies or employers who want to create health care plans have to negotiate with these hospital monopolies over rates. But insurers don't have the power to walk away from the bargaining table, because local hospital care is a must-have for their insurance plans. Knowing this, hospital monopolies become bullies. They dictate high prices, apply those prices across the board to every hospital in their massive systems, and tell insurers they have to take it or leave it.

A study by a team of economists recently found that hospital prices without competition will cost you 12 percent more than one in a hospital that faces competition. Another report, by the University of California, Berkeley's Petris Center on Health Care Markets and Consumer Welfare, compared hospital rates in Northern California, where the hospital market is highly concentrated, to rates in Southern California, where the hospital market is more competitive. Inpatient prices were 70 percent higher in Northern California, or 32 percent higher after taking into account cost-of-living differences.

Who do these hundreds of hospital mergers mostly benefit? Not patients. One study found a more than 3 percent increase in the mortality rate for heart attack victims after hospitals merge. Not health care workers either. Their wages rose only 8 percent between 2005 and 2015, almost 2 percent less than the national average. Even doctors aren't the biggest winners. When the price of hospital-based outpatient care rose 25 percent between 2007 and 2014, doctors' prices rose only 6 percent. Take a wild guess at who benefits the most from hospital mergers, in the New Gilded Age in which we live. You got it—CEOs! Major nonprofit medical center CEOs' pay has risen by 93 percent between 2005 and 2015. The richest of the rich keep getting richer, at everyone else's expense.

The FTC deserves credit for aggressively trying to block some hospital mergers. On occasion the FTC has succeeded, but often it has lost in court as judges accept the hospitals' arguments that their mergers will increase efficiency and reduce prices. To reiterate, the Clayton Act prohibits mergers that may lessen competition or tend to create a monopoly, and makes no mention of efficiency or prices. The perverse result of antitrust law's modern obsession with prices is that competition among hospitals has been destroyed and patients are getting soaked.

Hospitals are buying each other, and they're buying doctors' groups, more than 8,000 between 2016 and 2018. When hospitals buy doctors' groups, studies show that prices go up, but quality of care doesn't. Doctors charge an average of 14 percent more for the same services after they've been acquired, and even more when they are bought by a monopoly hospital, according to research.

You should remember this power structure when you go to the doctor, being aware of the financial incentives of doctors and hospitals. After I investigated a wide range of anticompetitive health care practices as part of my job as an antitrust enforcer at the New York Attorney General's Office, my eyes were opened to the business nature of medical care. I then used this knowledge as a patient. I remember once when a surgeon was eager to put me through every variation of invasive medical diagnostics without much discussion or in the end, need. When it came to the judgment calls about what procedures were necessary and what weren't, the surgeon's interests in making money ran counter to my interests in minimizing my suffering and avoiding the procedures' risks.

Every patient needs to be their own advocate. A procedure that benefits the hospital's or medical group's profits may not be the best decision for your health, so try to get a second or even third opinion before undergoing anything invasive, miserable, or risky. When I got additional opinions, I learned that less aggressive approaches were available to me and were perhaps far better for my overall health.

Fewer Options, Higher Bills

Although hospital mergers are the largest contributors to health care costs, mergers are rampant throughout every corner of the health care industry. Fresenius Medical Care and DaVita, for example, together control a 92 percent market share in the $24.4 billion dialysis industry. They gained dominance by buying up their competitors. And patients pay the price, with Fresenius recently sending a patient a half-a-million-dollar dialysis bill for fourteen weeks of treatment. Fresenius charged the patient $13,867.74 per dialysis session, which amounts to approximately 59 times the $235 rate that Medicare pays. Fresenius forgave the bill after it was publicly exposed, saying the patient was misclassified as out of network.

Large dialysis companies have raised prices while delivering worse patient care, according to a study out of Duke University's Fuqua School of Business. The study found that as large dialysis chains bought more than 1,200 smaller providers from 1998 to 2010, they cut skilled staff, took on more patients, changed drug regimens, and hurt patient health. Another study found a 19 and 24 percent higher risk of death at two large for-profit dialysis chains than at a nonprofit dialysis chain.

Rampant mergers have occurred in every nook and cranny of the health care business. Everything from medical device makers to syringe manufacturers are monopoly, duopoly, or oligopoly industries. Mergers in one part of the health care industry lead to mergers in another part, as companies bulk up to get greater bargaining power to negotiate against one another. Health insurance companies, too, have merged, in part to get more leverage in negotiating rates with hospitals, medical suppliers, drugmakers, dialysis centers, and other sectors that have merged like mad. Consolidation brings more consolidation in a merger snowball effect.

The Villains of Big Pharma

As drug costs skyrocket, it's easy to point the finger at individual personalities, as some pharmaceutical execs are almost caricatures of evil. Take former Vyera (now Phoenixus) CEO Martin Shkreli, a one-time hedge fund manager with no medical expertise, who bought the rights to a drug called Daraprim, which was developed in the 1950s. Daraprim was relied upon by AIDS patients, and Shkreli increased its price by more than 4,000 percent, from $17.50 to $750 a pill.

The New York Attorney General and the FTC sued Shkreli and his company in early 2020 for blocking lower-cost generic versions of Daraprim from coming on the market. Their lawsuit seeks repayment of illegally obtained profits and a lifetime ban on Shkreli working in pharma. Shkreli will defend the suit from prison because, after gouging AIDS patients to line his own pockets, Shkreli was convicted of securities fraud in an unrelated matter. At first Shkreli was free on bail, but his bail was revoked for making threats against Hillary Clinton. Now he allegedly runs Phoenixus from prison, using a contraband cellphone to strategize about stopping generic drug competition to Daraprim. Shkreli "plans to emerge from jail richer than he entered," reports the *Wall Street Journal.* Focusing on wicked personalities, though, distracts us from the structural problems of market power in the drug industry.

Instead of trying to eliminate evil—good luck with that—a more practical solution is to stop drug company mergers and anticompetitive behavior. My investigations at the New York Attorney General's Office covered a wide range of industries, from oil and gas to Wall Street. But the industry practices that disturbed me the most were Big Pharma's. Their ever-evolving tricks to squelch competition directly endangered human life. With billions of dollars at stake, Big Pharma executives get creative in the anticompetitive tactics they use to attain and preserve monopoly power.

The most basic of those techniques is buying up the competition.

"From 1995–2015, 60 pharma companies morphed into just 10 giants," tweeted FTC commissioner Rohit Chopra in November 2019, announcing his dissent to the FTC's approval of a $74 billion merger between drugmakers Bristol-Meyers Squibb (BMS) and Celgene.

Three Republican FTC commissioners approved the deal, while the two Democratic commissioners, Chopra and Rebecca Slaughter, both dissented. The dissenters took issue with the way the FTC analyzes pharmaceutical mergers, and rightfully so—the method the FTC uses has infuriated me for years. If both companies make or are developing drugs for the same condition, the FTC will require one of the pharma companies to sell off the pertinent division to a competitor, and that's pretty much it. The FTC satisfies itself that it has ensured competition for the drugs that both companies make and gives the merger the go-ahead.

Antitrust enforcers should be thoughtful about competitive consequences and not treat multibillion-dollar mergers with huge impact on public health as robotic exercises. This is another absurd result of the Chicago School takeover of antitrust law, because proving to a court that any single drug company merger will definitely raise prices is difficult. Cumulatively, the FTC's routine approvals of drug company mergers have led to a drastic reduction in the number of pharma companies competing on price and is a major reason we have drug shortages today. Plus these mergers cause innovation to go down because fewer drug companies are left to compete.

In his dissent, Commissioner Chopra noted that the BMS/Celgene merger appeared more motivated by financial engineering and tax considerations than any benefits to patients. Both dissenting commissioners expressed concern about the merging companies' histories of anticompetitive tactics and the merger's potential to exacerbate such behavior going forward.

More than ten years earlier, as an assistant attorney general, I saw what Chopra and Slaughter were referring to. I was working on a case involving BMS that seemed more like a mafia tale than the business dealings of a company dedicated to improving health. In 2003, BMS settled antitrust charges that it blocked the entry of lower-priced generic drugs for three of its top-selling drugs, including two anti-cancer drugs and one anti-anxiety drug. The FTC and several states alleged that BMS's behavior "protected nearly $2 billion in annual sales at a high cost to cancer patients and other consumers, who—being denied access to lower-cost alternatives—were forced to overpay by hundreds of millions of dollars for important and often life-saving medications." That settlement required BMS to submit any future agreements with generic drugmakers to the FTC and state attorneys general for approval.

The government wanted to review BMS's future agreements in part to make sure BMS didn't make any "pay-for-delay" deals with generic drugmakers. "Pay-for-delay" is when branded drug companies pay generic drugmakers millions of dollars to *not* make generic versions, so that the branded drug companies can keep charging high prices. Patents are government-granted monopolies, but when they expire, generic drugmakers can then offer lower-priced alternatives. Branded drugmakers' profits can drop by billions of dollars when generics enter the market, so they try to stop them.

Antitrust enforcers have successfully stopped pay-for-delay practices in court, but that doesn't stop drugmakers from trying a myriad of tactics to keep generic drugs off the market as long as possible. In pursuit of this goal, BMS entered into an agreement with a drugmaker in 2006 that sought to make a generic version of BMS's multibillion-dollar heart drug Plavix. Per its 2003 settlement, BMS was required to submit the agreement to the FTC and state attorneys general for approval. After the government pushed back on the agreement, then-BMS senior vice president Andrew Bodnar instead entered into an oral agreement with the generic drugmaker in order to hide it from enforcers. They say the mafia never puts anything in writing.

For deceiving the government, Bodnar was criminally prosecuted. "The prosecutions of BMS and its former senior executive, Andrew Bodnar, should send a strong message to the pharmaceutical community that attempts to undermine the federal government's critical role of ensuring Americans have access to life-saving drugs, like Plavix, at the most competitive prices will not be tolerated," said Scott D. Hammond, acting assistant attorney general in charge of the DOJ's Antitrust Division, in a press release. But in an absurd example of how rich white male corporate executives face few consequences for their actions, Bodnar pled guilty to a misdemeanor and the federal judge merely ordered him to pay a $5,000 fine, serve probation, and—you won't believe this—to write a book about the Plavix case as a cautionary tale to other executives. I'm writing a book right now, voluntarily, and I'm enjoying it! Bodnar did apparently write a book called *The First Question*, but it seems to exist only in case files, not a place where people will actually read it.

Given BMS's decades-long history of behaving badly, the FTC should have thought hard about how its massive $74 billion acquisition of Celgene could enable and worsen such behavior. The more muscle a monopoly has, the easier it can play puppeteer and prevent competition on the merits. As Commissioner Chopra eloquently stated in his dissent, "The financial crisis and the Great Recession taught our country a tough lesson: when watchdogs wear blindfolds or fail to evolve with the marketplace, millions of American families can suffer the consequences." The likely consequences of the BMS/Celgene merger, like those pharma mergers that came before it, are predictable—higher drug prices and less innovation.

85,000 Percent Shameless

For a stunning example of how buying up the competition lets pharma companies gouge patients, let's take a look at how the pharma company Questcor (now called Mallinckrodt) increased the price of one drug by 85,000 percent. Questcor bought Acthar—the only hormone product used to treat rare but serious infant seizures—from Aventis Pharmaceuticals in 2001 for a mere $100,000. Questcor then raised the price of Acthar from $40 per vial to $34,000 per vial in sixteen years. Imagine being a parent with a baby who is having seizures, and the only available medicine is priced at thirty-four grand per vial and typically requires three vials per treatment.

When a potential alternative emerged, Questcor bought it. The FTC and five states then sued Questcor for monopolization, eventually settling the suit by requiring Questcor to pay a $100 million fine and to license the synthetic drug Synachten to a competitor. "By acquiring Synachten, Questcor eliminated the possibility that another firm would develop it and compete against Acthar," said the government's complaint.

The FTC and the states deserve credit for bringing this case, but in the end a $100 million fine is nothing compared to the more than $1 billion in revenue Questcor made on Acthar in 2015 alone. The fine is a mere cost of doing business for Questcor, their anticompetitive conduct ended up making economic sense, and if given the chance, they'd likely do it all over again despite the fine. The penalties for violating antitrust laws are not high enough to overcome Big Pharma's financial incentives to break the law. Bad actors are not deterred by the threat of enforcement, and enforcers are left playing Whac-A-Mole as Big Pharma's anticompetitive tactics spring up everywhere.

A Monopoly-Made EpiPen Crisis

To understand the full gamut of anticompetitive tactics drug companies use to keep prices high, an antitrust lawsuit filed in 2017 by pharmaceutical company Sanofi against Mylan, maker of the EpiPen, is an illuminating read. Mylan bought the drug company Merck in 2007, thus acquiring the rights to EpiPen when it was priced at $100. A decade later in 2017, Mylan had increased EpiPen's average price to a whopping $600.

In its lawsuit that is ongoing at time of writing, Sanofi alleges that Mylan used a whole bag of tricks to shut out Sanofi's competing product, Auvi-Q. First, Sanofi alleged that Mylan, with 90 percent of the market, was able to jack up EpiPen prices above competitive levels. Mylan then used its monopoly profits to give lucrative rebates to pharmacy benefit managers, the middlemen that negotiate with drugmakers and pharmacies on behalf of insurance companies. But Mylan would only pay the rebates, which are essentially kickbacks, if the pharmacy benefit managers and insurance companies refused to cover Epi-Pen's competitor, Auvi-Q.

Second, Sanofi alleged that Mylan defrauded the federal government to pay for those kickbacks, pointing out that the DOJ had sued Mylan for Medicaid fraud and settled the suit for $465 million. Sanofi also accused Mylan of misleading consumers about the safety and effectiveness of Auvi-Q. Last, Sanofi pointed the court to Mylan's requirement that schools that wanted discounted EpiPens could not purchase any competing products. "No traditional competitor puts 'strings attached' to budget-constrained schools requiring them not to stock a single life-saving Auvi-Q if they also want the cheapest available EpiPen," wrote Sanofi in a court filing. Mylan had previously lobbied to get rules requiring epinephrine injectors in schools in the first place, adding lobbyists in thirty-six states between 2010 and 2014 according to the Center for Public Integrity.

Multiple senators and antitrust enforcers took issue with Mylan's exclusivity requirement for schools, and Mylan withdrew it under pressure. But just think about it: Mylan is a monopoly that deliberately excluded competition for a lifesaving product, but then can't itself meet the demand for that product. To explain shortages, Mylan has cited problems with the factory that makes its injector. But the real problem is that Americans at risk of fatal allergic reactions have all their eggs in one basket. Monopolized markets, as we saw with COVID-19, lead to life-threatening shortages.

New alternatives to EpiPens are finally gaining ground, but Americans should never have been in this dangerous and vulnerable position in the first place. In their quest to kick rivals out of the game, pharma monopolists put us all at the mercy of a limited number of suppliers. The FDA keeps a list of drug shortages, and at the time of writing, the list has more than one hundred and twenty-five entries, including epinephrine injectors like EpiPens.

Often the excuse to justify inaction against high drug prices is that research and development is so expensive that we need to make sure drugmakers are rewarded for the investment and risks they take, or drug innovation will suffer. But in the examples of Daraprim, Acthar, and EpiPen, the drug company that raised prices sky-high didn't even invent the drug. The price hikers bought old drugs, raised prices astronomically, and then used anticompetitive tactics to keep out lower-priced alternatives. Pharma monopolists seem to spend more energy crafting schemes to keep out competition than besting rivals based on superior therapies.

Americans Pay More for Less

Million-dollar hospital bills, crowd-sourced funding for lifesaving medicine, and health-care-induced homelessness happen in America, but not other industrialized nations. Compared to our counterparts around the world, we're getting robbed. The same appendectomy that runs about $3,800 in Australia costs $16,000 or more in the United States. Delivering a baby costs around $2,000 in Spain, but even without complications costs on average $11,000 in the United States, with expensive hospitals charging more than $18,000. Hospital stays in industrialized countries run $10,500 in the middle range, while a hospital stay in the United States costs more than double that at over $21,000, even though hospital stays in America are shorter than in most industrialized nations.

We tell ourselves that the quality of care in America is so much better, but the facts show otherwise. Our life expectancy is lower than Chile, Slovenia, and most of the European Union. "It's not that we're getting more; it's that we're paying much more," said Gerard F. Anderson, a Johns Hopkins professor who coauthored a study showing America spends a lot more money than every other country for less care.

And we pay on average over 50 percent more for the same drugs that other developed nations pay, and 80 percent more for cardiovascular, musculoskeletal, and nervous system drugs, according to global information provider IHS Markit. Even if it were true that the high prices you're paying went primarily to research and development rather than Big Pharma CEOs' bank accounts, how do you feel about funding innovation for the entire world? It's sure generous of you to take on so much financial stress for the French, who pay one-third of what you do for the same drugs. But then again, you really don't have a choice when you're living under monopoly rule!

Monopoly Overlords Make the Rules

When judges get antitrust wrong, as they have when they shut down the FTC's attempts to block anticompetitive hospital mergers, lawmakers have the power to step in and put judges back on track. Legislators could pass laws with clear rules that prohibit such mergers or that overrule wrongheaded cases that are getting in the FTC's way. But hospital monopoly money is flowing to lawmakers, discouraging them from taking steps that would protect patients. The Center for Responsive Politics, an organization that tracks the influence of money on politics and posts it on OpenSecrets.org, estimates that hospitals and nursing homes spent $102 million on lobbying in the 2018 election cycle alone.

Congress could also pass laws ensuring fair competition in pharmaceuticals. Rather than antitrust enforcers having to bring a lawsuit every time a drug company implements a new scheme to exclude competition, laws could prohibit the conduct in the first place and bring automatic fines that are big enough to deter the behavior. But Big Pharma spent $167 million last year on lobbying, and 573 of Pharma's lobbyists are former government insiders, according to Open Secrets.

On top of competition issues, major regulatory problems affect drug prices. Big Pharma lobbying led to a 2003 George W. Bush administration rule that the government can't negotiate with drug companies for Medicare Part D drug prices. Other countries don't just pay Big Pharma whatever they're asking. When it comes to health care, politicians are often beholden to medical monopoly money instead of you. As long as voters are in the dark, elected representatives can get away with it.

Let politicians know you're on to them. Check OpenSecrets.org to see if your representatives accept campaign contributions from Big Health Care. Then demand that your representatives put a stop to hospital mergers and acquisitions, and bar Big Pharma's pay-for-delay agreements and other competition-killing schemes. Fines should amount to double the illegally obtained profits. While you're at it, tell lawmakers to implement "Medicare Prices for All," an idea proposed by Phil Longman in *Washington Monthly*, which would apply the health care prices that the government does negotiate to all Americans, even those with private insurance. This measure alone would lower prices across the board and eliminate out-of-network overcharges.

Medical Monopolies Limit Your Career Opportunities

On top of taking our money, medical monopolies constrain our earning potential by making the leap to entrepreneurship even harder. I don't know about you, but I hate having a boss. No offense to the great bosses I've had in my life, but I just prefer to be the captain of my own ship. I grew up with two parents who ran their own small businesses, and I always thought I'd have the independence they enjoyed.

But whenever I calculate whether I can take the risk of leaving a steady paycheck, the cost of health care always puts me over the edge. Not only do I have to cover my monthly bills, but I've got to make sure I can cover tens of thousands of dollars in health care for my family. And then there's the entrepreneur's cost of paying for employees' health care, too.

I know I'm not alone in this. Imagine how much this obstacle to entrepreneurship drags down our economy. A study by the Kauffman-RAND Institute for Entrepreneurship Public Policy Studies shows that those with access to a spouse's health insurance plan are much more likely to become self-employed, and that self-employment rates rise when Medicare becomes available. Increasing the availability of affordable health insurance for the self-employed is important for entrepreneurship, the study concludes. A key to affordability is eliminating medical monopoly rents by ensuring free and fair competition.

Your Life, Better

The days of fragility and weakness in our medical system must come to an end. Now is the time to stop monopoly rule over health care and restore resilience and strength in our medical supply chains and infrastructure. At the very least, we owe it to our health care workers who risked their lives every day fighting COVID-19 without enough personal protective equipment and essential medical devices. Our health care system is fragile and expensive because of policy choices—it's not inevitable.

Imagine if the cost of health care didn't weigh you down. You would know what your medical procedure would cost before you get it done because the health care provider would post the standard Medicare Prices for All in a handy menu, like you get at a restaurant. When you receive an explanation of benefits, you relax because you know you're covered. You get health care and medicine when you need them, instead of stressing over costs. EpiPens cost $70, like they do in Europe, not $600. Prescription drug prices are down across the board. And the pharmacy doesn't run out! When your fellow Americans experience a medical emergency, they don't also face a financial crisis, compounding the trauma they are already experiencing.

If you spent the same percentage of your income on health insurance, deductibles, premiums, and drugs as Americans did in the 1980s, you'd get back the majority of what you're currently paying. Think of all the ways the cost of health care has stressed you out, constrained your freedom, or caused real hardship, and imagine them lessened, if not entirely gone. Much regulatory reform is needed to fix the morass that is the U.S. health care system, but a competitive health care marketplace alone would lighten the oppressive weight that health care costs are exerting on most Americans. And the travesty of 27.5 million Americans not being covered at all, a figure that predates the massive job losses of COVID-19, could easily be remedied if we reduced health care costs across the board by promoting competition and eliminating monopoly pricing.

We have the solutions. We just need our elected representatives to summon the will to fight the power of medical monopolies, and they need us to build a movement of people behind them. Members of Congress who want to pass needed reforms are up against the monopoly money being thrown at their colleagues and political opponents. Yet we as citizens who cherish our democracy must do the work of self-governance. We have to let policy makers who want to do the right thing know that we've got their backs, and we're not going to take medical monopoly rule anymore.

PEOPLE V. GIANT TECH MONOPOLIES

To understand the legal definition of monopoly, what types of behavior are illegal, and how there's hope that today's monopolies can be reined in by enforcing antitrust laws, it helps to take a look at the case the government brought against Microsoft more than two decades ago.

When the Department of Justice and twenty states sued Microsoft in 1998, Microsoft's Windows operating system had a 95 percent share of the market for "intel-compatible PC operating systems." Microsoft's Windows operating system was so dominant that companies that make personal computers didn't have much of a choice but to use it. Microsoft weaponized this dominance to illegally squash Netscape Navigator, a competitor of its Internet Explorer browser, using a slew of exclusionary tactics.

For example, Microsoft required personal computer makers to preinstall Internet Explorer in every PC that ran on Windows (which was pretty much all of them). Microsoft also technically integrated Internet Explorer into Windows so that using a non-Microsoft browser would be difficult and glitchy.

Messages between senior executives showed Microsoft didn't think it could win against Netscape if it just competed to be the best. A senior Microsoft executive wrote: "Pitting browser against browser is hard since Netscape has 80% market share and we have

20%. . . . I am convinced we have to use Windows—this is the one thing they don't have." He added that competing against Netscape to make a better browser wasn't enough, saying "we need something more—Windows integration." The exec planned to offer an upgrade to Windows that "must be killer" on computer shipments "so that Netscape *never gets a chance* on these systems" (emphasis added).

Even if Netscape offered a browser that was superior to Internet Explorer, Netscape didn't have a shot. Netscape lost market share, was acquired by AOL, and eventually shut down. Microsoft's anticompetitive practices not only allowed it to take over the browser market at that time, but also protected Microsoft's Windows monopoly power by eliminating a potential threat to the operating system. Navigator was emerging as an alternative platform around which to build apps and could in the future serve as a partial substitute for Windows. Microsoft was determined to use its muscle to kill that potential.

Monopolization Requirement #1: Monopoly Power

Being a monopoly on its own is not illegal—Sherman Act Section 2 makes it illegal to *monopolize*. Illegal monopolization has two requirements: 1) monopoly power, and 2) a company has "acquired or maintained" that monopoly power using "exclusionary conduct." Monopoly power is the ability to control prices or exclude competition. In other words, if a company has the power to kick a competitor out of the game or to set prices, it has monopoly power. Here Microsoft had the power to kick Netscape out of the competition.

monopoly power = ability to control prices or kick out rivals

The best way to prove monopoly power is through direct evidence: showing a company actually controlled prices or kicked out rivals. In the Microsoft case, there was direct evidence that Microsoft excluded competition from Netscape.

A second-best option for proving monopoly power is through indirect evidence, using market share and showing that barriers make it hard for competitors to enter the market. Contrary to popular belief, monopoly power doesn't require 100 percent market share or zero competitors. Under court decisions, a market share of 70 percent or more automatically qualifies as monopoly power, while lesser market shares can be enough, too.

Share of What Market?

The definition of the market is important. A market includes only those companies that customers are likely to switch to when prices go up or quality goes down a small amount. With Microsoft, for instance, Windows had a 95 percent share of a market defined as "Intel-compatible PC operating systems." The court didn't define the market as "all software." That's because the options for customers to switch to were quite limited. Operating systems for Macs weren't included in the product market because the customers at issue—the PC makers—could not switch to the operating system that only runs on Macs as a substitute. Without an alternative, PC makers had little choice but to accept Microsoft's requirement that they install Internet Explorer as the default browser.

Corporate defendants in antitrust cases typically argue that courts should define the market as broadly as possible in order to make their market share smaller. If Mac operating systems were included in the market definition, for example, then Windows' market share would be lower.

As a customer, your ability to switch to a substitute is important because having a choice empowers you and helps constrain companies from treating you badly. When you—as a consumer or a businessperson—don't have much of a choice but to deal with a company on terms that it dictates, monopoly power is the likely culprit. Competition gives you options. The ability to vote with your feet by walking away helps protect you from getting screwed.

Monopolization Requirement #2: Kicking Competitors Out of the Game

A thriving economy requires that companies duke it out to be the best, not act like wimps afraid of getting bested. The second requirement of illegal monopolization is called "exclusionary conduct," meaning that a company is trying to kick out rivals in order to get or keep monopoly power, rather than competing on the merits to be the best. The wimpy way out of a challenge is to try to stop opponents from even being able to play the game. People mistakenly think monopolizing behavior is aggressive and strong, but it's actually the chicken-shit, innovation-killing way to go.

Microsoft met this second requirement of illegal monopolization because it drove Netscape out of the game, rather than competing against Netscape to be the best.

One question gets at the heart of identifying illegal monopolization that violates Section 2 of the Sherman Act: *If a challenger puts forth a product or service that is equal to or better than a powerful company's offerings, do they have a shot at success?* If the answer is no, the market is not working and instead a monopolist is pulling strings like a master puppeteer, eliminating competition itself.

To summarize:

illegal monopolization = monopoly power + preventing rivals from competing based on merit

The antitrust case against Microsoft sadly came too late to save Netscape. But if the government never brought the case, Google may not exist because Microsoft could have used the same tactics against Google that it used against Netscape. After taking over the internet browser market, Microsoft could have required computer makers to use its own search engine, too. *U.S. v. Microsoft* made Microsoft curb its monopolistic practices, and competition and innovation flourished as a result.

But fighting monopolies requires constant vigilance. DOJ brought *U.S. v. Microsoft* more than twenty years ago, and it's long past time to bring back Sherman Act Section 2 in full force. Power wants to consolidate, and it's up to us, our elected representatives, and the law enforcers who work for us, to constantly combat the accumulation of excessive private power.

No One's Trying to Punish Companies for Being the Best

Bigness on its own does not violate the antitrust laws. The government did not sue Microsoft for having the best operating system or for having a large market share. If a company is a monopoly just because it's the best, and it stays a monopoly by outcompeting everyone else fair and square, that's cool. But dominant companies often focus more effort on keeping out competitors than on competing to be the best. It turns out that once companies have the power to squash competition, they use it. Especially because in recent years the consequences for breaking the antitrust laws, if any, have been small enough to be a rational cost of doing business.

The Monopoly Power of Today's Giants

U.S. v. Microsoft was my introduction to antitrust law. As a student intern at a law firm, back in the summer of 2001, I was assigned to update the antitrust group's legal manual with the Microsoft ruling. I spent a good chunk of my summer poring over the case. Fifteen years later, I could easily see that each tech giant—just like Microsoft—was leveraging its platform power to make fair competition impossible. In 2016, I began writing about how the Big Tech platforms were monopolizing markets just as Microsoft had done, predicting the tech giants would face antitrust trouble in America soon based on just how many illegal behaviors and mergers had been unchecked.

Now perhaps just like me, you too can begin to see how Google, Apple, Facebook, and Amazon are monopolies—and the potential cases against them for growing and maintaining their monopoly power through buying and kicking out rivals.

The tech giants started on their paths to dominance with innovation, but their monopoly power is not purely the result of competing on the merits or being the best. Though at one point start-ups themselves, they now have grown into entrepreneur-squashing behemoths through hundreds of acquisitions. Together Facebook and Google have bought over 150 companies just since 2013. Google alone has acquired nearly 250 companies since 2006. At last count, Apple has bought over 100 companies and Amazon nearly 90. Many of these acquisitions were illegal under the Clayton Act, Section 7, which, to say it again, prohibits mergers and acquisitions where the effect "may be substantially to lessen competition, or to tend to create a monopoly." Google acquired Android and YouTube; Google also bought up the digital ad market spoke by spoke, including Applied Semantics, AdMob, and DoubleClick, cementing its market power in every aspect of the ecosystem.

Acquisitions of competitive threats have allowed Facebook to amass and maintain market power. Instagram built a thriving social network with 27 million users on iOS alone, centered on sharing images. Then Facebook bought it.

WhatsApp too was a potential competitor before Facebook gobbled it up. Facebook bought an app called Onavo in 2013 that allowed it to detect early competitive threats and buy them or build its own versions. "Facebook used Onavo to conduct global surveys of the usage of mobile apps by customers, and apparently without their knowledge. They used this data to assess not just how many people had downloaded apps, but how often they used them. This knowledge helped them to decide which companies to acquire, and which to treat as a threat." These are the conclusions of a British Parliament committee after reviewing internal Facebook documents it had seized from a plaintiff in a private lawsuit against the tech giant.

In the documents, one executive was explicitly worried about mobile messaging apps as a competitive threat, and Onavo data identified WhatsApp as the top contender. Onavo data revealed that WhatsApp was sending more than twice as many messages per day as Messenger. Facebook even promoted Onavo as a way for users to keep their Web traffic private, yet it surveilled them and analyzed their usage.

Lack of antitrust enforcement against illegal mergers is half of the picture, leaving the other half, lack of enforcement against illegal monopolization. Big Tech has been following Microsoft's playbook, squashing challengers without antitrust enforcers or lawmakers stopping them. In chapter 3 I'll provide multiple examples of the tech giants kicking out rivals, which is direct evidence of monopoly power. The platforms ignore this direct evidence and focus on the indirect method for proving monopoly power, using market share. Direct evidence is stronger than indirect evidence as a legal principle, but the tech platforms want everyone to focus on market share and to believe their bogus definitions of what the relevant market is under antitrust law. Each giant tries to define their market broadly, as in "all e-commerce," "all social media," or "all mobile operating systems," to try to make their market share look small and hide their monopoly power.

Amazon maintains it doesn't have monopoly power because it defines the relevant product market as "all retail," which includes every single type of online and physical store in America. But remember, a relevant market under antitrust law only includes substitutes that consumers readily switch to in response to a price increase or reduction in quality. If Amazon raises prices for beauty supplies, the local hardware store is not a substitute! And what are the substitutes that customers can switch to if Amazon raises its Prime membership fees? Certainly not all retail! We shouldn't even need to define the product market because we have stronger proof of Amazon's monopoly power than the indirect evidence of market share—we have direct evidence that Amazon controls prices and excludes competition.

For example, Amazon doesn't just control the prices you pay on Amazon.com, but it can control the prices you pay on Walmart .com and Target.com and all across the Web. And it can make those prices higher. Amazon has forbidden sellers and brands from offering lower prices anywhere else on the Web than they offer on Amazon. After German and British antitrust enforcers investigated Amazon in 2013, Amazon dropped the requirements in contracts in Europe. Five years later, Connecticut senator Richard Blumenthal wrote a letter to the FTC urging it to investigate Amazon over these pricing requirements. Only in 2019 did Amazon quietly drop the contractual terms in the United States.

But sellers have since reported that Amazon is reaching the same ends through different means. Some sellers recently sued Amazon in a class action over its policies, alleging, "Absent Amazon's anticompetitive price policies, third-party sellers would have set a lower price on a platform with lower fees than Amazon or an even lower price on the seller's own website." This control over prices is just one of countless examples of Amazon's monopoly power.

Like Amazon, direct evidence shows that Facebook has monopoly power—chapter 3 will give examples of how it excludes rivals. But Facebook argues it doesn't have monopoly power, focusing on indirect evidence and wrongly defining the market as "all social media." All social media platforms are not substitutes for Facebook: you can't see baby pictures on LinkedIn, and you probably can't keep in touch with Grandma on Twitter. When Facebook users were mad about how the company had allowed their data to be used for Russian propaganda in the 2016 U.S. presidential election, many switched to Instagram—but Facebook had already bought its top substitute. Disgruntled users, however, did not switch to LinkedIn in any significant number. This means LinkedIn does not apply competitive pressure to Facebook, and LinkedIn should not be included in the market definition that is relevant for antitrust law.

People who question whether Facebook is a monopoly often ask me, "Can't people just stop using Facebook altogether?" Well, sure. It would be harder for some people, like business owners whose potential customers spend a lot of their time on Facebook or Instagram, or members of communities that treat Facebook, Instagram, and WhatsApp as primary means of communication. Personally, whenever I've launched a new venture or idea that I want to reach people, creating a Facebook page seemed a necessity, not an option. But the ability to #DeleteFacebook doesn't make Facebook any less of a monopoly. A company does not have to offer a mandatory product to have monopoly power. Anyone could decide to stop drinking milk, for example, but that doesn't mean there's no such thing as a milk monopoly.

Each tech giant provides useful, high-quality services to some portions of the public. But these benefits do not make monopolization okay, nor do they justify the exploitation of monopoly business models in ways that harm entrepreneurs, innovators, independent business owners, and employees. A factory that expels toxic smoke into the air can make a product that offers benefits to consumers, but that doesn't make pollution legal. Offering some benefits to consumers does not give Google, Amazon, Facebook, and Apple a free pass to break our antitrust laws. That they innovated and created something of value doesn't mean we should let the giants stop others from doing the same.

THREE

MONOPOLIES LOWER YOUR PAY AND CRUSH THE AMERICAN DREAM

"Regarding your compensation,
The Company firmly believes 'less is more'."

MONOPOLIES DEVOUR THE FRUITS OF YOUR LABOR

If you live your daily life like many Americas, you're working your butt off. From dawn until dusk, you barely stop. When your alarm goes off in the morning you roll out of bed and grab your phone in a single swoop. You check your work email and immediately start stressing about everything you need to do. You end your day as you began it, looking at your phone. You remind yourself to do all the things tomorrow that you didn't get to today and vow to do better. At the same time, you beat yourself up for not "living your best life" nor getting the rest and exercise your worn-out body needs.

The work-life balance gurus say you'd work smarter if you slowed down, but you can't seem to take your foot off the pedal. Deep down you're scared. What would happen if you ignored your work email? Would you get fired? Could you support yourself or your family? Life feels like a race you're not winning, but you can't stop running. You might wonder if you'll ever be able to retire.

If you were privileged enough to experience a comfortable middle-class existence when you were growing up, you may long to provide the same comfort for yourself or your family. But covering the bills requires a relentless pace of work, and you feel like the rug could be pulled out from under you at any time. What the hell happened?

Work Got Greedy Because It Could

At the same time that prices have gone up across the board, employee pay has flatlined. No wonder you feel squeezed. Corporate profit margins have doubled from around 20 percent in the 1980s to around 40 percent in 2017, while reduced competition from decades of mergers allowed corporations to extract wealth from consumers through higher prices. But corporations' extra dough has not gone to their employees.

Employee pay has been stagnating for forty years. From 1973 to 2014, most employees' pay went up only 9 percent when adjusted for inflation, a rate of 0.2 percent a year. Yet during that time productivity—the amount of economic output that results from an average hour of work—rose 72 percent, a rate of 1.33 percent a year, according to the Economic Policy Institute. Employees' share of the value of goods and services produced in America's economy (known as the gross domestic product, or GDP) has plummeted since the 1980s. The graph below plots the ratio of employees' pay over the value that was added for all industries, and it isn't pretty. Employees are getting a smaller and smaller cut of the value they help create.

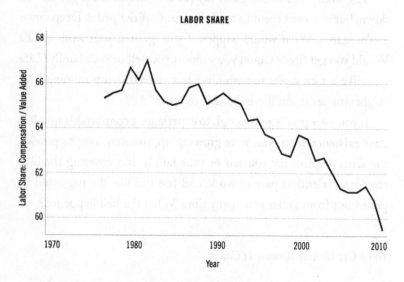

LABOR SHARE

Source: Emmanuel Saez and Gabriel Zucman, 2016. "Wealth Inequality in the United States since 1913: Evidence from Capitalized Income Tax Data," *The Quarterly Journal of Economics* 131(2), pages 519–578.

CEO pay at top firms, in contrast, has grown 940 percent since 1978. In 2018, CEOs were paid an average of $17.2 million, which is 278 times what employees were paid. Compare that to 1965, when CEOs made 20 times more than employees, or even 1989, when they made 58 times employees' pay. With CEOs being compensated predominantly with stock, they share in the monopoly gains that result from higher consumer prices and lower employee pay. As employees have become more productive, the gains have gone straight to corporate shareholders' and CEOs' pockets. This decline in employees' cut of the value they create, combined with rising prices under monopoly rule, is a main reason why your parents' generation probably had it easier than you do—you're not imagining it.

What changed since the 1980s that allowed corporations to share less of their gains with their employees? For one, competition for employees withered, as monopolies, duopolies, and oligopolies took over our economy. In most industries, your employer doesn't have to compete with a lot of other companies to hire or keep you because few companies are left after decades of anticompetitive mergers and behavior. With weak competition, employers can work you to the bone, taking a larger and larger percentage of the value you add. Work is greedy and more demanding because it can be.

Factors like globalization and technological change have also impacted pay, as has corporations' increased focus on short-term shareholder profits at the expense of all else. But the consolidation of our economy under the control of monopolies is a significant contributor to Americans' pay flatlining.

Let's apply the simple economics principle of supply and demand: Your labor is a service in limited supply—the more buyers you have for your labor, the higher the price you can charge for it. When our economy is highly concentrated, the number of buyers for your labor is lower than if each industry included dozens of potential employers (as many did in the past). Fewer buyers means you get paid less.

Companies can pay their employees meagerly without having to worry about losing them to competitors. One economic study found a 17 percent decline in wages when a labor market goes from the 25th percentile to the 75th percentile in concentration. It also found that labor markets across the country are highly concentrated on average. Such concentration "impairs the transmission of productivity growth into wage increases," found another study. In other words, monopoly rule means employees don't get paid more even when they're more productive.

Monopoly means a single seller has all the power, and "monopsony" is the term used for the other side of the coin, buyer power. Employers are the buyers, and monopsony power over labor means one or a few employers have outsized power over employees. Employees get lower pay or worse employment conditions than they'd have if lots of employees were competing to hire and retain them.

Given what we learned in chapter 2 about how monopolies are ruling health care, you won't be surprised to learn that health care employees are getting screwed over in their pay because of monopsony power. Take nurses. Even before COVID-19, nurses were in high demand, as many localities have a shortage of qualified nurses. The pandemic showed nurses are highly valuable, desperately needed, and vastly underpaid. In a competitive labor market, a shortage of nurses would mean higher pay. But most local health care markets have become monopolies or oligopolies, so nurses have seen their wages depressed. Average pay for a nurse is $68,000, but economists estimate that "a true competitive wage for a nurse would be at least $90,000, possibly as much as $200,000."

With high concentration being the nationwide norm, you may be getting robbed, too. Fewer companies in each industry decreases your mobility as an employee, that is, your ability to switch jobs. With less mobility, you have less power to bargain for higher pay. A common way that employees get raises is by receiving a competing offer from another employer and giving their current employer a choice: pay me more or lose me to the competition. But evidence shows employees are getting fewer offers to work at other companies, and this decline has contributed to stagnating pay. The "labor markets where mobility has decreased the most are the ones where earnings have as well," finds a Roosevelt Institute study.

Lower competition for employees is hitting Millennials and Gen-X hardest. The Great Recession of the late 2000s took a toll on Millennials' financial well-being through layoffs and unemployment for those already in the workforce, while drying up job openings for those about to enter it. Yet the worst part of the recession for Millennials may have been that it decreased the number of companies competing for their services. Boomers were less affected, in part because they change jobs less often. The negative consequences for younger generations' earnings are not abating and "appear to be increasing in magnitude over time," wrote Kevin Rinz, author of a 2019 study finding that the Great Recession's effects on competition for employees has led to a sustained loss of earnings for Millennials and Gen-X. This means the reduction of competition caused by the recession may actually be more harmful to younger workers over time than its job losses.

At time of writing, the first rounds of government bailouts in the COVID-19 crisis have repeated the government's mistakes of the Great Recession, sending millions of dollars to companies that are "too big to fail," without extending enough relief to small and mid-sized companies. Unless the government changes course, the pandemic will further concentrate our economy and have long-lasting damaging effects on Americans' earnings.

Monopolies reduce employees' pay in another way. If you are an employee of a company that supplies a product or a service to a monopolist or an oligopolist, you likely get paid less than you'd make if your employer could sell its offerings to more buyers. Monopolies can pay their suppliers low prices and demand they do business on unfair terms because their suppliers don't have other choices. When monopolies squeeze your employer, your employer squeezes you. The classic example is Walmart, which decimated the profit margins of consumer product brands, driving those brands to cut costs by reducing employees' pay. "Concentration can also affect workers further up the supply chain, as powerful buyers squeeze suppliers who in turn seek to reduce costs by holding down wages," explains Sandeep Vaheesan of the Open Markets Institute.

As monopoly rule squeezes you—charging you higher prices, reducing your pay, and, as we'll discuss below, working you to the bone—our society has become obsessed with "self-care." But this individualistic focus obscures the fact that we are getting screwed systemically. No matter how hard we try to handle stress in our own lives, our monopolized economy is working against us.

Mergers Kill Jobs

Mergers are a main reason we're in this monopoly mess, where few companies in each industry are competing to employ us. Mergers have skyrocketed since the time of the middle-class Boomers' comfortable existence, and mergers eliminate jobs. Take the 2013 merger of Kraft and Heinz, which led to 10,000 workers being laid off; the 2005 merger of Procter & Gamble and Gillette, which was estimated to result in 6,000 job losses; or the 2019 merger of Viacom and CBS, which led to layoffs within a single week and several rounds of ongoing layoffs. The American Airlines merger with US Airways that we talked about in chapter 1 didn't just lead to higher baggage fees for all of us; it also made people lose their jobs.

Under modern antitrust doctrine, firing workers is considered a good thing, and job losses weigh in favor of enforcers approving a merger! The idea is that when two companies merge, they can fire the workers who are doing the same job at each separate company. The merged company will thus save money by eliminating these duplicative workers and will operate more efficiently. The merged company will pass on these cost savings to consumers as lower prices, so says the Chicago School of Economics, making firing employees "efficient" and good for competition. But this promise—that mergers will lead to lower prices for consumers—hasn't panned out, as we saw in chapter 1.

Whether firings are efficient even under Chicago School standards is questionable, since laying off workers leads to loss of institutional knowledge and takes a hit on the morale of employees who remain. The failure rate of mergers and acquisitions ranges from 70 to 90 percent, according to studies. But even if merger-related firings were efficient, they still don't lead to lower prices for consumers.

The Chicago School's gutting of antitrust law has allowed thousands of anticompetitive mergers to go through, and countless anticompetitive acts to go unprosecuted, with the ultimate effect of both higher prices and lower pay for all. "Consumer welfare" has been an effective pretense for neutering the antitrust laws and ensuring that corporate power grows unfettered.

Labor economists suggest that the government's merger reviews should scrutinize whether deals would reduce competition for employees, instead of viewing firings as cost savings that are good for competition. In the past antitrust enforcers have blocked mergers because the deals would decrease the prices paid to suppliers of goods. Enforcers should do the same when mergers would lower the prices paid to suppliers of labor. When mergers kill jobs or lower employees' pay below competitive levels, these effects are bad for competition—not good for it!

Senator Sherman was concerned not only about concentrated power and freedom; he was also concerned about Americans earning competitive pay. In promoting his anti-monopoly law, Sherman explained that monopoly "commands the price of labor without fear of strikes, for in its field it allows no competitors."

Working for the Monopoly Man

Less competition for your labor doesn't just mean lower pay; it also means you'll have worse working conditions and crappier benefits. Just as when consumers lack alternatives and can't vote with their feet, monopolies can screw them over, the same is even more true for employees. Employees already have lower bargaining power than their employers, because they typically need their jobs more than their employers need them, and switching jobs is not easy to do even under the best of circumstances. But when you have fewer options of companies to hire you, you have even less bargaining power. Employers can take, take, take from you, working you to the bone, without fear of losing you to the competition.

Employee bargaining power affects things like health and retirement benefits, working hours, family leave, and even harassment or discrimination at work. Compared to most employees today, workers in the 1980s had a higher number of possible employers. It made business sense for employers to keep their employees happy, with a sane workday, good health benefits (which was also easier to do because monopolies didn't rule health care), and even pensions that allowed for secure retirement.

Labor unions have traditionally been a way for employees to join together to have more bargaining power against employers for better pay and better terms of employment. But as corporations have consolidated power, labor union membership simultaneously has dropped to the lowest it's been since 1964, when the Bureau of Labor began reporting the data. "In contrast to the 1950s when roughly a third of wage and salary workers were unionized, only a small percentage of workers are members of labor unions today—around one in ten among all workers, and one in sixteen among workers in the private sector," wrote Vaheesan.

Anti-labor policy is largely the reason for this decline, but monopolies actively fight unionization as well. "While Amazon has been diligently working to shut down any prospect of its workers unionizing, investigative journalists and activists have uncovered widespread abuses of workers," writes Michael Sainato for the *Guardian*. After Amazon warehouse employee Christian Smalls spoke out about dangerous risks of COVID-19 exposure at work at the start of the pandemic, Amazon fired him. His termination set off worker protests and an investigation from the New York attorney general for potential violation of whistle-blower laws. Meanwhile *VICE News* published leaked notes from an internal meeting of Amazon leadership, in which an executive called Smalls "not smart or articulate" and strategized to make him "the face of the entire union/organizing movement." Amazon workers continued to protest unsafe conditions during the pandemic, as the virus spread to over fifty warehouses, even painting a "Protect Amazon Workers" mural in front of Jeff Bezos's Washington, D.C., residence at the end of April. Just over two weeks earlier, on April 14, Jeff Bezos grew an estimated $6.4 billion richer when Amazon's stocks jumped due to increased demand during the pandemic.

Google, too, has been accused of wrongful termination and fighting unionization. At the end of 2019, five Google engineers filed complaints with the National Labor Relations Board (NLRB) accusing Google of illegally firing them for engaging in union-organizing activity. In a separate ruling in December 2019, the NLRB showed hostility to unions and ruled that employers may prohibit employees from using company email for union-organizing purposes, overruling its own 2014 decision that allowed such email use. Google had urged the NLRB to make this change. With the NLRB siding with Google, employees face an uphill battle in their quest to gain bargaining power against the tech giant. In a labor market that's not competitive, unions are needed now more than ever, for employees of all kinds, to bargain for fair pay and quality of life. But corporate giants' political power is making union organizing even harder.

More Than 35 Million Employees Aren't Allowed to Compete

On top of employees lacking bargaining power, employers are imposing contractual terms that take away what little power employees have left. At least 35 million employees are subject to noncompete clauses that prohibit them from leaving to work for a competitor. A rationale behind noncompetes is to stop employees from handing trade secrets over to a competitor, but noncompete clauses are used for employees who don't even have access to such valuable information, like fast-food workers. Noncompete clauses trap employees in their jobs, and in chapter 7 we'll examine how women and people of color are disparately impacted by these clauses.

FTC commissioner Rohit Chopra has written that the noncompete clause "dries up opportunities for employees to find better jobs using their skills and takes away their bargaining leverage in negotiations for advancement." Chopra added that these noncompete clauses also harm the economy as a whole because they hurt employees' ability to switch to the best-fitting jobs where they'd be most productive.

The Open Markets Institute, joined by a broad coalition of organizations, has petitioned the FTC to prohibit the use of noncompete clauses as an unfair method of competition. After all, the clauses have "noncompete" right in the name! Noncompete clauses lead to lower pay and lower rates of entrepreneurship, as employees are barred from striking out on their own in their industry.

Bosses Collude Against Employees

When Steve Jobs, then the CEO of Apple, learned in 2007 that a Google employee had attempted to recruit an Apple engineer, he emailed the CEO of Google at the time, Eric Schmidt. "I would be very pleased if your recruiting department would stop doing this," Jobs wrote. Schmidt forwarded Jobs's email internally, asking, "Can you get this stopped and let me know why this is happening?" The Google staffing director responded that the employee who contacted the Apple engineer would be fired within the hour, adding, "Please extend my apologies as appropriate to Steve Jobs."

In chapter 1, we talked about how the US Airways and American Airlines merger would reduce the number of airlines competing with each other and make it easier for airlines to collude to charge you higher fees. The same collusion happens in the labor market. The fewer companies in your industry, the easier it is for them to collude to keep your pay down. Such collusion occurs across the professional spectrum. Nurses have sued hospitals across the country for conspiring to keep their pay low, and shepherds have sued ranchers for conspiring to depress their wages. You'd think that tech employees would be guaranteed competitive pay, since demand for their skills far exceeds the trained workers available. Yet even they got screwed by their bosses' anticompetitive tactics.

Beginning around 2005, Apple, Google, Intel, and other major tech companies began agreeing not to recruit each other's employees. The DOJ investigated and concluded in 2010 that the companies had entered into illegal agreements that "interfered with the proper functioning of the price-setting mechanism that otherwise would have prevailed in competition for employees." The penalty that the Obama administration DOJ doled out, however, for this most serious, often criminally prosecuted, type of antitrust offense—collusion in violation of Sherman Act Section 1—was a slap on the wrist: don't do it again. The settlement prohibited the conspirators from breaking the law in the future, which is not a punishment at all. The companies had always been prohibited from breaking the law!

Private attorneys stepped in and brought class-action lawsuits against the colluding tech companies. The plaintiffs were able to overcome the procedural obstacles that courts have erected to antitrust class actions, a feat that defies odds. The court filings discussed a 2007 message from then–Intel CEO Paul Otellini that read: "Let me clarify. We have nothing signed." He added, "We have a handshake 'no recruit' between Eric and myself. I would not like this broadly known." Collusion among employers is often done in secret. On the rare occasions when employers are found out, enforcers need to bring the full weight of antitrust law to bear and dole out penalties that make engaging in such illegal behavior painful and unprofitable. The

DOJ settled its case for zero dollars, while the private class actions settled for $435 million.

Creators and Artists Get Robbed

If tech workers have it bad, the situation for creatives is much worse. "The middle class has been almost obliterated now," Helienne Lindvall, chair of the Songwriter Committee and board director at the Ivors Academy, a professional association for music writers in Europe, told me. These are "really desperate times for songwriters," she said. I have heard this same lament from artists worldwide.

"Starving artists" have always had a tough time making a living, but artists today face challenges they didn't encounter in the past. Artists and creators lack bargaining power against tech platforms that turn a blind eye to theft of their work or pay artists so little they're nearly stealing their work anyway. Google's YouTube pays "$0.0006 per stream to unsigned artists, and a fraction more to those with a record deal," writes competition journalist Ron Knox in *Global Competition Review*. To earn a month's worth of minimum wages, "artists would need their music to be streamed 2.4 million times."

YouTube pays a tiny portion of what other streaming services pay but accounts for nearly half of all digital music streams, so artists have little choice but to deal with YouTube on its terms. That YouTube has the power to set the price it wants to pay is evidence of its monopsony power.

Artists have resorted to using their music to promote their live shows and merchandise, which actually pay, but this option doesn't work for nonperforming songwriters (nor are live shows an option for artists during a pandemic). In Europe, songwriters get a small portion of the amount YouTube pays to recording artists per stream of their song. Songwriters are paid differently in the United States, where there's a statutory rate for songwriters to get paid. The rate was recently raised after years of stagnation, but Google, Spotify, Amazon, and Pandora have appealed the decision.

When Helienne first started out as a songwriter in 2000, she got a small advance from a publisher that was enough to sustain her, even though the publisher had no guarantee she'd make money. "My publisher took a risk in me," Helienne said. Advances are essential for songwriters to make ends meet because they don't get paid until after their songs are made and released. But now artists usually have to be proven to get advances because music publishers are getting squeezed by YouTube, too. Unlike publishers, YouTube takes its cut from musicians and songwriters without investing in their work. Songwriters put in the work and bear the risks, and then tech platforms collect a large part of the pay.

To make a living, songwriters now depend on brand partnerships or placing their songs in commercials or movies, where at least they can negotiate the rate. But this constraint means songwriters have to make music that's palatable for brands. And to make any decent money from monopoly platforms, artists have to make their music palatable to the widest range of people possible. Only hitmakers can survive. A small loyal following can't sustain artists who want to take risks or create interesting art that may not be easily accepted by the masses. Music is losing its political role of social critique.

Internet content of all kinds is molded to maximize its chances of ranking in Google's monopoly search engine, with an entire industry called search engine optimization dedicated to this effort. In music, the streaming business model means songs have to be shorter. In the first five seconds, a song has to grab people with a hook or they skip to the next free song. The album is almost over, with musicians releasing individual songs instead that they hope can gain online attention.

Traditional gatekeepers like record labels have had too much power and have been far from ideal, but writers and artists have even less say when it comes to distribution by platform monopolists.

Musicians can't refuse to be on YouTube because of its dominant share of the market and because musicians' work ends up on YouTube whether they put it there or not. Google has fought copyright laws worldwide in court and through lobbying, as creators—from musicians, to authors, to journalists—seek to have their work protected from being incorporated into products like Google News, Google Books, and Google Search. Copyright protection runs counter to Google's highly lucrative business model of showing people ads and collecting their data while they consume content created by others.

The current legal framework in the United States puts the onus on music artists to vigilantly guard against infringement on their work, not the platforms. But as soon as artists take songs down, the songs often just go right up again.

The digital age is supposedly a great time to be a creator. Anyone can just deliver their art to the world, without having to get through traditional gatekeepers. Kids want to be professional YouTubers when they grow up, and some people have made a great living doing just this. But don't let your kid drop out of school to film themselves playing video games just yet! A 2018 study showed that 96.5 percent of all YouTubers won't make enough money off advertising to crack the U.S. poverty line. In contrast, YouTube's net advertising revenues amounted to $15.1 billion in 2019. Google rakes in billions of dollars generated by the labor of creators of all kinds.

Tech platforms also adjust their user interfaces to steer customers to subscribe to their own unlimited offerings (which allow maximum revenue extraction from artists) rather than to purchase the art from individual artists (which still allows platforms to take a cut). One day I was trying to buy a song from an artist using my iPhone, but I kept finding myself steered to subscribe to Apple Music. Later that same day, I was trying to buy an individual book that was only available on Amazon, but Amazon kept channeling me to their subscription service, Kindle Unlimited. The pushes and nudges that platforms give to manipulate our behavior are called "dark patterns." These particular dark patterns are all about channeling the maximum amount of profits to the platform instead of the artist.

Digitization has helped YouTube frame their ads and surveillance around the work of others, work that used to be tangible, not digital. I'm a child of the 1980s, when buying an album was a big deal. Stores gave us clear visual cues that music wasn't to be stolen—cassette tapes were kept in long plastic anti-theft contraptions. The checkout clerk had a tool to unlock the device and liberate the cassette. I remember saving up my allowance to buy my first album. I headed off to Kmart with my family to buy Olivia Newton John's *Physical*, but my older brother convinced me to get Men at Work's *Business as Usual* instead. I immediately had buyer's remorse, but regardless of which album I chose, I fully expected that a good chunk of my hard-earned allowance money was going to the artist whose music I was buying.

I'm not suggesting we go back to the days of cassette tapes, but I am suggesting that we loosen the power of dominant gatekeepers like YouTube. If competition existed, musicians could say no to YouTube and platforms would have to compete to list musicians' songs by compensating them appropriately. Weakened monopoly power would translate to weakened political power and less influence over copyright law. Antitrust enforcement is more important than ever to make sure creators and makers of all kinds reap the fruits of their labor.

Musicians' and artists' organizations agree, and they have made antitrust enforcement a top priority. The Future of Music Coalition wrote in 2019, "Musicians have experienced ownership consolidation in nearly every part of our industry and in adjacent industries, and it interferes with our ability to reach audiences and be fairly compensated for their creativity and labor." Thus it's time for "fresh thinking and revitalized anti-trust enforcement at the Federal Trade Commission and Dept of Justice."

If today's robber barons are decimating the earnings of employees and creators, perhaps the best path to financial success is through entrepreneurship, you might think. But even entrepreneurs aren't safe from monopolists' tentacles.

MONOPOLIES CRUSH THE AMERICAN DREAM

Innovation Graveyards

In the early 1990s, Lillian Salerno and her business partner, Thomas Shaw, wanted to help people during the AIDS crisis. Lillian's friend was dying from HIV, and a twenty-four-year-old woman in her and Thomas's office contracted HIV from a boyfriend who was an injection drug user. So Lillian and Thomas called up the National Institutes of Health (NIH) and asked how they could make a difference. In Lillian's words, the NIH told her: "You know, we've got a real problem. The standard disposable syringe is a bad device in an AIDS epidemic because people reuse syringes, and nurses are frightened to treat AIDS patients because they are worried about contracting HIV. And the biggest manufacturer—Becton, Dickinson—they have no one working on this."

Thomas, a civil and structural engineer, bought a bunch of syringes from the local pharmacy and started throwing them at a dartboard to test them out. Lillian and Thomas began working with the county hospital in Dallas, Texas, that at that time had a staggering three full floors of HIV-positive patients. If nurses were scared to treat AIDS patients, Lillian and Thomas then asked them what they wanted from a syringe. Over a four-year period, Thomas invented a retractable syringe that would protect nurses from accidental needle sticks. But as Lillian explains it, their small company, Retractable Technologies Inc. (RTI), couldn't get its syringe into hospitals because a huge corporation,

Becton, Dickinson & Company, controlled more than 80 percent of the syringe market and blocked RTI's lifesaving devices at every turn.

Lillian tried to sell RTI's retractable syringes, which she says nurses overwhelmingly preferred to standard syringes, to hospitals and clinics. But she was dumbfounded that so many facilities were in long-term sole-supply contracts with Becton, Dickinson.

Lillian, an attorney, went to D.C. to ask the antitrust agencies for help. But because of Chicago School thinking, the agencies told her, in Lillian's words: "Lillian, it's about pricing. . . . We need these guys who are real big. They make a lot of stuff and we can get our costs down." Lillian would respond, "At the expense of who? Of the nurses who are treating HIV patients? Or the fourteen-year-old . . . who now has HIV instead of just being a drug addict?"

When antitrust enforcers and lawmakers failed to act, Lillian and Thomas took matters into their own hands. RTI sued Becton, Dickinson in 2001 for unfair competition. Becton settled the case for $100 million in 2004. But Becton continued to use anticompetitive tactics, so RTI sued Becton again in 2007. After a trial, the jury found that Becton had illegally attempted to monopolize the safety syringe market. The jury found that Becton engaged in false advertising that disparaged RTI's syringes and praised its own, including an untruthful claim that Becton's syringes had the "World's Sharpest Needle." An internal document presented at trial showed that Becton viewed this false claim as necessary to avoid losing market share, and to preserve the "10–30% price premium" that Becton enjoyed over the competition.

The jury awarded RTI $113 million in damages. That amount was then tripled—drafters of the Sherman Act thought deterring antitrust violations was so important that all damages must be multiplied by three.

Lillian and Thomas spent the better part of more than twenty years mired in litigation to try to bring their syringe to market, asking for help from their congressional delegations, the FTC, and the DOJ. "We've been denied every time," said Lillian.

The biggest harm of Becton's illegal behavior, however, was not revenue RTI lost because of illegal monopolization. Becton's "attempted monopolization of the safety syringe market injured the public by limiting the marketplace's access to retractable syringes," said the court, noting that Becton's practices limited innovation. "Innovation and market competition go hand-in-hand, and antitrust laws protect both," said the judge.

Health care monopolies, then, are not only gouging you on price. They're also creating innovation graveyards, depriving you and your family of the best medical solutions that the smartest minds, like Lillian and Thomas, have to offer. Allowing giants to rule based on a myth of low pricing—Becton's internal documents showed they charged higher prices—is not good for consumers. What's best for consumers and innovation is merit-based competition.

Like Lillian and Thomas, entrepreneurs across America are getting crushed by monopolies that have the power to shut them out of markets, copy their innovations, and compete unfairly. Investors know this and won't fund new ideas that tread on monopolists' turf. Even if you never aspired to entrepreneurship, all this dream-killing sucks for you, too. On top of making less money because fewer companies can get off the ground and compete to hire you, you miss out on innovation that would make your life better. You don't know it because these innovations never see the light of day.

When I was a journalist, I once investigated a merger of two companies that made cable boxes for TV. I was stunned to learn that cable engineers had been creating highly innovative cable boxes for years, but cable companies refused to roll them out! The high-tech boxes collected dust in innovation graveyards because cable companies knew they'd have to provide the boxes to customers once word got out of the improved version, and the cost of providing new higher-tech boxes to their customers would cut into their profit margins. Cable companies had a gravy train going, charging customers excessive monthly rental fees for cable boxes that looked like they were built in the 1960s. No need to invest in improving the product when there's so little competition!

Consumers only benefited from new innovative cable boxes when Netflix came along and competed against cable. Without competition, new innovations—from syringes that save lives to high-tech cable boxes that make lives just a little bit better—meet untimely deaths.

Dynamism Lost

With giant corporations across the country squashing innovators like Lillian and Thomas, entrepreneurship has plummeted. While our society has heralded the young geniuses who dropped out of college to build in their garages what have since become tech giants, they have in turn shut out opportunities for other aspiring entrepreneurs. Google, Apple, and Amazon are more than twenty years old, Facebook is more than fifteen years old, and all four have dominated their respective arenas for more than a decade.

Big Tech is only the beginning, and entrepreneurship is suffering across the economy. The share of employment accounted for by new companies has dropped by almost 30 percent over the last thirty years. And the share of companies less than a year old has declined by almost a half since 1980. Such a decline hurts both job creation and innovation.

"[T]he great burst of business activity in the 1980s and '90s was to a significant extent the result of actions taken by the federal government during previous decades of anti-trust enforcement," write Barry

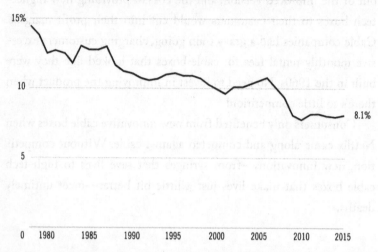

Share of Companies Less Than a Year Old in the United States

Source: Census Bureau; Ben Casselman, "A Start-Up Slump is a Drag on the Economy. Big Business May Be to Blame," *New York Times*, September 20, 2017.

Lynn and Phillip Longman of Open Markets Institute. So when antitrust went off the rails, starting in the early 1980s, the ability for future generations to succeed as entrepreneurs took a hit. A main goal of antitrust law is to stop established companies from shutting out entrepreneurs and smaller companies with new ideas. If entrepreneurs bring their hard work and the best ideas, products, and services forward, an open and freely competitive market should reward them with success and prosperity. This is the American dream.

As late Supreme Court justice Thurgood Marshall once wrote, the antitrust laws "are as important to the preservation of economic freedom and our free-enterprise system as the Bill of Rights is to the protection of our fundamental personal freedoms." He continued, "And the freedom guaranteed each and every business, no matter how small, is the freedom to compete—to assert with vigor, imagination, devotion, and ingenuity whatever economic muscle it can muster."

Squashing entrepreneurs by monopolizing markets is not just a terrible mess we've found ourselves in—it's illegal! We can begin to invigorate the American dream and help restore the engine of our economy if we strongly enforce the antitrust laws again.

Technological change can explain the decline of new businesses in some industries, like manufacturing and physical retail stores, but entrepreneurship in the tech sector has also declined. The number of businesses that are not at the mercy of Big Tech is declining every day, as the giants continue to expand into, or become gatekeepers for, almost all industries—including yours, most likely.

Tech Monopolies Prey on Entrepreneurs

The tech giants are following Microsoft's playbook, leveraging what I call "platform privilege"—the incentive and ability to favor their own goods and services over those of competitors that depend on their platforms. In antitrust speak, this behavior could also be called "monopoly leveraging," which means using monopoly power in an anticompetitive manner to create a dangerous probability of monopolizing a second market, another type of antitrust case that the Chicago School has made harder to win. Platform privilege means that competitors don't get a fair shot because the platform monopolists get to both play the game and control it, too.

Because Google, Amazon, Facebook, and Apple each have monopoly power and engage in exclusionary conduct to acquire or maintain that power, I believe that each platform is illegally monopolizing in violation of Section 2 of the Sherman Act. This is bad for every entrepreneur—bad for those who must rely on their services, and bad for those who create an innovative product or service only to see it stolen from them or choked off in favor of a product owned by the platforms. This distorted playing field strikes at the heart of the American dream, and it deprives consumers of the choice, innovation, and quality that come from real competition. Companies of all sizes can get decimated at the will of the kings of tech, so your livelihood is at risk even if you're an employee.

Google's Don't Be Evil

Google is not a single monopoly, but rather has monopolies in multiple markets. Google Search accounts for approximately 92 percent of internet search globally, and Google Android accounts for more than 85 percent of the world's smartphones. In 2019, Google's ad revenue alone was nearly $135 billion. Google has seven products with more than a billion users each:

1. Search
2. Android
3. Chrome
4. YouTube
5. Maps
6. Gmail
7. Google Play

Just as Microsoft used its monopoly in PC operating systems to kick Netscape out of the competition in internet browsers, Google used its monopoly power in mobile operating systems to kick out entrepreneurial makers of mobile apps. The European Commission fined Google $5 billion in July 2017 for abusing its dominance—the European equivalent of monopolization—by requiring phone makers using Android, with its 80 percent market share in Europe, to pre-install Google's apps, like Google Search, Chrome, Gmail, YouTube, and Maps. The commission ordered Google to stop its anticompetitive contracts in Europe and to offer consumers a choice of what apps are installed on their phones, and Google has appealed.

Just like the PC makers dealing with Microsoft, phone makers

didn't have the power to disobey Google's anticompetitive requirements because they lacked a viable alternative for an operating system.
Google's anticompetitive exclusion of competition allowed Google
to extend its monopoly power in Search and Chrome on computer
desktops into phones as the world went mobile. Entrepreneurs who
wanted to challenge any of a suite of Google apps didn't have a shot
at getting pre-installed in 85 percent of the world's phones.

Android users could still install competing apps after they got
their phones, but users don't tend to do that when they already have
the same type of app on their phone, a phenomenon known as default
bias. Default bias is so powerful that Google paid Apple $12 billion
in 2019, according to Goldman Sachs estimates, to be the default
search engine on Apple devices, like iPhones, iPads, Apple Watches,
and Macs.

Search is what Google is most known for, and its monopoly in
this area has given it control over the internet itself, disadvantaging
entrepreneurs and creators of all stripes.

At a House Judiciary Subcommittee hearing in summer of 2019,
Google was asked if it's true that less than 50 percent of total U.S.
mobile and desktop Google searches result in clicks to non-Google
websites, as research had shown. When Google's representative gave
an unclear answer, the subcommittee followed up with written questions that requested a "yes or no" answer and even provided check
boxes. Google ignored the "yes or no" instruction, and responded by
saying, among other things, that Google has "long sent large amounts
of traffic to other sites." But in the same letter, Google answered a
different follow-up question with a straightforward "no," making its
failure to answer this question with a "no" telling. The subcommittee
is still investigating the issue at time of writing. With over 90 percent
of search market share worldwide, sending such a large percentage of
traffic to its own sites amounts to Google colonizing the internet—
and the flow of information around the globe.

Google's control of internet traffic means nearly any entrepreneur could get crushed if Google decides to enter their market. Husband-and-wife pair Adam and Shivaun Raff, founders of a Britain-based service called Foundem that helps consumers compare products when shopping online, met this exact fate.

In 2017, eight years after the Raffs filed a complaint, the commission fined Google $2.7 billion for abuse of dominance, finding that Google buried its competitors in the comparison shopping market on page four, on average, of Google search results. The commission ordered Google to treat its competitors equally as it treats itself in search.

Google has made changes but the Raffs say Google is still not complying with the European Commission's requirement of equal treatment. Google has also been accused of prioritizing its own reviews, maps, images, and travel booking services in its search results, excluding competition in what are collectively called "vertical search" markets. Google has rejected claims that it uses its muscle to crush competitors, and has appealed the decision.

Google's platform privilege doesn't just destroy the dreams of entrepreneurs; it also means you are getting worse service and less innovation as a consumer. "The Commission is concerned that users do not necessarily see the most relevant results in response to queries—this is to the detriment of consumers and rival comparison shopping services, as well as stifling innovation," read a European Commission press release about the Google comparison shopping case. One study concluded that Google degraded its search quality results in order to prioritize its own services or content that keeps users on Google search pages.

And the requirement that entrepreneurs and businesses of all sizes pay Google to appear at the top of searches for their business name is effectively a tax, which wouldn't be necessary if Google consistently delivered the most relevant results. A small tech company called Basecamp pays upwards of $72,000 a year on Google ads just to be a top result when people search for its trademarked name. One of the few companies outspoken about Google's monopoly power, Basecamp runs the below ad copy:

> Basecamp.com | We don't want to run this ad. ⓘ
> [Ad] www.basecamp.com
>
> We're the #1 result, but this site lets companies advertise against us using our brand. So here we are. A small, independent co. forced to pay ransom to a giant tech company.

Back in the early 2010s, the United States also investigated Google for monopolization, but it did not take action. An FTC staff memo on the investigation that was mistakenly released and then obtained by the *Wall Street Journal* said that Google's "conduct has resulted—and will result—in real harm to consumers and to innovation in the online search and advertising markets." The staff recommended the FTC sue Google, but the FTC's Bureau of Economics, composed of economists trained in Chicago School ideology, had recommended against it. We don't know why the FTC dropped the case. Many also suspect that politics may have played a role, even though the FTC is supposed to be an independent agency.

A 2016 article written by David Dayen for the *Intercept* called "The Android Administration" detailed the close ties between the Obama administration and Google. "Google representatives attended White House meetings more than once a week, on average, from the beginning of Obama's presidency through October 2015," wrote Dayen. "Nearly 250 people have shuttled from government service to Google employment or vice versa over the course of his administration."

Six years after the FTC's initial Google Search investigation, Google's use of platform privilege has not subsided and has grown.

The FTC and DOJ, fifty-one states and territories, and the House Judiciary Antitrust Subcommittee are all investigating Google at the time of this writing.

Digital Advertising Is a Googlopoly

In 2007, Brian O'Kelley founded AppNexus, a software company that helped companies buy ads on the internet. His company was a huge success, valued at $1.2 billion in 2014. Then Google kicked AppNexus out of the game, prohibiting companies from buying ads on YouTube using outside software like theirs. Because of YouTube's monopoly power over video, O'Kelley could no longer offer customers access to the vast majority of online video advertising. "It's not a supply-and-demand problem. It's a 'You just broke our entire business' problem," O'Kelley told *Bloomberg*.

The European Commission has fined Google nearly $1.5 billion for abusing its dominance in the market for the brokering of online search advertising. Like the other two Commission decisions, Google has appealed.

Google has far-reaching monopoly power in digital advertising because it acquired every spoke of the ecosystem, while exercising platform privilege. In 2007, when Google bought DoubleClick, a marketplace for buying and selling digital advertising, the FTC did only a cursory investigation and cleared the deal. But one FTC Commissioner at the time, Pamela Jones Harbour, dissented. Her predictions about how the merger could harm competition and threaten privacy have since come true.

"I am convinced that the combination of Google and Double-Click has the potential to profoundly alter the twenty-first-century internet-based economy—in ways we can imagine, and in ways we cannot," wrote Jones Harbour in her dissenting statement. She argued the FTC should take a closer look and answer several questions, including whether any other companies will have the ability to compete meaningfully in the market after the merger. The deal has potential to "harm competition, and it also threatens privacy," she wrote. "By closing its investigation without imposing any conditions or other safeguards, the Commission is asking consumers to bear too much of the risk of both types of harm."

Twelve years after Jones Harbour's dissent, in 2019, Texas AG Ken Paxton spoke about Google's advertising dominance when he announced the 51 states and territories' investigation into Google. Paxton said, "They dominate the buyer side, the seller side, the auction side, and the video side with YouTube." If Google had not bought DoubleClick, and in 2009, Admob, the leading mobile advertising company, plus a slew of other adtech companies, things could have been different. These acquisitions violated Clayton Act Section 7's prohibition of acquisitions that may substantially lessen competition or tend to create a monopoly. Ignoring Jones Harbour's concerns and allowing Google to amass the monopoly power that lets it squash entrepreneurs was a choice, not an inevitability.

King Bezos and His Ever-Expanding Amazon Empire

Before COVID-19, Amazon accounted for roughly one out of every two dollars spent online. It counted an estimated 112 million Amazon Prime customers in the United States by December 2019. For perspective, America had almost 129 million households in 2019, with an estimated 12 percent of the U.S. population living in poverty. If most households have a single Prime account, then nearly all U.S. households above the poverty line are Prime members. In 2019, Prime members spent on average $1,400 on the platform. During the pandemic, demand for product delivery skyrocketed and undoubtedly drove these numbers even higher.

Amazon, too, is following the monopolist's playbook, picking and choosing which products consumers discover and determining which entrepreneurs and businesses get to compete on its platform. Amazon has become the infrastructure for brands and retailers to reach customers, giving it "the power to dictate the terms by which its competitors and suppliers operate, and to levy a kind of tax on their revenue," reads a 2016 report by the Institute for Local Self-Reliance. Even investors see that Amazon has monopoly power. "We believe there is a multi-trillion dollar monopoly hiding in plain sight," said Chamath Palihapitiya, founder of Social Capital, at the Sohn Investment Conference in May 2016. Palihapitiya also reportedly described Amazon Web Services, Amazon's cloud infrastructure service, as "a tax on the internet." Under monopoly rule, entrepreneurs don't just pay taxes to the government, they pay taxes to Big Tech.

Amazon does not merely control its marketplace. Amazon acts as a retailer, buying products at wholesale and selling them on its platform (those are the products that say "sold by Amazon," also called "first-party" products). It thereby pits itself against those small, mid-sized, and large businesses that sell products on Amazon.com (known as "marketplace sellers"). Amazon also acts as a brand, selling its own private label products, both "AmazonBasics" products and products under more than 400 Amazon house labels.

Every entrepreneur who sells on Amazon is both competing against the giant and dependent on it. Many brands and small- and mid-sized retailers have no choice but to sell on Amazon if they want to stay in business. No entrepreneur or businessperson wants to be dependent on their competitor, who can disadvantage them, take a cut of their profits, knock them out of the competition, or knock them off. That's not how the American dream is supposed to work.

Amazon leverages its platform privilege to pick and choose what markets it wants to dominate, markets like skin care (91 percent share of retail e-commerce as of the first quarter of 2018), batteries (97 percent share), or even golf (92 percent). They are "constantly looking to cut you out," a marketplace seller told me (who asked to remain anonymous, as nearly all do out of fear of retaliation), and "they've been locking the [product] categories down."

Amazon often justifies excluding competition on its platform as needed to police counterfeits. But one marketplace seller told me he was kicked off the platform under the guise of counterfeits, only for Amazon to turn to him for supply of the same supposedly counterfeit items. And David Barnett, the CEO of PopSockets, maker of PopGrips for phones, submitted testimony to Congress saying "on multiple occasions we found that Amazon Retail was itself sourcing counterfeit PopGrips and selling them alongside our authentic products." Amazon would only address the problem of counterfeit PopSockets on its platform in exchange for the company committing to spend nearly $2 million on retail marketing programs, said Barnett.

When Amazon doesn't kick the competition out entirely by prohibiting marketplace sellers from listing certain products and brands, it pulls a number of levers to distort competition in its favor. Amazon has given its own private label products and first-party products advantages over competitors in a number of ways, from elevating its own products to the top of Amazon search results, to giving itself premium advertising placement not available to others, to targeted marketing to Amazon customers based on data collected about them that only Amazon has, to exclusive customer reviews that competitors can't access. Sellers and brands cannot market to their Amazon.com customers, or know much about them, because Amazon controls the relationship with customers.

Whether Google puts its shopping competitor on page four of its search results or Amazon buries its brand or retailer competitors, the result is the same. The giants are taking their monopolies in one market and leveraging them to take over new markets that depend on their platforms, destroying competition itself. They claim monopolies for themselves in the secondary markets, while maintaining and growing their monopoly power in their primary markets. The platforms crush entrepreneurs and businesses of all sizes in the process. Employees of those businesses lose jobs or get paid less. And the platforms degrade the quality of their offerings to consumers, who expect to get the most relevant search results, not results that prioritize Amazon's or Google's profits.

As Amazon rolls out Alexa—in 100 million devices as of January 2019—it's creating an entirely new and extreme version of platform privilege. The problems of Amazon and Google putting themselves first will be way worse when voice search brings only one or a few search results. Forget about being on page four of Google search or the bottom of Amazon's search ranking; if an entrepreneur's product or business is not answer 1, 2, or 3 in voice, it will be as if they don't even exist.

On top of its opaque product ranking algorithm, Amazon also has control over the "buy box," the area to the right of the product description that contains the "Add to Cart" yellow button, which yields an estimated 90 percent of sales. "If you don't have the buy box," meaning the product you are selling isn't the one that will automatically be put in someone's cart when they click buy, "and you're the same price as Amazon, you get zero sales," one marketplace seller explained to me. "You basically have to liquidate your inventory." Amazon is picking the winners and losers of commerce, and the winner is . . . Amazon.

Most Amazon marketplace sellers do not consider other online marketplaces to be viable alternatives to switch to if Amazon imposes prices or terms they don't like, because Amazon accounts for such a large share of online spending. This means marketplace sellers lack bargaining power, and Amazon can dictate the terms of dealing, including the fees it takes, how long Amazon waits to pay them for their sales, and sellers' recourse (or lack thereof) when Amazon decides to prohibit them from selling a particular item.

Amazon has reportedly kicked entrepreneurs out of the competition in yet another way—by knocking off their ideas. Take the laptop stand innovator who one day discovered their sales had plummeted when Amazon knocked them off and then ranked above them in Amazon search results. Or the innovator who is pretty sure Amazon's Echo Show is the video intercom he had invented. Executives of Sonos, the speaker company, say Amazon and Google both stole their technology, but they could only risk suing one of the two. They sued Google in January 2020, alleging theft of intellectual property and antitrust violations. Sonos's lawsuit is bold given Google's tremendous litigation budget and ability to pick the winners and losers of the internet, which is why the giants can usually get away with stealing entrepreneurs' ideas. Google has responded by suing Sonos back.

You may wonder how Amazon making its own copies of products is different from the long-standing practice of stores making their own generic version of a product. When a retailer that is not dominant has its own brands, like a local grocery store, it doesn't violate the antitrust laws because it doesn't have monopoly power. Makers of the knockoff won't get decimated because there are many other stores available to sell their product. The types of conduct that are exclusionary and illegal when a firm has monopoly power are not illegal when a firm does not have monopoly power. (Remember, illegal monopolization = monopoly power + preventing rivals from competing based on merit.)

The tactics that Amazon employs to harm competition on its e-commerce platform are only the half of it. Amazon pulls the same types of anticompetitive levers in its cloud computing arm, Amazon Web Services (AWS), to co-opt innovations of others, a practice some call "strip-mining," reports the *New York Times*. "It has given an edge to its own services by making them more convenient to use, burying rival offerings and bundling discounts to make its products less expensive," writes Daisuke Wakabayashi. Yet just like Amazon's e-commerce marketplace, rivals don't feel like they have a choice to walk away from AWS because of its market power.

Knowledge Is Power

Amazon doesn't merely control the platform, it controls the data and can peek inside entrepreneurs' businesses. At time of writing, the DOJ, FTC, and House Judiciary Antitrust Subcommittee are investigating Amazon, with the European Commission undertaking a years-long investigation into whether Amazon uses data anticompetitively. Curious what the commission was likely to find when I was working as an investigative journalist in 2018, I spoke to former Amazon employees, who asked to remain anonymous due to concerns about their careers.

"Everybody has access to all the seller data," one former midlevel employee told me, which means Amazon employees can "data mine all the bestselling products and go make a private label." He went on to say, "I had access to a data warehouse as an employee at Amazon and could literally pull up any transaction from any seller. I had access to every single sale and was data mining the hell out of it for my job."

He then laid out a hypothetical of what he would do if he were proposing a new private label product at Amazon: "Let's say Amazon wants to get into folders. I would find all of the [listings] that are being sold on the website now. I'd pull up the history. I'd look at the volumes, price points. Regardless of whether it was sold wholesale or third party, I'd pull it all together. I'd look and see what's the hottest product. What's the hottest variation in color? We'd have these folders in these colors at this price point, and we'd go off and make it ourselves."

Another former Amazon manager told me, "If Amazon owns a product, it's almost impossible for anyone to compete. . . . Even if you make a better product, you can't market it to anyone—Amazon owns the customers, pricing, merchandising, marketing, and all the data to know which products to build, to whom, and when."

The most valuable data Amazon collects, according to this second source, is who has searched for a particular product in the past. This "consideration data" allows Amazon to "target their private label products with perfect precision," he explained.

Entrepreneurs and businesses of all sizes that don't have access to comparable data can hardly compete against Amazon. And because keeping their products off Amazon's platform is nearly impossible, these entrepreneurs are defenseless in handing over their proprietary business information to their competitor.

Price-Cutting to Squash Entrepreneurs

Yet another wrinkle Amazon presents is that it can eliminate entrepreneurial rivals easily because it can forgo revenue for as long as it takes. Amazon followed in Walmart's path of monopolization through a low pricing strategy that is not just about competing with rivals but rather aims to drive them from the market entirely, a tactic also used by the original robber barons. This practice is called predatory pricing and is illegal under the antitrust laws, but judges, under the influence of the Chicago School of Economics, have erected standards that made winning a predatory pricing case a losing proposition. Without enforcement, Amazon was able to evade antitrust laws, which antitrust scholar Lina Khan, then a law student, detailed in her influential 2017 paper "Amazon's Antitrust Paradox" for the *Yale Law Journal*.

Predatory pricing is quite effective at eliminating competition and was part of the DOJ's charges against Microsoft. "We are going to cut off their air supply. Everything they're selling, we're going to give away for free." These are the words of Paul Maritz, a former vice president at Microsoft, speaking to executives about Netscape, as quoted in the *New York Times*. "Microsoft invested hundreds of millions of dollars to develop, test, and promote Internet Explorer, a product which it distributes without separate charge," reads the DOJ's complaint.

Amazon has a well-documented track record of pricing below cost to drive out competition. One example of predatory pricing was Amazon's weakening of upstart competitor Diapers.com to force its 2010 sale to Amazon by pricing diapers at a loss. Brad Stone's book *The Everything Store* discusses the chain of events in detail, saying Amazon was on track to lose $100 million in three months on diapers alone before buying Diapers.com. By 2017, Amazon announced it was shutting down the company. Amazon's ability and willingness to sustain temporary losses, paired with lack of enforcement on predatory pricing, allowed it to eliminate an entrepreneurial challenger.

Amazon can use other arms of its business, like its highly profitable AWS cloud computing business, to fund any short-term losses that fortify its long-term dominance. Any company that makes or sells products now has to compete against a giant that can predatory-price them out of existence. We need to fix and enforce predatory pricing laws, otherwise no entrepreneur, brand, or retailer—no matter how efficient, innovative, or high quality—stands a chance at competing against Amazon, or any other monopoly.

Entrepreneurs Get "Sherlocked" by Apple

Relative to Google, Amazon, and Facebook, Apple seems like a warm and fuzzy monopolist. Its business model depends on selling luxury devices, and it has focused less on surveillance or controlling commerce than have its fellow tech giants. But Apple still has monopoly power because there's no real substitute for the App Store for iPhone owners, as we saw in chapter 1 with the 30 percent "Apple tax" on app sales. Apple's ability to control prices through tax-setting is direct evidence of its monopoly power.

As Apple grows into new lines of business, it has the same platform privilege as these other companies, to the detriment of entrepreneurs and businesses. For example, Apple has been accused of discriminating against Spotify and giving favorable treatment to Apple Music. Spotify recently sued Apple in Europe, arguing that Apple leveraged its platform to distort competition with unfair app store terms. The general counsel of Tile, a company that helps people find misplaced items using an app that pairs with physical "tiles," made similar claims when testifying before Congress in January 2020. Apple launched an app called FindMy, which is pre-installed and cannot be deleted, that competes directly with Tile. On top of its own app benefiting from default bias, Apple pulled a number of anticompetitive levers to disadvantage Tile, according to the testimony, including kicking Tile's products out of Apple's physical stores, making Tile harder to find on the iPhone, and making it difficult for iPhone users to activate their Tile devices, among other things. As Apple plans to enter more and more markets, including streaming TV, credit cards, and online gaming, Apple will increasingly play the game and control it, too.

When Apple introduces a new version of its iPhone operating system iOS or its macOS operating system, it often incorporates the features of the most popular apps that other innovators built, usually without paying them for it. Apple has been doing this for so long that developers have named the phenomenon getting "sherlocked." That term dates way back to the early 2000s, when Karelia Software developed a competitor to Apple's Sherlock search tool and named it Watson. Apple simply added Watson's functionality into the next version of Sherlock, killing its rival Watson.

Sherlocking is still alive and well today. In Apple's developer conference in spring of 2019, Matt Ronge, cofounder and CEO of Luna Display, which extends a Mac's display wirelessly to the iPad, learned that his innovation had been sherlocked. "Apple used us for market research," Ronge told *AppleInsider*. He described how Apple invited his company to demonstrate their product to Apple. "They expressed their support and told us to contact them if they could help (we emailed multiple times and never heard back)." Apple then bought dozens of Luna Display units when it launched in 2018. But in 2019 Apple launched its own version of Luna Display, called Sidecar.

Even if Luna Display tries to compete against Sidecar, competing against the platform is never a fair competition. Ronge explained to *AppleInsider* that Apple has access to functionalities that third-party developers don't, including technology that "prioritizes their Sidecar traffic over others." Ronge added, "This is certainly not a level playing field for developers."

Sure sounds a lot like what Microsoft did to Netscape. Monopoly power plus kicking rivals out of the game amounts to illegal monopolization. Just because Apple created the iPhone doesn't mean it should be allowed to take over all markets that depend on its platform without competing fair and square.

Entrepreneurs have no choice but to put up with this abuse, especially since Apple's App Store is the dominant revenue source for apps. Like Amazon for product innovators, Apple's App Store provides a must-have sales volume for entrepreneurs' businesses to survive. The U.S. Supreme Court in *Apple v. Pepper*, the case we talked about in chapter 1 that held consumers could sue Apple for charging them a 30 percent commission on every app purchase, also noted the possibility that "app developers will also sue Apple on a monopsony theory." The Court acknowledged that Apple has market power over app entrepreneurs, who could potentially also bring an antitrust case against Apple. Antitrust enforcers in the United States and Europe have recently opened investigations into Apple as well.

Monopsony, as you've seen, is a huge problem in an economy

where tech giants serve as gatekeepers that set the terms and conditions for suppliers and creators to do business. Ask any Amazon marketplace seller, for instance, if they can negotiate the fees they pay to Amazon—they'll think you're out of your mind. App developers can't negotiate the 30 percent Apple Tax that is charged to buyers of apps, nor do they have the power to stop Sherlocking.

Facebook's Platform Privilege

Like Google, Facebook picks the winners and losers of internet content, as we saw in the 2016 U.S. presidential election and beyond. Because Facebook's platform privilege manipulates us and harms democracy, we'll talk about Facebook's global control over the flow of information—and disinformation—in chapters 4 and 5. So here we'll explore how Facebook squashes new companies that could compete against it and changes entrepreneurs' fortunes just by altering its algorithm.

Facebook has a history of taking entrepreneurs' ideas when they refuse to sell their companies to the platform. As the *Wall Street Journal* explains it, Facebook CEO Mark Zuckerberg met with the founders of Snapchat and Foursquare and gave them two options: either hand over their companies at the price he proposed, or the tech giant would imitate their features and make it harder for them to operate.

When the founders didn't cave, Facebook copied Snapchat and Foursquare's popular features. Instagram's knockoff of Snapchat Stories grew bigger than the original innovation because Facebook applied the feature to its 2.3 billion users, a number that dwarfs Snapchat's 210 million users. Over the years, Snapchat lawyers kept track of tactics by Facebook that they consider anticompetitive in a file called Project Voldemort, named after the villain from Harry Potter. Snapchat reportedly shared the evidence with the

FTC as part of its antitrust investigation into Facebook that began in 2019.

Companies, especially small businesses, can find their fortunes change with the flip of a switch when Facebook makes algorithmic changes that harm their ability to reach their customers. I experienced this firsthand back in 2012, when I cofounded a web start-up called The Parent Maze that helped busy parents find trusted recommendations for parenting services. At the time, Facebook encouraged businesses to create Facebook pages, and then invest in ads to get people to become fans of the pages. Fans would then see content posted by the Facebook business pages, and the investment would pay off as a marketing channel.

But after businesses of all sizes invested in growing their fans, Facebook simply changed the terms. Now businesses would have to pay for their fans to see their content. For my start-up, investment in ads to build our Facebook following had consumed a large part of our shoestring budget because our potential users spent a lot of time there, which, after Facebook's bait and switch, felt like wasted money. Businesses were angry, particularly because Facebook was not forthright about the change, but they lacked bargaining power to do anything about it.

Must Winners Take All?

Pundits say tech markets are "winner take all," or monopolistic by nature, and they point to a principle called network effects. Network effects arise when a user's value from a product increases as others use it. People want to be where their friends are, for example, making a social network without your friends not much use.

But the same was true for the AT&T monopoly since a phone network would serve no purpose if you couldn't call your friends. Government regulators didn't just throw up their hands and say, "Ah well, it's a winner-take-all market with network effects." Instead, the government broke up the AT&T monopoly and required interoperability, making AT&T connect with competing networks in order to open up competition in long-distance calling.

For Big Tech, interoperability would allow users to authorize networks to securely communicate and interface with each other, like how people with different email services can send emails to one another. On top of enforcing the antitrust laws, interoperability is one of several practical, doable solutions that can help revive entrepreneurship, which we'll discuss in the book's final chapter.

Even if it were true that network effects mean there can only be one dominant social network, search engine, video service, mobile operating system, ad tech company, e-commerce platform, mobile app store, and browser, and that Facebook, Google, Apple, and Amazon are natural monopolies, what does the government do to natural monopolies? It labels them utilities and it regulates them. Traditionally, utilities are required to provide equal access to competitors on fair and reasonable terms and prices.

By allowing illegal acquisitions and monopolization, and by abandoning rules and regulations that decentralize communications networks, the government has created monopoly markets—these were policy choices. The government can make the opposite choice and start reviving the American dream. It's up to us to demand government take action.

Your Life, Better

Thomas Philippon, leading economist and author of *The Great Reversal: How America Gave Up on Free Markets*, estimates that bringing competition back would increase employees' income by about $1.25 trillion. Weakening monopoly and oligopoly power could lift that pervasive cloud of financial fear and insecurity that surrounded us even before the COVID-19 pandemic's economic damage. We think life has to be like this, but it doesn't.

In a world free of monopoly rule, you may just be able to pursue that innovative business idea, get it funded, and build a company that doesn't get crushed by powerful companies protecting their turf. Small and big companies could say no to giant corporations' extractive and unfair terms of dealing, stay in business longer, and pay their employees better.

Instead of innovation graveyards, increased antitrust enforcement would create a new burst of innovation, like the one that came after the government took action against AT&T. Imagine what innovation could look like if a handful of companies weren't charting its course.

The defenders of the status quo want us to believe that these problems are too complicated to fix and nothing can be done. But it's not that complicated. We just need to demand that government use the tools it already has to restore a competitive marketplace for employees and entrepreneurs.

FOUR

MONOPOLIES SPY ON AND MANIPULATE YOU

"The house is free, but they own your life."

MONOPOLIES ARE WATCHING YOU RIGHT NOW

You were gifted an Amazon smart speaker for the holidays, and you gave the gadget a go. But then Alexa started talking out of nowhere, when you hadn't even summoned your new "assistant." Exactly what is Alexa listening to, you start to wonder, and what might it be doing with your personal information? You hear on the news that Amazon employees listen to recordings from Alexa, and Apple and Google have people listen to voice audio, too. Maybe you felt better when a robot controlled by a trillion-dollar corporation was listening, but real humans? Did they hear you having sex? Did they eavesdrop on that far-from-perfect parenting moment?

On top of that, online ads are stalking you. Sometimes a shirt you decided against buying follows you wherever you go on the Web, and other times an ad for the exact brand of coconut and chocolate swirl ice cream you bought from the grocery store shows up in your Facebook newsfeed. Last night you offered that ice cream to a guest in your home. Is Facebook listening to you, too?

When you need to get to the bottom of an embarrassing medical condition, you turn to the directory of the world's information, Google. Perhaps you cringe as you hit search, divulging even more personal secrets to the one company that knows the most about you. Google probably doesn't need your search to already know a lot about your health; according to reports, Google has gathered millions of Americans' health records straight from a medical provider without telling patients or their doctors. It feels like nothing is sacred anymore.

Don't Blame Baby Pictures

If you don't want to be tracked, you shouldn't put your whole life online, so goes the typical victim-blaming. All you have to do is stop using social media if you want privacy. This trope is so off base that it exposes deep deception by the companies that track us.

What you knowingly and willingly share, like a post on Facebook, is a tiny fraction of what Facebook knows about you. What you search for on Google is an even smaller percentage of what Google knows about you. Escaping Big Tech's prying eyes is a nearly impossible feat. You're under ubiquitous surveillance, and it's not your fault.

Tech giants have an all-encompassing view of what you read,

think, do, believe, buy, watch, where you go, who you're with, even how many credit lines you have and what you invest in. The companies track you across millions of websites, devices, tech wearables, and offline, and combine the data they collect on you with data from other companies, like data brokers, or your smart TV maker. Seventy-six percent of websites have hidden Google trackers, and Google collects your information through its own services like Search, YouTube, Maps, Android, Chrome, Google Play, Gmail, and Google Home. In one study, an Android phone that was stationary and not in use, but had the Chrome browser open in the background, communicated location data to Google 340 times in twenty-four hours. Google even has trackers on 74 percent of pornography sites.

Facebook tracks you across the Web, including approximately 8.4 million websites with the Facebook "like" button and 16.4 million websites with Facebook login as of 2018, plus any website that uses Facebook analytics or ad tools. Even if you don't use Facebook, Instagram, or WhatsApp, Facebook has created a "shadow profile" of you, tracking your internet browsing history and your social connections by accessing the email contacts of your friends who use Facebook. Facebook uses this data in part to sell targeted ads across thousands of mobile apps and websites through its Facebook Audience Network. Facebook also uses facial recognition technology to identify you in pictures that others take of you, even if they don't tag you in the photo. Amazon, too, is a surveillance giant.

Instead of faulting social media users, we should fault our elected officials who have failed to protect us from a privatized spy net. Life is hard. People have to work all day and feed their families, and they literally couldn't hold down a job if they read every privacy policy that came their way. The task of being endlessly vigilant about our data rights is so daunting and overwhelming that most of us become hopeless and give up altogether.

Award-winning journalist and editor Julia Angwin, author of *Dragnet Nation: A Quest for Privacy, Security, and Freedom in a World of Relentless Surveillance*, tried multiple experiments to protect herself from tracking. Ultimately Angwin concluded, "I'm in an arms race I'm not going to win." The onus to stop surveillance cannot be on the people. The onus must rest on our democratically elected leaders, who can pass strong privacy laws and ensure competitive markets that empower consumers.

Spying Is Social Control

Digital surveillance is relatively new, but surveillance itself is not. Throughout its dark history, surveillance has been used by the powerful to control and persecute innocent people. Take the story of Vera Lengsfeld, who was organizing for peace and human rights in East Germany in the early 1980s. East Germany's communist government, and its secret police force the Stasi, labeled Vera a threat to the state. The Stasi gave her the code name "Virus," tapped her phone, and began recording her meetings. They arrested Vera and threw her in jail when she was carrying a poster that read, "Every citizen has the right to express his opinion freely and openly."

In an act of psychological torture, the prison wardens would play Vera's favorite symphony to remind her of her home and her beloved children, whom she missed dearly. How did the wardens know Vera's music tastes? The Stasi had watched Vera's every move. When the Berlin Wall came down, twenty large files the Stasi had amassed about "Virus" were released. Vera was "quite astonished" to learn that forty-nine regular people—friends, family, and acquaintances—were unofficial Stasi collaborators who kept tabs on her. Among her betrayers was her own husband, with whom she had borne and raised two children. Big Data would be a dream come true for the Stasi.

You're a good, law-abiding person, so you've got nothing to hide, right? Wrong. As we saw with Vera, something as innocuous as your favorite song can be used against you. You may think you don't need to worry because you're not an activist. But someday, if not today, you might become one. These tumultuous times have made clear our democracy and basic human rights are not guaranteed to us. If you're not the type to rise up and resist, you still don't want to live in a world where others cannot. When people know they're being watched, they conform, obey, stay in line, and self-censor.

Yeonmi Park escaped from North Korea's oppressive regime at the young age of thirteen and wrote about her experiences in her book, *In Order to Live*. As a young child, Park's mother taught her that "even when you think you're alone, the birds and mice can hear you whisper." Park learned to not even think critically, and certainly not to speak up. Like the birds and mice Yeonmi's mom warned her about, surveillance giants are watching us even when we think we are alone.

China is giving each citizen a score based on their surveilled obedience, and it's tracking the Uighur Muslim minority with facial recognition technology. A disturbing video surfaced at the end of 2019 that shows Chinese police interrogating a man for apparently criticizing a police officer in a "private" group on WeChat, China's social media network. The man is restrained in a "tiger chair," a torture device that shackles the victim's entire body and is known to bear the slogan: "Truthfully confess and your whole body will feel at ease."

If you don't like being told what to do, having arbitrary rules imposed on you, being controlled in ways you may not even know, or living your life the way other people think you should, then you should guard your privacy with all you've got.

Build It and They Will Come

Big Tech focuses on profits and pays far less attention to the dangers of building an architecture of surveillance that can enable government oppression. In an interview on the *Land of the Giants* podcast, Recode journalist Jason Del Rey asked Amazon executive Daniel Rausch, vice president of Smart Home, whether teams at Amazon look at people's concerns about Alexa. Rausch replied only that Amazon is "deeply optimistic" about what Alexa can do for customers.

In other words, Amazon isn't thinking about the consequences of the surveillance technology it deploys at breakneck pace. The consequences are for the rest of us to bear. The least powerful in our society will suffer the worst consequences of surveillance, as they always have, and Amazon executives safely can get richer knowing deep down they'll be the last ones to pay the price. Amazon's facial recognition technology is already being used by police departments, despite widespread concerns about the technology's discriminatory bias and inaccuracies. A coalition of activists' groups including Fight for the Future and EPIC advocate for a total ban on facial recognition technology, saying it can control and oppress us by enabling "automated and ubiquitous monitoring of an entire population" that "is nearly impossible to avoid." Amazon provides cloud storage for Immigration and Customs Enforcement's deportation operation, ignoring calls by an alliance of 500 Amazon employees and repeated protests about Amazon's government contracts. Amazon has shown it is willing to employ its technologies against the most vulnerable.

Most tracking by tech giants is designed to target us with ads and sell us stuff, which may seem harmless. Whatever data Big Tech collects, however, the government can get. Occasionally we hear a case about a tech platform refusing to cooperate with the government, like when Apple refused to crack open an iPhone from the scene of a 2015 mass shooting in San Bernardino, California. But those examples are in the minority. What we don't hear about are the thousands of secret requests that Big Tech doesn't protest, and that often come hand in hand with a gag order. In fact, between July and December 2018, Apple received nearly 8,500 government requests for customer data and complied with more than 80 percent of those requests. Google received 26,964 government requests for data involving 74,619 customer accounts in a mere six months between January and June 2019, and provided data in response to 82 percent of those requests. In most cases, tech giants would lose in court if they refused to comply. The laws keeping information that tech platforms collect about you out of the hands of the government are incredibly weak. Citizens have no voice in the process and usually don't even know their data is being handed over, all in the name of national security or law enforcement and hidden under the paternalistic umbrella of protection.

Big Tech says that surveillance is good for us because we get relevant ads targeted to us. But never before hypertargeted ads came along did I wish for the convenience of companies spying on me twenty-four hours a day, seven days a week, and then deciding what products I discover. I don't buy that the meager benefits of highly targeted ads outweigh the dangers they bring.

History Repeats Itself

You may think oppression through surveillance can't happen here in America, but it already has—and does. In the late 1940s and early 1950s, Senator Joseph McCarthy used anticommunist hysteria to perpetuate a reign of terror known as McCarthyism or the Second Red Scare. The U.S. government used spying, wiretaps, and infiltration of political groups to accuse anyone with politically left views of being communists and to blacklist them from jobs, or worse.

The FBI director J. Edgar Hoover even labeled Martin Luther

King Jr. a communist and used invasive surveillance to monitor him long after the Second Red Scare had subsided. More recently, the Department of Homeland Security monitored members of the Black Lives Matter movement, continuing America's disturbing and persistent record of surveilling black activists. The surveillance state itself is dangerous to democracy, and Big Tech's spying eyes are making it worse.

If McCarthyism occurred today, it could use the surveillance architecture built by Facebook, Google, and Amazon. Instead of communism, pick any belief you like—feminism, conservatism, anticorruption, or environmentalism. If, for example, the government decided to label people who want to stop the climate crisis as political enemies and blacklist them, it wouldn't need to use spies as it did in the McCarthy era because it could simply use the surveillance Big Tech is already doing.

From search and Web tracking data, the government has the ability to learn who searched for articles and visited websites about climate change. From the purchase data tracked by Amazon, Google, and Facebook, the government can know who purchased energy-efficient products. From Facebook and Google group data, the government is able to identify the members of environmental groups and see their discussions with one another about how to organize for change. Location data tracked by Big Tech can tell the government if you went to a climate march or other activist event, and the government can get your photos from the event, too. Google calendar data reveals plans for future events.

Amazon purchase data and Kindle tracking data can identify people who have bought books about the environment and even what e-book pages they read and what passages they highlighted. People who have written or received Gmail or Facebook messages, watched YouTube videos, or written Google Docs about climate change can all be easily identified thanks to Big Tech's surveillance architecture.

Devices with Alexa, Google Home, or other voice assistants can even offer a live feed into your home to listen to any climate crisis talk.

Big Tech also makes assumptions about you based on the data they collect, known as inferences or correlations. Sometimes these inferences are correct and sometimes they are not. For example, Big Tech could assume you are an environmentalist because you bought Birkenstocks and vegan burgers, and these inferences could land you on our hypothetical government blacklist, too.

Unfortunately, our government has already grown cozy with Big Tech. Amazon has forged partnerships with police departments to use its Ring smart doorbells, which offer surveillance footage surrounding a user's home, to effectively create a spy net in America's neighborhoods. Now not only can your nosy neighbor know all your comings and goings, but so can the police. Ring even created a custom portal for police to easily request Ring footage, touting in a video, "It's like having thousands of eyes and ears on the street."

Google location data is being used to identify everyone in the area of a crime. An innocent man, Jorge Molina, spent nearly a week in jail after his phone was one of many identified by Google data as being in the area of a crime, the *New York Times* reported. Molina was at home at the time of the crime, two miles from the scene.

Our Fourth Amendment right set up to protect us against unreasonable search and seizure is getting weak. The online world has escaped laws intended to protect us in the real world, and these two worlds are melding into one.

Blame Monopoly Power

You may be wondering what smart speakers eavesdropping on you, online ads stalking you, Google knowing your deepest medical secrets, and surveillance-enabled political persecution have to do with monopoly. After all, lots of companies that are not monopolies spy on you and invasively collect your personal information. Yet privacy and monopoly are intricately related, with monopoly power allowing Big Tech to abuse your privacy without losing your business, keeping you in the dark about the ways it abuses your privacy, and buying off lawmakers so they don't pass robust privacy laws.

It works the other way, too. Massive data collection allows giants to strengthen their monopoly power. Big Tech uses that power to shut out privacy-protecting start-ups. Surveillance-based business models are a choice, not an inevitability of the internet, and loosening the giants' monopoly grip could promote competition among business models. Pro-privacy, pro-democracy innovators need the opportunity to break through the monopolists' gates without being crushed by anticompetitive tactics.

Largely, I don't fault tech monopolists as much as I fault the government for failing to act. I'm critical of decisions Facebook CEO Mark Zuckerberg has made, for example, but focusing too much on his character is a distraction. Demonizing individual CEOs confuses the fact that monopoly problems are structural and systemic. We must demand better from our government, and we must not forget that corporations by design are profit-maximizing entities.

Ordinarily, two things constrain corporations from pursuing profits in ways that cause harm: 1) competition and 2) regulation. Tech giants have had neither. Without competition, Big Tech can hurt people without losing profits, and choose dangerous and harmful business models. It is our government leaders who have failed to adequately enforce the antitrust laws, or protect citizens with regulation. This is not a job we can leave to corporations, and putting any faith in Big Tech self-regulation is doomed to fail. Government should not *ask* corporations to do better, it should *make* them do better. Both privacy regulation and competition, created through strong antitrust enforcement and other anti-monopoly polices, must make it unprofitable for corporations to make business model choices that threaten our fundamental rights.

In April 2020, when large corporations sucked hundreds of millions of dollars out of the COVID-19 bailout fund meant for small businesses, comedian and political satirist Trevor Noah said on *The Daily Show* that government should have created rules instead of just letting companies take taxpayers' money in a free-for-all. After all, he said, "companies gonna company." Just the same, government should have created rules instead of letting companies take Americans' data as they pleased. Surveillance giants gonna surveil—unless we make our government stop them.

Monopolies Don't Lose Profits When They Abuse You

Monopoly power allows Big Tech to abuse your privacy without losing your business. Treating customers badly doesn't risk profits when customers don't have anywhere to go. We already talked in chapter 1 about how tech giants are charging you monopoly rents of data, an excessive price rather than the price competition would yield. On top of price-gouging, hidden and invasive surveillance means you're getting a lower quality service. Competition makes companies vie for your business by offering better-quality services. Like the monopoly cable operator that can make you wait eight hours for the set-top-box repair person to show up, monopoly tech platforms can provide poor-quality service, invading your privacy without the risk of losing you to competitors.

At its start, Facebook competed against the then-leading social media platform MySpace on privacy grounds. Former advertising executive Dina Srinivasan has detailed the history of Facebook competing against MySpace as the more privacy-protecting alternative in a paper called "The Antitrust Case Against Facebook," published in

2019 in the *Berkeley Business Law Journal*. For the first ten years of its existence, Facebook promised not to track users for commercial purposes. Facebook even promised users they could remove information Facebook had about them whenever they wanted. Srinivasan details how Facebook's surveillance increased in tandem with decreases in competition over time. With Facebook's competition eliminated, the pressure to protect users' privacy fell away.

When Facebook users learned Facebook had allowed the digital analytics firm Cambridge Analytica to access their personal information, which was used to target users with deceptive propaganda intended to influence the U.S. 2016 presidential election, they were angry. But, as we discussed earlier, this abuse of customer privacy didn't threaten Facebook's profits because disgruntled Facebook users mostly switched to Facebook-owned Instagram.

If Facebook had never bought Instagram, or antitrust enforcers had blocked this, in my opinion, illegal acquisition, Facebook would face competitive pressure. Instead of making only minuscule changes, Facebook would be motivated to stop invading users' privacy.

Facebook's business model must change to fix its privacy problem—small tweaks here and there will not suffice. In 2018 and 2019, Facebook made *more than a billion dollars a week* by collecting data and then targeting ads at individuals based on that data. Risk of profit loss would force Facebook to change its business model more than risk of regulation, which Facebook knows its lobbyists can influence.

Monopolies Can Keep You in the Dark

People need to be able to switch to privacy-protecting alternatives, while also needing to understand how their privacy is being violated. The giants haven't made it easy to know what types of information they are tracking, where and how they are tracking you, and what they are doing with it. Under pressure, both Google and Facebook have unveiled ways to find out what information they've already collected about you, but the tools tell you about all the spying the platforms have already done on you, instead of alerting you to spying in real time. Facebook's and Google's entire business models are built around getting your attention and influencing you with messaging, yet they don't deliver messages clearly announcing, "We are tracking you right now, and here's how."

Big Tech is doing a terrible job informing you because transparency runs directly against their profit motives. Surveillance giants know that if they alerted you in real time, in a way that is understandable, quick, and easy, you might refuse their tracking. Profits lie in their deception, and billions of dollars in revenue depend on a global fraud on the world's citizens. Competition could help shed light on Big Tech's privacy abuses. The privacy-protecting search engine DuckDuckGo, in a bid for your business, provides education through its newsletter on the ways Google and other companies violate your privacy. Just as a sneaker company draws attention to the poorer quality of its competitors' shoes, so could competitors highlight the privacy invasions of Big Tech if markets were free and fair.

Big Tech Uses Their Might to Shut Out Privacy-Protecting Start-ups

Privacy-protecting innovators are waiting in the wings, and they just need a fair opportunity to break through the digital gatekeepers and serve you. But Big Tech controls the infrastructure of business and are the gatekeepers who decide who gets to play the game.

Take the privacy-protecting Brave browser and search engine DuckDuckGo from above. They have been locked out from being the built-in default browser and search engine on Google Android phones, which have a more than 85 percent global market share. This is a huge barrier to privacy-protecting start-ups reaching users because of default bias. Personally, I took the uncommon step of overcoming default bias and installing DuckDuckGo as the primary search engine in my devices, which provided me a calming sense of freedom.

Privacy-protecting start-ups not only have to overcome default bias, but they also have to get through Big Tech's gates to reach users. A company called Candle has set out to create the "privacy-friendly smart home of the future," and has announced a launch of its prototype. But exactly how would such a privacy-protecting voice assistant reach consumers? Amazon, Google, and Facebook each could exert their platform privilege. The giants have the incentive and ability to bury this upstart challenger to their voice assistants, demoting Candle in search listings and newsfeeds by tweaking their algorithms. If enforcers and policy makers unlocked Big Tech's gates and promoted competition, privacy-protecting innovation could flourish.

Data Helps Big Tech Grow and Keep Monopoly Power

While lack of competition allows Big Tech to collect excessive data without losing profits, the data the platforms collect simultaneously shore up their monopoly power. Margrethe Vestager, the European commissioner for competition and the digital age, has explained that "having the right set of data could make it almost impossible for anyone else to keep up." Regulators "need to keep a close eye on whether companies control unique data, which no one else can get hold of, and can use it to shut their rivals out of the market," said Vestager, particularly "data that's been collected through a monopoly."

Facebook, for example, has used its control of data to try to shut out rivals. Leaked internal Facebook documents revealed that Mark Zuckerberg personally kept a list of strategic competitors, who were not permitted to access the Facebook Graph API. (API is short for application programming interface, which allows two applications to talk to each other.) In Facebook's words, the Graph API is "the primary way to get data into and out of the Facebook platform." When Twitter launched its video service Vine, emails show that Zuckerberg approved cutting Twitter off from Facebook's API because Vine was competing with a Facebook "core functionality."

Such behavior is known as a "discriminatory refusal to deal" in antitrust law, which is a type of illegal monopolization under Section 2 of the Sherman Act. Ordinarily, companies do not have obligations to deal with their competitors. But if a monopoly refuses to offer a service to a competitor that it offers to others, or if a monopoly has done business with the competitor and then stops for anticompetitive reasons, such behavior amounts to illegal monopolization.

In another leaked document, a Facebook employee suggested cutting off access to Facebook's API to a competitor and justifying the move as protecting privacy. Although we want Facebook to protect users' privacy, we do not want Facebook to use privacy as a pretense for monopolization. Facebook seems to define privacy as keeping our data out of others' hands, but we also need privacy protection from Facebook itself! Internal documents detail Facebook's aggressive snooping in ways consumers would never expect, including collecting Android users' calls and text records without their knowledge.

Mergers allow dominant companies to acquire data that strengthens or grows their market power. Take Amazon's purchase of Whole Foods. Simplistic antitrust analysis that just looks at the grocery market would conclude the deal doesn't harm competition because Amazon had a small market share in groceries. The FTC quickly approved the deal without doing an in-depth investigation. But antitrust enforcers should try to see the forest for the trees and not undertake such a narrow analysis. I was aghast when I heard from an FTC decision maker that they didn't view the merger as involving data. A former Amazon insider once told me that Amazon is "a data company that happens to sell stuff." To say that any merger involving Amazon doesn't involve data is to fundamentally misunderstand Amazon's business.

If you shop at Whole Foods, have you forked over your data to Amazon yet by logging in as a Prime member? Your data may be more valuable than the Whole Foods discount you receive, but you wouldn't know it. With a tremendous overlap between Whole Foods customers and Amazon Prime members, the merger allowed Amazon to gather even more personal information about its Prime customers. Unlike the Amazon purchases we don't really need, we have to buy food all the time. Acquiring Whole Foods gave Amazon many more opportunities to interact with us and learn about us. What we eat can tell a lot about who we are.

Data that enhances Amazon's ability to precisely target and market to Prime members strengthens its existing online monopoly power. The FTC at the very least should have investigated how the data Amazon would acquire could harm competition and increase barriers for any other company trying to enter Amazon's monopoly markets. The deal also allowed Amazon to terminate Whole Foods' partnerships with delivery company Instacart, an emerging competitive threat to Amazon's core offering of fast delivery. Remember, Clayton Act Section 7 prohibits any merger that may substantially lessen competition or tend to create a monopoly.

Google's acquisition of FitBit causes the same problems, fortifying Google's existing surveillance-based dominance of online advertising. As Amazon and Google expand into health care, our personal data can be used against us in countless ways. Think Amazon expanding into health insurance, and then using your Whole Foods purchase history to decide how much to charge you, or whether to cover you at all. Not enough kale, too much ice cream and beer? Denied! Or picture Google getting into health insurance, and your FitBit showing only one workout a month. High GoogleCare prices for you!

Big Tech Uses Its Monopoly Power to Fight Privacy Laws

Big Tech monopolists are throwing millions of dollars at lawmakers to keep abusing your privacy. As the giants' economic power grows, the companies buy up increasing amounts of political power.

In the years leading up to the 2016 passage of Europe's privacy law, the General Data Protection Regulation (GDPR), Facebook and Google lobbied hard against it. When they lost that battle, the talking heads on Big Tech's payroll, spanning from think tanks to academia, spread a common talking point in unison: Europe's privacy law would strengthen the giants' monopoly power because it would impose burdens on smaller companies.

Huh? If Europe's privacy law was so good for Big Tech, it wouldn't have spent millions of dollars lobbying against it! If the privacy law worked as intended—and why they fought it—it would weaken Big Tech's monopoly power because Facebook and Google's 360-degree view of the user is the source of their dominance in targeted online advertising. But so far the GDPR hasn't really worked, largely because tech monopolies are so powerful they can interpret the law how they choose and wait for government to try to force them to change their practices. Europe is still struggling to get Facebook and Google to comply, with the French data protection commissioner fining Google in 2019 and inquiries into the two companies ongoing.

The United States still lacks a comprehensive consumer privacy law at the federal level. California became the first state to pass such a law in 2018, which went into effect on January 1, 2020. The law puts forth a different legal framework than the GDPR but shares the same goals, giving citizens the right to know what personal information is collected, used, shared or sold, the right to delete personal information held by businesses, and the right to opt out of sale of personal information. Polls show the citizens of California overwhelmingly support the privacy law, but that doesn't stop their elected representatives from putting forth amendments to weaken it on a regular basis. Some of the amendments propose exceptions that would undo the law, like an exemption for digital advertising, the main driver of surveillance.

While relentlessly attacking California's privacy law, Big Tech lobbyists are pushing for a weak federal privacy law, which could override California's law, as well as the laws that any state passes to ensure its citizens' privacy. The monopolists' tentacles extend into government institutions and bend them to their will, away from the will of the people.

The FTC has long been the privacy cop for the American people, primarily using consumer protection laws that prohibit companies from deceiving their customers. But the FTC has failed to stop tech companies from deceiving consumers over and over again. When Big Tech breaks the law, the FTC gives them a slap on the wrist. If the platforms can make tens of billions of dollars a year violating your privacy, and then have to pay a few billions as a fine every decade, it makes economic sense to keep doing it. Paying a fine is just a cost of doing business.

The FTC fined Facebook $5 billion in 2019 for violating a privacy order dating back to 2011, with the two Democratic FTC commissioners dissenting on the ground that stronger measures were needed. Five billion sounds like a lot but consider that Facebook made over $70 billion in 2019 alone by spying on you and then selling advertisers the ability to target you. The FTC's 2011 order was imposed on Facebook for violating users' privacy and required that Facebook "not misrepresent . . . the extent to which it maintains the privacy or security of [personal] information," and establish a comprehensive privacy program that protects the confidentiality of personal information.

For eight years, Facebook basically ignored this order. The only consequence was it had to pay a little over a month's revenue as a penalty. As Commissioner Rohit Chopra stated in his dissenting statement, the settlement will not fix the problem because it did not require Facebook to change its business practices. When the $5 billion fine was announced, Facebook's stock surged.

Our time to demand real privacy laws and enforcement, as well as antitrust action against surveillance monopolists, is short. Federal antitrust enforcers and lawmakers have only begun to exhibit the political will to rein in the powerful and wealthy Silicon Valley giants, and their surveillance-based business models. But as government increasingly grows dependent on Big Tech's surveillance in the name of policing and national security, it will be even less willing to stop it.

Not only can surveillance be used to persecute the innocent, but personal information can be used to screw you over in countless ways, from charging you higher prices than other people pay for the same stuff because your data shows how much you're willing and able to pay, to shutting you out of job opportunities based on personal characteristics, which we'll discuss in chapter 7. And as the following chapters will show, surveillance is also what allows monopolies to hyper target and manipulate you, warp elections, and defund the press.

We can stop the surveillance by demanding our political representatives pass strong privacy laws and enforce the antitrust laws to weaken giant platforms' power and to open up competition to pro-privacy innovators.

MONOPOLIES MAKE YOU SCARED, ANGRY, AND ADDICTED

These are scary times, but some tech monopolies are making them even scarier. For Facebook and Google, your anxiety maximizes profits.

When it comes to harmful content, most people think Facebook and YouTube's main problem is they can't take millions of posts down quickly enough. But both platforms actually *boost* hate and disinformation. Their algorithms prioritize "engagement" (that is, clicks, likes, comments, and shares) to keep users on their platform longer because content that provokes fear and anger—the most incendiary content—"engages" humans the most.

The more time people spend on Facebook's and YouTube's platforms, the more data the platforms collect, the more ads they show, and the more money they make. On Facebook's first quarter 2016 earnings call, CEO Mark Zuckerberg announced that users spend on average more than fifty minutes a day using Facebook, Instagram, and Messenger, up ten minutes from the number reported in 2014. Facebook reports to investors how much of your time and attention it can hoard because that's what fuels Facebook's targeted advertising business model. Advertising accounted for approximately 84 percent of Google's revenue and 98 percent of Facebook's revenue in 2019.

Giving incendiary content top priority best serves Facebook's and YouTube's business models because "engagement" makes them the most money. Their amplification of hateful content is not an inevitability of the internet or human nature—it's a business decision.

In 2017, I interviewed NYU Stern professor and author Scott Galloway, and he said he often gets the question from media about whether it's possible for the platforms to police their content. Galloway said he thought that was such a strange question, given their tremendous cash flow. "We're not talking about the realm of the possible here," said Galloway, "we're talking about the realm of the profitable." He added that "when big tech starts making noises that old media and the government seems to buy into that something would be impossible, that's Latin for we would be less profitable if we did this."

Prioritization of the types of content that rake in the most dough means the platforms' newsfeeds do not neutrally reflect the content people post. Consider the trials and tribulations of Women You Should Know, a pioneering online publisher that has been telling empowering women's stories for years. The site's founders, Jen Jones and Cynthia Hornig, built their small business with Facebook at its core, growing their Facebook fan base to more than 400,000 loyal followers. Their digital ad-supported business thrived, with their Facebook followers regularly clicking to read their articles on WomenYou ShouldKnow.net.

But the site's founders began getting confusing messages from their Facebook fans, messages criticizing Women You Should Know for straying from their positive brand by only sharing negative stories of violence against women. Jen and Cynthia were baffled. Sure, they occasionally shared a story about gender-based violence, an important issue, but the uplifting stories immensely outnumbered those articles. Jen and Cynthia checked their Facebook statistics and realized that Facebook's algorithms—programmed to prioritize engagement—often were not showing followers their positive stories, but rather serving up the stories that provoke fear and anger. Jen and Cynthia wanted to empower women, but Facebook made women afraid instead.

Rather than blaming profit-maximizing algorithms, we tend to blame humanity itself. Humans are the ones who post incendiary content, and humans are terrible for being drawn to this content. But the algorithms prioritize a much bleaker picture than reality reflects, because they bury the middle-of-the-road, reasonable, and even-toned content.

A major reason that humans are drawn to scary content, why it's more "engaging" for us, is our survival instinct. A post reporting a pedophile loose in your neighborhood, whether true or not, will go viral because of humanity's genetic programming to protect our young. We shouldn't feel bad about our survival instinct, but instead fault the giants who profit by setting it off, getting our cortisol pumping, and getting us clicking and sharing. Yes, the current political climate is toxic, but engagement-prioritizing algorithms make it even more so. No wonder we're all so agitated and stressed out!

You may strive to live a calmer life where you are less reactive to the content that barrages you daily, but the richest and most powerful companies in the world have designed their technology to make us do the exact opposite! Clicks, likes, shares, and "being engaged" are reactions that serve Big Tech business models and maximize profits. Facebook and YouTube could prioritize what content is served up to people in countless other ways besides engagement, including simple chronology. Users could even control what types of things are prioritized in their newsfeeds.

Addiction for Profit

When tech companies' profits depend on how much of our time they can hoard, they build addiction into their design. Stanford University even created a program called the Persuasive Technology Lab, where students learned how to build technologies that addict and manipulate.

Tristan Harris, a former Google design ethicist and cofounder of the Center for Humane Technology, explained some of the tricks tech companies employ to addict users in written congressional testimony in January 2020. "'Likes' and 'filters' *exploit teens' need for social validation and approval* from others," wrote Harris, while notifications condition us to expect "frequent rewards." Infinite feeds are "designed to operate like slot machines, offering 'intermittent variable rewards' as you check for notifications, maximizing addiction," he continued. These tricks are rooted in the work of psychologist B. F. Skinner, who learned how to manipulate the behavior of mice back in the 1950s.

Sean Parker, Facebook's founding president, has explained of the social media platform, "It's a social-validation feedback loop . . . exactly the kind of thing that a hacker like myself would come up with, because you're exploiting a vulnerability in human psychology." And

Chamath Palihapitiya, who was Facebook's vice president for user growth, said in an interview that "the short-term, dopamine-driven feedback loops we've created are destroying how society works."

In the same interview, Palihapitiya said he feels "tremendous guilt" for his involvement in building Facebook and noted that his own children "aren't allowed to use that shit." Parents in Silicon Valley reportedly put tight controls on their own kids' use of technology, while many work for companies that profit from addicting other people's kids. Sean Parker has said of Facebook, "God only knows what it's doing to our children's brains."

Harris, too, has sounded the alarm about how addictive technology is affecting our kids. "We are raising a generation of children who are more distracted, less creative, more narcissistic, and more vulnerable to bullying and teen suicides than in the last few decades," wrote Harris. He pointed to a 170 percent increase in high-depressive symptoms for 13–18-year-old girls between 2010 and 2017, which NYU researchers link to social media usage.

Simultaneously, suicide rates in the United States have skyrocketed, doubling for girls aged 15 to 19 between 2007 and 2015. Definitively proving that social media causes increases in depression and suicide is nearly impossible, as causation is notoriously difficult to prove. But it's not a stretch to conclude that social media is harming mental health.

And while forbidding your kids from using social media seems like the solution, it's easier said than done. Teens don't communicate with their friends over email or by calling on the phone. They use platforms like Instagram. Cutting them off from communicating with their friends is a challenge, to say the least, at a developmental stage when peers' opinions mean everything.

As a parent myself, I think about how much easier it was for parents in the 1980s. As a child growing up before call-waiting was even invented, I would call my friend to play and be greeted by a busy signal while her teen sister held up the line for hours. I'd eventually give up, hop on my bike, and fetch my friend in person. Parents in those days merely had to yell "Get off the phone!" without having to battle against billion-dollar corporations who have the exact opposite goal they do.

Extremism Is Engaging

Engagement-maximizing business models don't stop at stressing us out and addicting us—they also foster extremism. As she explained in her TED Talk, "We're building a Dystopia Just to Make People Click on Ads," University of North Carolina associate professor and techno-sociologist Zeynep Tufekci viewed Donald Trump rally videos on YouTube as part of her research. YouTube next served up to her videos of white supremacy through its auto-play feature, which is designed to capture attention. Tufekci watched a video about vegetarianism, and YouTube auto-played her videos about being a vegan. "The algorithm has figured out that if you can entice people into thinking that you can show them something more hardcore, they're more likely to stay on the site watching video after video going down that rabbit hole while Google serves them ads," said Tufekci. Seventy percent of what people watch on YouTube is determined by recommendation algorithms.

YouTube has said it made changes to its algorithm in January 2019 to address concerns about the content it auto-plays. But reporter and producer Emily Gadek tweeted in September 2019 about her experience watching a documentary video produced by *The Atlantic* about rats in New Zealand on YouTube. She left the video running on mute when a meeting began, and within three hops the algorithm had auto-played her a Fox News clip about illegal immigrants entering

America. Was the algorithm drawing a connection between rats and immigrants?

The Mozilla Foundation conducted a campaign to collect You-Tube users' stories about its recommendation engine leading down "sometimes dangerous pathways." Among the stories collected were LGBTQ+ youth watching empowering videos only to be barraged with homophobic content, and a ten-year-old girl's search for "tap dance videos" leading her to body-shaming content that her mother worries has triggered the beginnings of an eating disorder.

Facebook's and YouTube's algorithms take fear-mongering to the extreme by targeting content at individuals based on all the bits of data the platforms have collected about them. The algorithms know exactly how to push your particular buttons because of the platforms' spying on you. Facebook and Google have so much data on you and people who are like you that the algorithms know what content is likely to make you react and know how to target you based on your particular vulnerability.

These giants take all the information they gather on you and crunch it together with the data of billions of other people, so that they can infer things about you that you don't even know about yourself! This means what Facebook and Google know about you is not limited to the tremendous amount of data they've collected about you, but their algorithms draw inferences about you based on the data of billions of other users—that you of course don't have access to. The scale of the data they collect is the problem because they have so much information about so many people that they can know the most personal things about you that you have not in any way disclosed. They can target and manipulate users based on these inferences, knowing what types of messages they are most susceptible to.

Fear, anger, addiction, and extremism are monopoly problems for the same reason privacy is a monopoly problem: monopolies don't lose profits when they abuse you, they can keep you in the dark without the sunlight that competition brings, they buy off lawmakers to stop regulation of harms they cause, and they can shut out innovators with better business models.

Because of their sheer scale, Facebook and Google have outsized control on the flow of information worldwide. If competition existed, purveyors of hate, fear, and disinformation wouldn't have as much of an impact. They wouldn't be able to reach potentially 2.3 billion users on a single platform that boosts their hate. And if digital markets were more competitive, Facebook and Google would have less influence on the worldwide distribution of content.

Just as tech giants can abuse privacy because people can't vote with their feet and switch to alternatives, so too can they push all our buttons and make us angry and fearful without competitive constraint. If competition existed among algorithms and the way content is prioritized and delivered to us, users could choose platforms that don't worsen anxiety and polarization.

Some say an open market would just lead to a race to the bottom as companies competed with one another to addict us. But regulation that incentivizes better business models and makes addictive ones unprofitable or illegal could prevent such an outcome. We can demand our political representatives take action.

Polarizing Media Is Also a Monopoly Problem

Big News also amplifies polarization in America. News companies have always tried to freak us out to get our attention and sell ads. "If it bleeds it leads," was the slogan of newspapers from long ago. But America used to have rules that preserved diversity in the marketplace of ideas and limited how much power one company could have over the flow of information. The rules that remain have been under attack, as the Federal Communications Commission has pursued monopoly-friendly deregulation under its Trump-appointed chairman, Ajit Pai. On top of rubber-stamping the Sprint/T-Mobile merger, the FCC under Pai rolled back long-standing rules that limited the number of stations broadcasters can own. A federal court of appeals invalidated the FCC's rule change, and the FCC has appealed to the Supreme Court.

Pai led the effort to relax broadcast ownership limits after he and his staff had several meetings with executives of Sinclair Broadcast Group, a giant in broadcasting. Sinclair owns and operates 191 broadcast television stations in 89 markets, and has in the past used shell corporations to evade broadcast ownership limits. Sinclair has spread its right-wing viewpoint across the country, including racist and anti-Muslim propaganda. During the 2016 presidential election, Sinclair reportedly ordered its stations to air a video segment that suggested voters should not support Hillary Clinton because the Democratic Party was historically pro-slavery.

In cable, Fox News has a strong grip on the dissemination of information to a large portion of the country. News outlets that reach viewers who are information-poor have greater "media power" and influence, according to researchers. If measured by "attention share," they concluded, "Rupert Murdoch is the most powerful U.S. news owner, both because Fox News has a large viewership and because its viewers are information-poor: they access a smaller number of other sources than users of most other sources." Comcast, which includes NBC, MSNBC, and CNBC, and Time Warner, which includes CNN, each had less than half the attention share of Fox's owner News Corporation.

Such concentrated control of news is not only politically polarizing but can also be dangerous to public health, as we saw at the onset of the COVID-19 pandemic. Fox News has come under fire for minimizing the virus and referring to it as a hoax that was politically motivated to attack Trump. Seventy-four journalism professors wrote a letter to Fox asking the network to urgently "help protect the lives of all Americans—including your elderly viewers—by ensuring that the information you deliver is based on scientific facts." Exposure to different viewpoints is lacking not only on social media, but also in media at large. When media is in the hands of a few owners, information oligopolists can more easily manipulate public opinion.

Your Life, Better

An alternate reality from relentless spying is possible. In that reality, meaningful privacy regulation, not crafted by monopoly lobbyists, curbs surveillance by default. Big Tech is no longer exempt from norms and laws against spying that have long existed in the offline world, like the prohibitions on reading someone else's mail or recording a phone call without consent. Antitrust enforcement brings competition and ensures you have the option of voting with your feet if a company dares abuse your privacy.

You're free to talk to Alexa and control exactly what information Amazon gathers about you and how it's used. Maybe you can even talk to Alex instead—perhaps new competitors don't make all assistants be women by default. Dystopia through surveillance is the stuff of novels like *The Handmaid's Tale* and *1984*, not real life.

When you check social media, you see a range of ideas and outlooks on current affairs that are even-toned and thoroughly researched. Competition and privacy regulation could go a long way to making us feel calmer, safer, more united, and more connected. The needed changes may not be profitable for Big Tech, but they are indeed possible.

For now, a few privacy-protecting alternatives could bring you at least a bit of peace. They include DuckDuckGo for privacy-friendly searching, Brave for private browsing, Protonmail for encrypted email, and Signal for encrypted messaging. DuckDuckGo provides a range of privacy-protecting options on its website spreadprivacy.com. The site also gives tips for adjusting the settings on your devices to maximize privacy and for opting out of online tracking.

FIVE

MONOPOLIES THREATEN DEMOCRACY AND YOUR FREEDOM

"Tonight, Americans find out which candidate
the social media algorithms have selected."

MONOPOLY POWER ENDANGERS OUR ELECTIONS

Facebook's business model is harming political discourse and elections around the world. Ever since the 2016 U.S. presidential election, Facebook has promised to work on its disinformation problem, yet has offered only minor, ineffective Band-Aids. Lies are also spreading on YouTube, Twitter, TikTok, and other platforms, but Facebook likely is the biggest threat because of its massive scale and its micro-targeting features. The problem is not solved—Facebook fueled disinformation in the 2019 British election and the 2020 U.S. Democratic primary.

Drastic, urgent action must be taken against Facebook's surveillance-based, hypertargeted advertising business model, or our democracy risks being subverted to Facebook's financial interests in the 2020 U.S. presidential election and beyond.

Truly fixing Facebook's threat to free and fair elections would require fundamental changes to its business model, but Facebook is not going to upset its gravy train unless it's forced to do so.

By 2016, the digital analytics firm Cambridge Analytica had developed psychological profiles of every American voter, it asserted, using Facebook data. Working hand in hand with Facebook employees, Cambridge Analytica targeted "persuadable" American voters in swing states with propaganda intended to help elect Donald Trump, whose campaign paid the company nearly $6 million. Alexander Nix, Cambridge Analytica's then-CEO, was caught on film pitching the company's disinformation services to reporters, who posed as potential clients interested in changing the outcome of the Sri Lankan elections. "It doesn't have to be true, it just has to be believed," said Nix. Cambridge Analytica has claimed credit for helping to elect far-right leaders around the globe, from Tobago to Kenya to Brazil.

According to congressional testimony by whistle-blower Chris Wylie, Cambridge Analytica cofounder Steve Bannon oversaw the company's campaign to suppress African American voting before leaving the company to become the Trump campaign's CEO. In an interview, Wylie said, "Steve Bannon was looking for ways of fighting a culture war." The weapons are disinformation, and just like a missile or a gun, these weapons need a targeting system, explained Wylie. "So in a culture war, your payload is a narrative, and your targeting system becomes data and algorithms in order to fire at culture, where he needed to literally treat it like a war." Once Steven Bannon and alt-right hedge fund billionaire Robert Mercer learned of the warlike capabilities of the company then called SCL, they bought into it with $10 million to start Cambridge Analytica.

SCL's expertise "was in 'psychological operations—or psyops—changing people's minds not through persuasion but through 'information dominance,' a set of techniques that includes rumour, disinformation and fake news," reports Carole Cadwalladr, the *Guardian* journalist who exposed the Facebook Cambridge Analytica scandal. SCL previously had been hired by the U.S. government's Defense Advanced Research Projects Agency (DARPA) to develop profiling tools. "So all of a sudden," said Wylie, "all of the people who were there when we were looking at research on how to defend Britain, defend America, the tools and the weapons and the things that we were looking at in order to defend the people was now acquired by people who wanted to invert them on those same people and treat an American voter in the same way that we treat a radical Islamist terrorist."

Surveillance done in the name of keeping us safe can easily be turned against us.

Leading up to the 2016 presidential election, Cambridge Analytica harvested the personal data of a reported 87 million Facebook users with a personality quiz that collected users' personal data, and the data of their friends, without their knowledge. This data harvesting operation was led by a Russian-American researcher at the University of Cambridge, Dr. Aleksandr Kogan. Wylie's written testimony said that while Dr. Kogan was working with Cambridge Analytica, he was simultaneously building algorithms using Facebook data for psychological profiling for Russia in St. Petersburg. The Russian project focused on the traits of "narcissism, Machiavellianism and psychopathy," testified Wylie.

Cambridge Analytica, similarly, "sought to identify mental and emotional vulnerabilities in certain subsets of the American population and worked to exploit those vulnerabilities by targeting information designed to activate some of the worst characteristics in people, such as neuroticism, paranoia and racial biases," testified Wylie. He continues, "This was targeted at narrow segments of the population."

What Cambridge Analytica did, however, wasn't a hack on Facebook. Cambridge Analytica played fast and loose with Facebook data, breaking a rule that Facebook failed to enforce. A ton of other apps got access to our personal data, so Facebook hiding behind its meaningless rule is like a bank pointing the finger at robbers when it left its vault open. Overall Cambridge Analytica used Facebook exactly how it is intended to be used—as a manipulation machine.

Through ubiquitous tracking, compiling the data sets of billions of people, and algorithmic inferences, Facebook learns what messages people are susceptible to—whether advertisements, extreme political propaganda, or election meddling. Just as Facebook enables advertisers to influence people's purchasing decisions, it enables propagandists to influence people's political decisions. Facebook made Cambridge Analytica's work easy by spying on us, by programming its algorithms to amplify incendiary content, and by developing micro-targeting that allows propagandists to individually target voters based on highly granular data it has gathered about them. This is still how Facebook's business model works today. In April 2020, *The Markup* reported that Facebook was allowing advertisers to target ads at people it classified as being interested in "pseudoscience," a particularly dangerous proposition amid the rampant disinformation surrounding COVID-19.

In 2017, *The Australian* obtained access to an internal Facebook document that explains how the platform can target "moments when young people need a confidence boost." "By monitoring posts, pictures, interactions and internet activity in real-time, Facebook can work out when young people feel 'stressed,' 'defeated,' 'overwhelmed,' 'anxious,' 'nervous,' 'stupid,' 'silly,' 'useless,' and a 'failure,'" reported the newspaper. Prepared as part of an advertising pitch to one of Australia's big banks, the document stated that detailed information on young people's emotional states is "based on internal Facebook data," according to *The Australian*. The Facebook document includes information on when young people exhibit emotions related to "conquering fear," or moments related to "looking good and body confidence," and "working out & losing weight." When *The Australian*'s report prompted an outcry, Facebook released a statement saying it "does not offer tools to target people based on their emotional state."

But Cambridge Analytica did target users based on emotional vulnerabilities using Facebook data and Facebook micro-targeting. Facebook has even tried to patent psychological profiling, applying for a patent on "determining user personality characteristics from social networking system communications and characteristics."

Facebook rents out its manipulation machine to anyone who will pay, even if their customers are paying for U.S. political ads with rubles. In 2016, the year of the U.S. presidential election and the United Kingdom's Brexit vote, Facebook's ad revenue jumped by nearly $10 billion.

Facebook knew at least as early as 2015 that Cambridge Analytica had harvested users' data, but it didn't warn those users. When the tech giant learned the *Guardian* was going to break the Cambridge Analytica story, Facebook threatened to sue them. Facebook only warned users in 2018, three weeks after the *Guardian*, the *New York Times*, and Channel 4 made the story public. It kicked the whistle-blower, Christopher Wylie, off the Facebook, Instagram, and Whats-App platforms, leading Wylie to ask: "*What happens to our democracy when these companies can delete people at will who dissent, scrutinize, or speak out?*"

Move Fast and Break Democracy

Senator Elizabeth Warren has spoken out against Big Tech and called for the breakup of Facebook, Google, and Amazon. That's a bold thing to do, since Facebook and Google control the flow of information, politicians don't have much of a choice of whether to use them to reach voters, and Facebook is the manipulation tool of choice for elections around the world. In an internal Facebook meeting in July 2019, Mark Zuckerberg predicted that if Warren were to become the next president, "I would bet that we will have a legal challenge. . . ." He vowed to fight such a challenge, saying "at the end of the day, if someone's going to try to threaten something that existential, you go to the mat and you fight."

A few short months later, in the fall of 2019, Mark Zuckerberg had two unannounced meetings with Donald Trump. In mid-October, the week before the second meeting, Zuckerberg gave a speech at Georgetown University stating that although regular ads were not allowed to contain false or deceptive information, "We don't fact-check political ads."

Anyone who speaks out against the monopolist can be punished by the monopolist. Such punishment may come through Facebook business moves that appear neutral on their face. In changing its policies to allow false political ads, which favored Donald Trump, Facebook bought itself protection against getting broken up. Trump probably didn't want to break up Facebook anyway—he wanted to control it. He wanted to use the manipulation machine to spread hate-mongering propaganda.

We cannot allow one guy's decisions to influence the election of our nation's leader. I didn't get to vote for Mark Zuckerberg, did you?

Zuckerberg's Georgetown speech justified Facebook's political ad policy as grounded in free expression. But free expression is impossible when one company controls the flow of speech to more than 2.3 billion people, using algorithms that amplify disinformation and surveillance-based ad tools that allow micro-targeting of voters. Facebook picking and choosing what information users see based on how much money the content makes the platform—with "engaging" content being most profitable—is the antithesis of free expression. Deceptive political ads that spread fear and anger, and deceptive content intended to inflame tension and divide Americans on cultural issues, are favored content, boosted by Facebook's business model.

Michelle Obama's slogan, "When they go low, we go high," is not compatible with Facebook's disinformation-amplifying algorithms. Countering hateful propaganda with positive messaging is not possible because Facebook's algorithm will amplify the hate and bury the unifying message. Without Facebook changing its algorithm, being hateful is one of the most effective ways to spread your message and reach voters.

Free expression also requires a public sphere of debate, not individualized feeds of content targeted at people based on information learned about them through surveillance.

In her TED Talk, Zeynep Tufekci talks about how engagement algorithms make the public sphere private: "As a public and as citizens, we no longer know if we're seeing the same information or what anybody else is seeing, and without a common basis of information, little by little, public debate is becoming impossible." This problem of information being siloed and individualized is widely referred to as filter bubbles or echo chambers. When we don't see the same information or if we do, it's presented from the polar opposite perspective, it's no wonder we can't find common ground with each other.

An important principle of First Amendment law is the counterspeech doctrine. Supreme Court justice Louis D. Brandeis established the doctrine in the 1927 case *Whitney v. California*, saying, "If there be time to expose through discussion, the falsehoods and fallacies, to avert the evil by the process of education, the remedy to be applied is more speech, not enforced silence." Brandeis's solution to deceptive or harmful speech is to counter it with speech that sets the record straight or conveys a different message, rather than censoring it. But with targeted social media feeds, users don't see counterspeech. Instead of censorship, one solution is to loosen Facebook's control over the flow of information through competition, as antitrust enforcement could make way for pro-democracy innovators. Another is to prohibit Facebook's surveillance-based, hypertargeted digital advertising business model.

Don't think that Instagram is a disinformation-free alternative to Facebook. A 2018 report by the cybersecurity firm New Knowledge, commissioned by the Senate Intelligence Committee, details the attempts by Russia's Internet Research Agency (IRA) to influence U.S. political discourse. "Instagram was a significant front in the IRA's influence operation, something that Facebook executives appear to have avoided mentioning in Congressional testimony," the report said. "Our assessment is that Instagram is likely to be a key battleground on an ongoing basis."

What's Monopoly Got to Do with It

Facebook is not the only culprit threatening our elections, as a nefarious web of actors are attacking democracy across the globe. But Facebook's scale and lack of accountability make it particularly dangerous, and its political power stands in the way of needed reforms.

Revisiting an earlier point here, what constrains corporations from pursuing profits in ways that cause harm are: 1) competition and 2) regulation. Without either of these, Facebook can choose a business model that endangers our elections, and it doesn't have to worry about losing customers or profits. It can choose to spy on us, program its algorithms to boost incendiary content, and allow propagandists of

all kinds—whether advertisers, foreign governments, or lying American politicians—to individually target us based on invasive profiling.

Facebook doesn't have to worry about users defecting to a competitor because Facebook bought its closest substitutes. It can use
its monopoly power to shut out potential competitors that would do
better, competing by offering different algorithms or business models.
Facebook can use its political power to stop lawmakers from making
the needed fixes. On that front, the GOP leadership seems to favor
Facebook's interests in allowing election interference, believing any
interference would be to their advantage, and being willing to trade
democracy for political gain.

I've focused on Facebook, but Google's YouTube is also a threat
to elections because of its engagement-prioritizing algorithms and
2 billion users. An in-depth report by the *New York Times* looked
at YouTube's role in the election in Brazil of far-right president Jair
Bolsonaro. "In a country driven to the edge by economic and political crises, YouTube's algorithms may have played a decisive role in
Bolsonaro's rise." The sheer scale of Facebook and Google's surveillance, the manipulation they allow, and their massive reach means the
dangers they cause are a direct result of lawmakers allowing them to
morph into monopoly monsters.

Facebook's and YouTube's power must be checked and their dangerous business models dismantled to save our elections.

Winning this battle will take time, but immediately one simple
measure could make a difference in our elections—banning or heavily restricting micro-targeted advertising. As Wylie points out, the
weapon in the war against the American voter is disinformation,
and disinformation needs a targeting system just like a missile or a
gun does. Facebook's own employees have called for restrictions on
micro-targeting in a letter to management that included other com-
monsense measures, like imposing a silence period before elections

when no political ads can run. Facebook's former chief security officer has also proposed limits to micro-targeting as a solution, as has Ellen L. Weintraub, a Democratic commissioner of the Federal Election Commission.

Micro-targeting must be banned across the board, not just on Facebook. Digital strategies also include "geo-fencing," using people's IP addresses to identify whether they attended a Trump rally or church, for example, and to then target their devices with text messages or app alerts.

The number of tools to spy on and manipulate us is proliferating, and fixing Facebook won't fix everything. But it'll be a damn good start. People will say the solutions of ending surveillance and micro-targeting are too simplistic, unrealistic, naïve, and not possible. Those are the people who benefit from the status quo and have something to lose by changing it, who want us all to throw up our hands and say "it's too complicated" to do anything. But don't listen! Our democracy is worth fighting for, and monopolies' profits are not worth its sacrifice.

Monopoly power threatens our elections in another way. Russian hackers targeted voting machines in twenty-one states in 2016 and breached systems in two states, according to Special Counsel Robert Mueller's report. Yet a voting machine duopoly stands in the way of securing our elections from hacking. Two companies, Election Systems & Software (ES&S) and Dominion Voting Systems, together supply more than 80 percent of America's voting machines. Several of their lobbyists reportedly made contributions to Mitch McConnell's campaign and joint fund-raising committee, soon before McConnell made clear he would not allow any of the bipartisan bills proposing voting machine reform to reach the Senate floor.

MONOPOLIES RAVAGE THE FREE
PRESS ESSENTIAL TO DEMOCRACY

Politicians who are supposed to represent you and your fellow voters are doing the bidding of big business instead. How do they get away with it?

Your local hometown newspaper closed up shop. They'd been around forever and were the only ones keeping tabs on local politicians and writing about what's happening in your community. The local paper just couldn't keep up in the digital age, people say.

Or perhaps your hometown paper still exists but is a shell of its former self. Most of its content is nationally syndicated, with a small local section that's a far cry from hard-hitting news.

Now your favorite online news company is also closing its doors. Tech-savvy Millennials ran that media outlet, and everyone said the founders were so innovative. Innovation apparently wasn't enough to keep their reporting alive, either. Real news is becoming an endangered species, at the same time that "fake news" is booming. Where are the watchdogs that help hold local and federal governments accountable, while helping us know more about our community, by informing, recording, and commenting on what's going on?

The Internet Didn't Kill the News, Monopolies Did

With disinformation running rampant, we desperately need a strong press. But at the same time that Facebook and Google are boosting deceptive propaganda, they're decimating journalism. Facebook and Google are monopolizing ad revenue, while using the content that publishers create as fodder to fuel their platforms. Newspaper employment fell about 47 percent between 2008 and 2018, and more than half of America's counties now don't have a daily local paper. This means thousands fewer reporters and editors are covering the news. By April 2020, thirty-three thousand employees of news companies were furloughed, had their pay slashed, or were laid off as the COVID-19 pandemic reduced advertising revenues and worsened the collapse of local news.

Many people think Craigslist is to blame for the destruction of local newspapers because it pocketed the classifieds ad revenue that had long supported news. While this disruption did undercut a traditionally important source of journalism's funding, Craigslist cannot be blamed for media outlets' inability to get their share of the multibillion-dollar digital ad market. In the digital age, online advertising could support journalism just as regular advertising did in the past. But Facebook and Google account for 85 to 90 percent of the growth of the more than $150 billion North American and European digital advertising market, according to Jason Kint, CEO of Digital Content Next, a trade association for publishers. Facebook and Google make a ton of money from the content publishers create—without having to pay the content creators or invest in creating the content themselves. Just like how the platforms extract wealth from creators like songwriters, Facebook and Google extract the fruits of journalists' labor.

Facebook and Google are publishers' competitors, vying for user attention, user data, and ad dollars. But news publishers must get through Facebook's and Google's gates to reach readers due to the two platforms' concentrated control over the flow of information globally. More than 68 percent of American adults get some news from social media, according to Pew. And Facebook is now the second-largest news provider when measured in terms of share of Americans' attention.

Facebook, however, has long maintained it is a neutral platform and not a publisher, so that it can avoid liability for false or harmful content under a safe harbor law called Section 230 of the Communications Decency Act. Section 230 gives Big Tech wide-reaching legal immunity for content posted on their platforms. News publishers have to compete against Facebook and Google while being held to stricter legal standards.

Like third-party sellers competing against Amazon on Amazon.com or app developers competing against Apple in its App Store, news publishers are in the lose-lose position of competing against the platforms they must use to reach customers. Facebook and Google exploit their gatekeeper positions to divert ad revenue away from publishers and into their own pockets. As Jason Kint explains it, "Google and Facebook have put themselves between news institutions and their readers, often replacing valuable editorial decisions with algorithmic decisions." But, says Kint, "They act as absentee owners often missing local context in their understanding of and impact on communities," and "capture outsized profits without the risk of liability for content and programming decisions."

Once again, the platform monopolists are controlling the game and playing it, too.

Cut Off with the Flip of a Switch

Because Facebook and Google have concentrated control over the internet, which at its start was wonderfully decentralized, news publishers became dependent on them to reach users. But over time both platforms have adjusted their product design to keep more and more internet traffic for themselves. Google and Facebook both have business incentives to keep users on their platforms to collect more data and show more ads. More than 70 percent of Google's revenue came from ads on its own properties in 2018. The platforms pull technological levers that keep users within Facebook's and Google's digital walls, reducing traffic to news publishers' properties and depriving publishers of the ad revenue that funds journalism.

Facebook has the ability to hoard more user attention, data, and ad revenue simply by tweaking its algorithm. Facebook changed its algorithm in 2018, promising to show more posts from friends and family. This flip of a switch decimated news publishers of all sizes, threatening the survival of outlets like *Mother Jones*, *Vox*, and *Slate*. *Slate*'s traffic from Facebook plummeted 87 percent from a peak of 28 million in January 2017 to less than 4 million in May 2018. Even the small media company that I mentioned earlier, Women You Should Know, is still fighting for its survival after the 2018 algorithmic change caused its Web traffic to plummet.

Women You Should Know is a digital native, with almost half a million followers on Facebook, not an old crusty media outlet that couldn't keep up with the digital age. Failure to innovate in the face of disruption is not the problem. Neither are *Vox* or *Slate* old-fashioned dinosaurs. The problem, instead, is Facebook's consolidated gatekeeper power over the internet. Because of Facebook's centralized power, its changes—even purportedly well-intentioned ones—determine the winners and losers of content, including news publishers' very existence.

Publishers never had a fair shot, nor do they have bargaining power against the platforms.

Facebook and Google can pursue profit-maximizing tactics and hurt the profits of real news companies without constraint because the normal checks and balances of a free, competitive market do not exist. Weak antitrust enforcement set the stage for these platforms to extract the fruits of publishers' and journalists' labor, much as monopolies are extracting wealth across most sectors of our economy. If publishers have no choice but to deal with monopolists because they have become the infrastructure of information flow, monopolists can extract wealth and undercut publishers' ability to bring important and diverse viewpoints to the world.

With the ability to control the distribution of information, ad money, and the relationship between the reader and the news outlet, tech platform monopolists now have unprecedented power over reporters and news publishers themselves. In yet another instance of monopolists giving with one hand and taking a whole lot more with the other, Facebook and Google have begun giving grants to news organizations. These grants only increase the platforms' power over journalists and don't fix the real problems.

Spies Like Us

On top of Facebook and Google hoarding internet traffic, a main problem is that Facebook and Google each built an architecture of surveillance—with the help of anticompetitive mergers—that sustains their duopoly power over digital advertising. Publishers and content creators that don't read your email, know your internet searches, track your location, know who your friends are, know every YouTube video you've watched or what you've purchased across the Web, for example, can't really hope to compete with Google and Facebook, who are tracking you in all of these ways and more, for targeted advertising dollars.

Advertising used to be done based on context (you'd see a fishing pole ad next to an article about fishing), rather than by tracking people across the Web and offline to target ads at them (instead you see a fishing pole because a tech platform spied on your fishing trip last weekend). This context-based advertising was a better deal for news publishers and content creators, and for you. Banning hypertargeted advertising would help level the competitive playing field for digital ad dollars, while lessening problems like election interference and user manipulation that we've already discussed.

Monopoly Corruption with No One Watching

A financially frail and smaller press means politicians can cater to monopoly money in the dark. They can represent huge corporations' interests instead of yours, without being held accountable for it.

Kevin Riley, editor of the *Atlanta Journal-Constitution* (*AJC*), testified before Congress about the role his paper has played in protecting the people of Georgia: "At times, the AJC's reporters appear to be among the only journalists covering the bills, the lobbyists and the political developments," wrote Riley. The *AJC* has a reporter who has been covering the state budget for decades, helping to ensure that budgets serve the people instead of powerful corporations. Incidentally, it was the *AJC* that investigated and exposed Georgia's incorrect—some argued misleading—reporting of coronavirus case numbers, while Governor Brian Kemp swiftly reopened the state. Kemp later publicly apologized. When local papers can no longer make ends meet due to monopoly power over digital ad revenue, politicians become unaccountable to the public.

In chapter 4, we discussed how Californians overwhelmingly support privacy legislation, but yet their elected representatives keep proposing amendments to destroy California's new privacy law. In the 2019–20 legislative session, lawmakers proposed more than a dozen amendments to try to weaken the law. Big Tech has limitless funds to throw at local legislators willing to sell out their people in order to fund their next reelection campaign. This reelection strategy only works if voters don't know what their representatives are doing, which is why the destruction of local news is a critical component to the corruption.

As Big Tech exerts political leverage to try to decimate the will of the people, few local journalists are left to expose the politicians acting at Big Tech's behest. And because Big Tech has used its monopoly power to starve journalism, the people of California often don't know their representatives are working for Big Tech instead of them.

Even privacy activists have a hard time keeping up with all the proposed amendments to California's law. They have a limited amount of time to respond, so not knowing about a bill stops them from being able to fight it. The more adept Big Tech is at thwarting privacy regulation, the more it will continue to starve journalism and the more it will be able to influence government under the cloak of secrecy.

Effective privacy laws would go a long way toward opening up competition and leveling the playing field between Facebook and Google on one hand and news publishers on the other. Strong privacy legislation would help save journalism and weaken Facebook's and Google's monopoly power. Yet it risks being thwarted because of that very monopoly power.

Your voice can help make strong privacy laws and antitrust enforcement against platform monopolists happen. Politicians can stand up to corporate power if a movement of people—who refuse to take it anymore—has their back.

Real News Gets Buried

We've talked about how Facebook and YouTube amplify content that makes us fearful and angry, giving a boost to incendiary propaganda and "fake news." This boost means legitimate news that is not incendiary is de-prioritized, pushed to the bottom of newsfeeds or not shown to users at all. Since disinformation that says Hillary Clinton is running a child sex ring out of a pizza place is more "engaging" than a Pulitzer Prize–winning well-researched article, the real article gets buried. As Maria Ressa, CEO and executive editor of the Philippines' *Rappler*, said in a 2019 speech: "Newsrooms are born to compete, but what we're not seeing is that we're no longer competing against each other—we're competing against disinformation networks. We're competing to tell the facts."

If Facebook's algorithms show the content created by legitimate news publishers less often, then Facebook is tipping the competitive playing field against the publishers it competes with for ad revenue and in favor of content that keeps users on its platform. Such exclusionary behavior is not much different than Google sending competing comparison-shopping services to page four of its search results or Microsoft eliminating Netscape as a browser option on computers in favor of its own Internet Explorer. Burying real news is not only terrible for democracy, it's also a form of monopolization.

Your Life, Better

We can no longer tolerate foreign governments, unscrupulous politicians, and alt-right billionaires being able to psychologically profile us and individually target us with deceptive propaganda. We must demand that lawmakers and enforcers dismantle Facebook's manipulation machine, pass tough privacy laws, and ban surveillance-based targeted advertising, particularly micro-targeting around elections. Only we, the people, can save our elections and our democracy.

When the internet is no longer consolidated into the hands of a few gatekeepers, a robust set of open, interoperable platforms can provide consumers varied options for getting their news, and losing referral traffic from Facebook or Google is no longer such a big deal for news publishers. Public discourse is not subject to the whims and profit motives of monopolists, who can no more extract a tax on or silence everyone else's ideas, creations, and whistle-blowers' and watchdogs' important work. We can see what speech others are seeing, and we can respond to any speech we don't like with counterspeech, as the

First Amendment requires. When politicians act on behalf of their monopoly overlords instead of their voters, their betrayals make the front-page news. Knowing they'll face consequences on election day, politicians become more accountable to the people. This reality is less profitable for big tech, but it *is* possible.

SIX

MONOPOLIES DESTROY OUR PLANET AND CONTROL YOUR FOOD

"I don't care what the 'experts' say.
I'm not budging."

MONOPOLIES RUIN HUMANITY'S HABITAT

Perhaps you've given up plastic bags, straws, and bottles. Maybe you stopped eating meat, drive an electric car, or even use a bike as your means of transportation. But you wonder what good it all does when the Environmental Protection Agency has been gutted and the United States has pulled out of the Paris Climate Accord, which most countries weren't complying with anyway.

If you're a parent, you ache to tell your kids that everything is going to be okay and that you will protect them. Your children wonder why you aren't fixing it. Kids are taking matters into their own hands, walking out of school for climate marches and trying to convince the world's political and business leaders to act. Swedish teenage climate activist Greta Thunberg displays the courage that adults lack.

Experts say that if we continue on our current course, the future will be ridden with dangerous weather, a major reduction in global food supply, rampant political conflict, and millions of climate refugees, with entire cities and even countries dropping into the ocean or becoming uninhabitable. It's so terrifying to think about that you probably want to stop reading this right now, but there is reason for hope.

We Know What We Have to Do

We've already caused irreparable damage to our habitat by warming it by one degree Celsius, but if we limit the warming to 1.5 degrees Celsius, we can avert extreme catastrophe. What needs to be done is not a mystery, but rather is a matter of global consensus among scientists (apart from those who are being paid by Big Oil to lie to us). Young Thunberg spelled it out as clear as day at the World Economic Forum at Davos in 2020:

> When we children tell you to panic, we're not telling you to go on like before . . . And let's be clear, we don't need a low carbon economy, we don't need to lower emissions. Our emissions have to stop if we are to have a chance to stay below the 1.5 degree target. And until we have the technologies that at scale can put our emissions to minus, then we must forget about net zero. We need real zero. . . .
>
> We demand that at this year's World Economic Forum, participants from all companies, banks, institutions, and governments immediately hold all investments in fossil fuel exploration and extraction, immediately end all fossil fuel subsidies and immediately

and completely divest from fossil fuels. We don't want these things done by 2050 or 2030 or even 2021; we want this done now. It may seem like we are asking for a lot and you will of course say that we are naive, but this is just the very minimum amount of effort that is needed to start the rapid sustainable transition. So either you do this, or you're going to have to explain to your children why you are giving up on the 1.5 degree target, giving up without even trying. . . . Your inaction is fueling the flames by the hour, and we are telling you to act as if you loved your children above all else.

We have the solutions to the climate crisis. Like so many other problems discussed in this book, we tie ourselves up in knots trying to find solutions that the behemoths in power will accept. We are told the actual solutions are unrealistic and naïve because they won't fly with the monopolies that run our economy and our government. Solutions that won't work are billed as "realistic" because they won't meaningfully impact monopoly profits. But if something doesn't work, it's not a solution at all. What's more naïve than pursuing nonsolutions when trying to avoid global catastrophe? In Thunberg's words, even worse than doing nothing are "empty words and promises which give the impression that sufficient action is being taken."

Just like when Big Tech says change is *not possible* what it really means is change is *not profitable*, the same is true for Big Oil. The people who say that stemming the climate crisis is not possible are the ones who have something to lose. Rex Tillerson, the former CEO of ExxonMobil and former U.S. secretary of state under Donald Trump, feigned ignorance of scientific consensus on the climate impact of cutting emissions in February 2020, saying "whether or not anything we do will ultimately influence [climate change] remains to be seen." He added, "One day we'll know the answer to that, but our ability to predict the answer to that is quite complicated."

There it is again. The old "it's complicated" do-nothing trap again used by those in power who don't want anything to change. It's not that freaking complicated!

As Naomi Klein writes in *On Fire: The (Burning) Case for a Green New Deal*, "If you are part of the economy's winning class and funded by even bigger winners, as so many politicians are, then your attempts to craft climate legislation tend to be guided by the idea that change should be as minimal and as unchallenging to the status quo as possible." Eliminating emissions and meeting the 1.5 degree target is possible. It's just not profitable for the select few who are reaping the spoils of the status quo.

When we let big corporations rule the world instead of people, short-term thinking fixated on maximizing profits for the next quarter determines what is possible and what is not. Michael Mann, one of the world's leading climate scientists, told the *Guardian*, "The great tragedy of the climate crisis is that seven and a half billion people must pay the price—in the form of a degraded planet—so that a couple of dozen polluting interests can continue to make record profits."

Meeting the 1.5 degree target is actually profit-maximizing for most everybody else. From 2017 to 2019, climate disaster events across the United States cost more than $460 billion, according to government reports. Citibank puts the cost of climate inaction at $44 trillion by 2060, while estimating the cost of investing in renewables as lower than the costs of continuing on the current path. Even most of the monopolies in this book see the climate crisis as bad for business. A 2019 report shows that major corporations expect the climate crisis to cost them $1 trillion over the next five years, while estimating opportunities to address climate change could bring in more than $2 trillion.

Greta Thunberg is not the naïve one. What could be more unhinged from reality than flushing trillions of dollars down the toilet while endangering the future of humanity? Governments are planning to produce 120 percent more fossil fuels by 2030 than meeting the 1.5 degree target requires, according to a 2019 report. Talk about being unrealistic.

Opportunity in Crisis

To stem the climate crisis, we must make drastic changes to the way power is structured that will enrich 99 percent of Americans. This gives reason for hope.

This book is all about how concentrated power is ruining our lives. Nowhere is that clearer than in the threat to humanity posed by the climate crisis. Monopolized America is unsustainable, and concentrated power, most literally, will be the end of us unless we act now to break it down and redistribute it. A transition to renewable energy sources would do exactly this. The transition, like all drastic change, will be difficult, but ultimately it will make our lives better, while preserving humanity's habitat. A deconcentrated economy is good for everyone.

And as Naomi Klein explains, "We will not get the job done unless we are willing to embrace systemic economic and social change." For this reason, the Green New Deal doesn't just call for eliminating emissions; it also calls for universal health care, education, and day care and calls for green jobs to be unionized. Some have criticized the Green New Deal approach for focusing on economic and social justice, saying it makes climate action harder to politically achieve. But rather than "weighing it down," the social and economic components of the Green New Deal "are precisely what is lifting it up," writes Klein.

Any plan that passes on the costs of the transition to sustainability to working people is destined to fail, Klein posits, pointing to French president Emmanuel Macron's attempt to increase a fuel tax in 2018. The tax led to protests and riots by workers in yellow safety vests, who were already under intense economic strain. Macron was forced to roll back the tax. "The Green New Deal, however, is already showing that it has the power to mobilize a truly intersectional mass movement behind it—not despite its sweeping ambition, but precisely because of it," writes Klein.

We can't save humanity unless we make people's lives better because, like the yellow vests, Americans already stretched thin, or devastated by COVID-19, cannot withstand greater economic strain. But, as I hope this book has convinced you, attempts to make people's lives better will fail unless we deconcentrate power and stop monopolistic extraction of wealth from us all.

With humanity's future hanging in the balance, then, we have no choice but to fight monopoly power. The Green New Deal recognizes this, including a provision for "ensuring a commercial environment where every business is free from unfair competition and domination by domestic or international monopolies."

The Green New Deal has the potential to democratize power. Open Markets Institute's Sandeep Vaheesan explains how Franklin Delano Roosevelt's New Deal gave loans and support to rural residents who wanted to electrify their communities through cooperation. The program, administered by the Rural Electrification Administration, revolutionized rural America and brought electricity controlled by the people to farms across the country. "Like its 1930s counterpart, the Green New Deal should champion democratic cooperation in electricity," writes Vaheesan. Such a plan "would help put the United States on a path to clean power controlled not by unaccountable and short-termist corporate and financial interests, but by all of us."

The United States Climate Alliance, a bipartisan coalition of twenty-five state governors, announced in November 2019: "we have demonstrated that economic growth and climate action go hand-in-hand. Alliance states have reduced emissions faster than the rest of the country while growing per capita GDP three times as fast. Climate action is a driver of—not a deterrent to—innovation and economic strength."

We're all so accustomed to monopoly rule that we've forgotten what America can achieve when our government works for the people instead of giant corporations.

Oligopolies Brought Us Here

Fossil fuel giants are the epitome of the extractive business model, literally extracting resources from earth while extracting wealth from everyone else—and much worse, extracting the future from humanity.

Chevron, Exxon, BP, and Shell are together behind more than 10 percent of global carbon emissions since 1965, reports the *Guardian*. Together with Total, they invested over $1 billion on misleading climate-related branding and lobbying against climate-motivated policy in the three years following the Paris Agreement, according to the nonprofit InfluenceMap. Five out of the top ten largest global companies by revenue are oil and gas companies. Yet the United States government pays $20 billion in direct fossil fuel subsidies annually, giving a taxpayer handout to the richest companies in the world to destroy humanity's habitat.

Oil and gas giants knew they were endangering humanity long before we did. Exxon actively suppressed research beginning in the 1970s about the effects of fossil fuels on the viability of our habitat. In the early 1990s, Koch Industries joined Exxon in promoting a counter-narrative to climate change. These giants effectively own members of Congress, predominantly in the Republican Party. From 2019 to 2020, sixteen of the top twenty recipients of oil and gas donations were Republican, according to Open Secrets. Mitch McConnell ranked number five and Donald Trump ranked fourth in dollar amount of donations received.

Koch Industries is consistently the top oil and gas donor, donating to Republican politicians and conservative groups. As journalist Christopher Leonard detailed in his book *Kochland*, the Koch brothers built a lobbying powerhouse that included "think tanks, university research institutes, industry trade associations, and a parade of philanthropic institutions to support it financially," known as the "Kochtopus."

To make matters worse, Big Finance and Big Tech are in bed with Big Oil. "The 'big three' asset managers have massive holdings of coal stocks, and the world's largest asset manager, BlackRock, alone holds nearly $61 billion in equity in four of the largest global oil companies," writes Graham Steele for the Great Democracy Initiative, a nonprofit organization developing policy solutions for a rigged economy. Steele proposes that financial regulators use existing legal authority to stop Big Finance's funding of the climate crisis, which poses significant risks to financial stability. Steele notes that the corporations polluting earth are currently being treated as "too big to fail," and concludes, "Instead, it is our planet, not the big banks or Big Oil, that we cannot afford to let fail."

As for Big Tech, they're climate hypocrites. Journalist Brian Merchant exposes the dishonesty in Big Tech's public commitments to sustainability in a piece for *Gizmodo* titled, "How Google, Microsoft, and Big Tech are Automating the Climate Crisis." Google, Merchant writes, is a "veritable innovation arm of the fossil fuel extraction industry," that is "using machine learning to find more oil reserves both above and below the seas, its data services are streamlining and automating extant oilfield operations, and it is helping oil companies find ways to trim costs and compete with clean energy upstarts."

Amazon even has an oil and gas division that pitches its Amazon Web Services to fossil fuel companies! When Amazon employees spoke out against it, Amazon threatened to fire them. "Empowering Oil & Gas with AI," was the theme of Microsoft's November 2018 exhibition at one of the world's largest trade events for oil and gas in Abu Dhabi. Take a minute and contemplate the absurdity of "empowering" companies that are among the most powerful on earth, whose unrelenting quest for profits threaten the future survival of humanity.

On top of Microsoft rolling out its AI to help optimize drilling, Microsoft Azure has a contract with Chevron that is rumored to be worth more than a billion dollars to help it more efficiently destroy planet earth. Microsoft Azure also counts BP, Shell, and an Exxon subsidiary as clients, reports Merchant.

Facebook, for its part, earns tens of millions of dollars on disinformation advertising by Big Oil. InfluenceMap estimated that oil and gas companies and their trade groups spent $17 million on political advertising on Facebook in the United States alone, just between May 2018 and October 2019. This number doesn't include all the deceptive Facebook groups funded by Big Oil, like "Texans for Natural Gas," which has spent up to $750,000 on political social media advertising. InfluenceMap adds that "social media tactics have particularly supported the oil sector and their trade groups' attempts to block or rollback regulation that impacts their sector at the state-level."

Big Oil, Big Finance, and Big Tech are in cahoots, and we must beat them (as well as Big Ag, which we'll talk about in the next section) to save humanity's future. Similar to how monopoly and privacy abuses are intricately related, so too are monopoly power and climate change. Concentrated corporate power allows these companies to destroy earth and hurt us all without losing profits, to choose dangerous business models, to keep us in the dark about the ways they are destroying earth, and to buy off lawmakers to keep them from passing robust environmental laws. Climate-destroying business models are not inevitable. Sustainable, affordable alternatives exist. Big Oil uses their market power to shut out green innovators, and if lawmakers and enforcers would loosen the oligopolists' grip on the rules of the game, it would give green innovations a chance to break through.

But we don't have time to wait for an antitrust case to break up fossil fuel companies. We need to break out everything else in the anti-monopoly toolkit. We need to attack corruption, insist on regulation, and remove financial support for fossil fuels. We need to pass the Green New Deal, or a similar legislative platform. We need to act immediately not just at national and international levels, but also locally.

Consumerism Won't Save Us

The ideological primacy of the consumer over other aspects of humanity has not just destroyed antitrust law (while price-gouging us all in the name of "consumer welfare"), it has endangered humanity itself. We've been operating on a climate-destroying model of economic growth driven by consumption, a model increasingly questioned by economists who fall into two main camps. One camp thinks economic prosperity is possible without growth, by shifting spending from accumulating stuff to services, such as health care and child care. The other camp strives for "green growth"—growth driven by things like sustainable infrastructure investment, without carbon emissions.

Consumerism has been both this country's economic model and our drug. In our monopoly-based system that extracts wealth and power from us and puts us under relentless stress, shopping has been the opiate of the masses. So have the dopamine hits we get from notifications and posts on social media, and quite literally, opioids. These opiates distract us from the robber barons stealing from us and numb the pain of those who suffer the worst consequences of their extraction.

We've been so indoctrinated into the cult of the consumer that we've forgotten how much power we have as citizens. We tend to look for solutions in consumerism but buying metal straws is not the answer. No one can solve this problem individualistically.

Meeting the 1.5 degree target requires collective action. Collective action is daunting when we are all time-starved. But if you reduced your shopping and social media usage, you'd be surprised how much room you actually do have for flexing your citizenship muscle by participating in green groups like Earthjustice, Greenpeace, or local groups in your community. It's not about saying "no" to stuff that makes you happy, it's about saying "yes" to a better life—and a brighter future for our children. Because, let's face it, that stuff never made you happy in the first place. We throw stuff into an unfillable hole left by a life under pressure, a life without enough community and purpose. Civic engagement actually can fill that hole. And whether to be an active citizen is frankly no longer optional.

Humanity will rise to the occasion because it must, and now. The Sunrise Movement championing the Green New Deal is just one example of the type of collective action that, together with movements around the globe, can simultaneously defeat monopolistic extraction, create an economy that works for all, and save humanity's home. The most important obstacle to overcome is the belief—sowed by those who benefit from the status quo—that change is not possible. Don't listen to their nonsense. We will only be able to meet the 1.5 degree target if we believe we can and take action accordingly.

MONOPOLIES CONTROL YOUR FOOD

Only four companies—Bayer-Monsanto, Corteva (formerly part of Dow-Dupont), Syngenta Group, and BASF—control the vast majority of the world's supply of seeds and agricultural chemicals. Among them, Bayer-Monsanto is the world's largest vegetable seed company, cotton seed company, herbicide company, and owner of intellectual property for seed traits. It locks farmers into "platforms" of seeds and herbicides that only work together. If a farmer doesn't use Monsanto's seeds that are formulated to resist its herbicide Dicamba, for example, crops die when Dicamba blows over from a neighboring farm. And Monsanto has sued farmers for patent infringement if it finds Monsanto plants growing in their fields, even though many farmers say their fields were contaminated with Monsanto's seeds without their knowledge, due to wind and rain. Farmers ultimately are left with little choice but to use Monsanto's seeds and Monsanto's herbicides.

Monsanto was already exerting monopoly rule when it merged with the agro-giant Bayer in 2018, yet the world's antitrust enforcers let it happen! Opposing the deal, the National Family Farm Coalition wrote that the combined company's dominance in seeds and pesticides "means that more and more farmers will be compelled to plant these crops and spray more and more toxic herbicides throughout farm country."

Bayer-Monsanto is a dominant tech platform, too, using sensors in farmers' fields and farmers' equipment to track them and using algorithms to manipulate their farming practices. With data-driven agriculture, Bayer-Monsanto tells farmers how many seeds to plant and how much herbicide to use, while also selling farmers the seeds and herbicide. Talk about a conflict of interest.

With four platforms controlling the world's supply of seeds, the consequences of every decision these ag giants make—which are geared toward profit maximizing and shareholder return—are felt worldwide. Merely four companies decide what chemicals and practices farmers use that have tremendous impact on what we eat, on public health, and on the earth.

What could go wrong? Glysophate, the active ingredient in Bayer-Monsanto's Roundup, has ended up in our drinking water and breakfast cereal, for one thing. In June 2020, Bayer-Monsanto agreed to pay $10 billion to settle thousands of people's claims that Roundup caused their cancer but plans to keep selling the product without a warning label. For another thing, our food supply has become increasingly fragile, with every limit to farmers' choices limiting eaters' choices, too.

And it's not just seeds. An in-depth Open Markets Institute report, "Food and Power: Addressing Monopolization in America's Food System," by Claire Kelloway and Sarah Miller, details how every aspect of the food supply has concentrated into a few hands in recent decades: chicken, beef, pork, dairy, seeds, herbicides, farm equipment, grain processing, grocery stores, food brands, cafeteria operators.

By consolidating our food supply, all of our eggs are in a few baskets. Big Ag mergers risk food shortages the way that we've seen Big Pharma mergers lead to drug shortages. Early on in the novel coronavirus pandemic, farmers were dumping up to 3.7 million gallons of milk per day, a single chicken processor was smashing 750,000 eggs each week, and farmers were destroying their produce. Meanwhile, America plunged into a hunger crisis. COVID-19 exposed that a consolidated food supply chain is a fragile one.

"Beginning in the 1980s, the federal government allowed more agribusinesses to merge and grow largely without restraint in the name of efficiency—before, antitrust and other policies helped keep these industries decentralized and competitive," wrote Kelloway for *Washington Monthly*. University of Missouri professor Mary Hendrickson explained in the article, "If you pull out one little thing in that specialized, centralized, consolidated chain, then everything crashes." The consequences have been severe during the pandemic. "Now we have an animal welfare catastrophe, an environmental catastrophe, a farmer catastrophe, and a worker catastrophe altogether, and we can trace a lot of this back to the pursuit of efficiency." When giant plants closed because of COVID-19 outbreaks, farmers began euthanizing their animals by the thousands. Consolidation of the food supply chain leads to massive bottlenecks and locks farmers into contracts for dominant buyers, meaning that farmers can't redirect their products to other plants or purposes.

One of America's biggest COVID clusters occurred at a Smithfield pork processing plant in South Dakota. The workers are mostly immigrants and refugees, and the work is grueling. Union representatives told the BBC that Smithfield had failed to adequately protect its workers, ignoring requests for personal protective equipment, incentivizing sick workers to keep working, and withholding information about the virus's spread. A Chinese conglomerate owns Smithfield, the largest pork producer in the world, which slaughters 1 in every 4 hogs raised in America. Kelloway told me in an interview that Smithfield is "using American land and resources," and "exporting a really dirty form of production to the U.S., growing these hogs, making money on them in the U.S., but also shipping them back to China." An estimated 550 farms send their pigs to this one Smithfield plant in South Dakota. If the industry was less concentrated, these farmers would have more options and flexibility to respond to a single plant closure by sending their pigs elsewhere.

Beef is no better. About 85 percent of beef slaughter is controlled by four companies: Tyson, JBS, Cargill, and National Beef. Consolidation in all aspects of the industry means ranchers cannot get a fair price from monopolist buyers, and an average of nearly 17,000 cattle ranchers have gone out of business every year since 1980. The low prices paid to ranchers have not led to low prices for consumers. The prices of beef and pork went up 41 percent between 2000 and 2010. As of June 2020, DOJ is investigating the beef giants for price-fixing, and has indicted four poultry industry executives for conspiring to set chicken prices. Price-fixing, you'll remember, violates Section 1 of the Sherman Act, and it is easier to do when fewer companies rule an industry.

Merger mania hasn't been good for food quality or safety, either. In 2017, for example, JBS was accused of bribing meat inspectors and exporting rotten meat to the United States. Concentrated control over our food supply leads to massive recalls, like all romaine lettuce, because of the reach monopolies have.

"Food markets are so heavily concentrated today that the big behemoths are eating each other, and what's caught in the middle is the consumer and the farmer, and they're being crushed," said Joe Maxwell, president of Family Farm Action and former Missouri lieutenant governor, at a February 2020 conference hosted by the *Capitol Forum*, noting that Walmart recently opened a beef plant in Georgia. He added that "over a three-year period of time the cattle prices dropped 13 percent and there was an increase to consumers by 4 percent. There was not an increase in cost of production, there was simply more profit made by the largest packers in the world, and they put that money in their pocket."

Big Tech's exploitative relationship with businesses of all sizes looks like a partnership compared to the tyranny of the Monsanto platform over the farmer, or the Perdue platform over the chicken-raiser. Monopoly rule means that three out of every four poultry farmers live below the poverty line, as of a 2001 study. One point eight billion dollars of Americans' tax money was used between 2012 and 2016 to back up loans for poultry farmers from the Small Business Administration, even though poultry farmers are not really small businesses at all but rather operate under near total control of large corporations. Poultry farmers get locked into exploitative contracts with poultry giants that require them to take on debt to build expensive chicken houses, and dictate nearly every aspect of their business operations. According to a 2014 study, poultry farmers who run small operations earn an average hourly wage of $11.50.

Farmers are so powerless that farmer suicides are now a regular occurrence. The nonprofit Farm Aid said in 2018 that increased calls to its hotline "confirm that farmers are under incredible financial, legal, and emotional stress. Bankruptcies, foreclosures, depression, and even suicide are some of the tragic consequences of these pressures." When Brad Pfaff, Wisconsin state agriculture secretary, spoke out about farmer suicides in 2020, the Wisconsin Republican Senate—so controlled by monopoly money—ousted him from office.

Farmers are merely seeking to break even, said Patty Lovera of the Campaign for Family Farms and the Environment at the *Capitol Forum* conference. "The folks I work with are looking for independent family farms to be able to participate in a marketplace where they can get a fair price for what they grow," said Lovera. The reason they don't get a fair price, she said, is "because of the excessive consolidation that we have in literally every step of the food supply from the inputs—from the seeds—all the way to the retailer." Agriculture policy has focused on band-aids, she added, like loans and insurance for farmers, but "the root cause we are not dealing with is that these markets are so consolidated it is not possible for them to work fairly." The groups she works with want to be independent, not locked into working for Big Ag. "They don't want to be gig workers for Smithfield, JBS, or Tyson."

Small farms that want to use better production methods and run diverse, sustainable farms "are entirely cut out from the grocery store in ways that get more and more stark every day," Kelloway explained. "You have big retailers partnering with big food distributors, who are partnering with big food processors, who are partnering with big farms." In order to have a market, farmers are locked into a regime of production methods that is prescribed by the dominant monopoly buyer.

Monopolies even dictate to farmers what hormones and how much feed they have to use, and require them to use highly unnatural techniques. "Because farmers are in such a squeeze, they have no choice," said Kelloway. That means eaters have fewer choices for hormone-free, natural food, too.

In thirty-eight regions across America, Walmart has more than a 70 percent share of the grocery market, reports the Institute for Local Self-Reliance. With fewer and fewer grocery stores, Walmart has the power to demand crazy concessions just for food to get on their shelves. "If you want a prime spot on the shelf, you're going to have to pay Walmart for it, or you're going to have to pay Kroger for it," Kelloway told me. Some oligopoly food processors, like Kraft Heinz, give so much money to these retail chains that they get to be what's called a "category captain." They actually get to decide where their competitors sit on the grocery store shelf! If a small start-up has a great organic product, the category captain will stick them on the very bottom shelf or the very top shelf. Sounds a lot like Google and Amazon being able to make their competitors almost disappear, doesn't it? Speaking of Amazon, Whole Foods is not much better than the big grocery store chains because it has market power in organic grocery.

As a small act of rebellion, and to increase your odds of getting quality food, try shopping the very top and bottom shelves next time you go to the grocery store!

When it comes to food, American taxpayers once again pay the price for monopoly power. For example, U.S. taxpayers pay gigantic corn subsidies—$113.9 billion from 1995 to 2019—which directly benefit Big Ag and indirectly subsidize the meat industry and Coca-Cola and Pepsi. These subsidies make the wrong kinds of food very cheap, and we pay for it in our health care system and in Big Ag pollution, Kelloway said.

Bigger doesn't always mean better when it comes to farms. Farms are expected to be more efficient the bigger they get because they can buy seeds and other inputs for lower prices, but a study of Kansas farms' economic performance showed that once farms reach a certain size, getting bigger doesn't offer advantages. The current system is really only efficient for monopoly profits. As we learned with COVID-19, efficiency is in tension with resiliency, and leads to fragility when pursued above all else.

Big Food Blocks Healthy School Lunches

Imagine if every child got proper nutrition at school, which is far from the current reality with Big Food's control over school lunch, and billions of taxpayer dollars going to food monopolies. For those kids who have no choice but to have school lunch, proper nutrition would go a long way to improving children's ability to learn, improving their health outcomes, and reducing obesity.

The importance of this issue is why Michelle Obama made it a top priority as first lady. Mrs. Obama introduced her campaign as a move to alter policy, requiring changes in food formulations to no longer use excessive sweeteners and fats. But as ThinkProgress pointed out in "How Big Food Corporations Watered Down Michelle Obama's 'Let's Move' Campaign," she ultimately redirected her focus to "exercise and personal fitness—a position favored by processed food companies to divert scrutiny of their products." The article continues, "This avoidance of policy change may have something to do with the food lobby's influence in Obama's White House. According to a 2012 Reuters analysis, 50 food and beverage groups lobbied to a tune of $175 million during the first three years of the Obama administration, dwarfing the $83 million they spent in the last 3 years of the Bush administration.

Journalism professor and author Michael Pollan details every twist and turn of the saga of monopoly power defeating the Obama administration's goals in his *New York Times Magazine* article, "Big Food Strikes Back: Why Did the Obamas Fail to Take on Corporate Agriculture?" "Whenever the Obamas seriously poked at Big Food, they were quickly outlobbied and outgunned," Pollan writes. "Why? Because the food movement still barely exists as a political force in Washington."

No politician can take on monopoly power without the support of a movement of people. You can help defeat Big Food's lobbyists and nourish America's children by adding your voice to the food movement. A list of groups working in this area can be found at MonopoliesSuck.com/action.

The modest gains made by the Obama administration were rolled back by the Trump administration, which claimed the reforms were too burdensome for schools. But Kelloway disagrees: "The number of schools struggling to meet the requirements was actually quite small, and frankly, there's no other way to interpret this but as a handout back to the large processing companies that make so much money off the school lunch program."

People think that providing healthy school lunches would be too expensive and is not realistic. Yet other countries around the world manage to do it just fine. If America cut the billions of dollars of monopoly fat in our budgets, from health care to defense, and stopped subsidizing monopoly profits, the seemingly impossible could be possible.

Big Ag Is Destroying the Planet, Too

The same monopoly power that endangers our health also endangers our habitat. "With the adoption of more regenerative, organic farming practices, for example, today's industrial agriculture could go from being a major source of pollution to a major means of sequestering carbon and achieving other environmental benefits," explains the *Corner* newsletter by the Open Markets Institute. "Yet anyone who wants to reform today's industrial food system must deal with the power of agribusiness giants like chemical maker Bayer-Monsanto and slaughterhouse monopolist JBS, as well as with food retail and processing behemoths like Walmart and Kraft Heinz, who all have a deep interest in maintaining the status quo."

Unlike Big Ag, farmers want to be part of the climate change solution and conversation, said Family Farm Action's Joe Maxwell, speaking on a panel. "Farmers look out their back door; they know something's wrong; they call it different things but something's going on," said Maxwell. "They're in harm's way and on the front line."

In order to "have a meaningful impact on climate change we will have to confront agribusiness, which spends more on lobbying in the United States than even defense lobbyists," writes Timothy Wise, author of *Eating Tomorrow: Agribusiness, Family Farmers, and the Battle for the Future of Food*, in *Wired*. "A good first step in the United States would be to break up agribusiness giants that have virtual monopolies in regional seed, chemical, and meat markets," he writes, including unwinding Monsanto's merger with Bayer.

Instead of being part of the problem, agriculture can actually become part of the solution. "Agriculture is a huge contributor to carbon emissions but it also offers a huge opportunity to reduce carbon emissions and to capture carbon," Anja Geitmann, a professor at McGill University's plant science program, told Canada's CBC News. Farmland can sequester carbon into the soil through the process of photosynthesis, and the earth's existing farmland has the power to absorb all of the world's greenhouse gas emissions for the next 100 years, according to a report by Canada's agriculture department.

A Canadian cattle rancher, Paul Slomp, told CBC news that his farm has already moved away from chemicals and artificial feeds, and his cows graze on grass. He said he's now making more money than before. "Because we're reducing the amount of input that we need to purchase, we're actually able to generate a much better profit margin," said Slomp. "The cows are meant to do this; they thrive in a system like ours, and it can be quite profitable."

Such changes are only achievable for farmers if they are not already hanging on by a thread and beholden to monopoly rule. Just as we need to remove tech gatekeepers so that privacy-protecting pro-democracy innovators can break through, farmers need a way to get to market without having to pass through food giants' gates.

Your Life, Better

Our planet and our food are too important to leave to monopoly rule. Change may not be profitable for Big Oil and Big Ag, but it is possible. "The climate crisis is not only the single greatest challenge facing our country; it is also our single greatest opportunity to build a more just and equitable future," said Bernie Sanders in a written statement. We put people on the moon fifty years ago, and we "can sure as hell transform our energy system away from fossil fuels to 100 percent renewables today and create millions of jobs in the process," reads his website.

We must demand that our government end Big Oil subsidies and investments, divest from fossil fuels, require Big Oil to help fund the transition to sustainability, and open up opportunity to green innovators. The new climate movement is about saying "yes" to shared prosperity and a more equitable distribution of power.

By joining a grassroots movement applying pressure on lawmakers and regulators to do their job or get fired, you would no longer feel helpless.

When the people prevail, your climate anxiety wanes. You enjoy the political stability that comes with your fellow Americans having good green jobs and hope. Most important, you can tell your kids that the world's grown-ups are doing everything they possibly can to protect them.

When you go to the grocery store, you know the food being sold is safe and healthy for you and your family. Children who eat school lunch get the nutrition their young bodies need to learn and to grow into healthy adults. Your food supply is diversified and safer, recalls are smaller in scope, and farming helps save the future of humanity rather than endanger it. This vision of what life could look like may seem unrealistic, but the alternative—staying the course under monopoly rule—is far more so.

SEVEN

MONOPOLIES RAMP UP INEQUALITY

"Shall we play a game?"

The ultrarich are thriving in America, with the rest of us watching their indulgences on social media or bombarded by advertising that idolizes excess. Billionaire Kylie Jenner posted on Instagram a photo of her one-year-old daughter carrying a mini Hermès handbag that retails for over $8,000. The post got more than 4.7 million likes.

With a steady stream of wealth porn around you glorifying the rich, it wouldn't be surprising if you felt a need for more. Whether consciously or unconsciously, some of us are trying to literally "keep up" with the Kardashians, not just "the Joneses" next door. Comparing yourself with those who have more inevitably makes you feel not good enough.

We rarely compare ourselves with those who have less than we do, perhaps because the poor barely exist in our public consciousness, in a world curated by social media. If you're reading this book, you're probably not among the 40 percent of Americans who can't pay an unexpected $400 expense without borrowing money or selling something. When you hear such dire statistics—and that one's from 2018, before COVID-19's financial devastation—you're at a loss for what you can do about it. Like so many other Americans, you're consumed with your own stresses, working long hours to pay high overhead costs, to cover health care monopoly prices, and to save for college or pay off college debts.

You certainly don't *feel* like you have it easy, and the fear of things getting even harder fuels a relentless drive for more. You're not trying to buy designer handbags for your toddler, you just want financial security. But at what dollar figure will you have *enough* to feel secure?

Maybe you are among the few who do feel financially secure. Perhaps you haven't worried much about inequality because you're on the winning side of the equation. No matter how hard you may have worked to get there, don't get too comfortable or expect to stay. Inequality is a conveyor belt, running on an endless loop that will eventually come for you. Unless we do something to stop it, that is.

Inequality hurts even the most fortunate because it destabilizes democracy. If you live in a bubble of privilege, you may be unaware of the hopelessness of large swaths of America. In your head you know the desperation exists, but you may not know what it really feels like. Yet you know what it feels like to be scared. The world feels unbalanced, unstable, and unsafe.

Inequality takes a toll on us all, but our rigged economy deepens existing societal inequities even further. If you're a woman, person of color, LGBTQ+, and/or a member of other marginalized groups, monopoly rule makes your uphill climb even steeper.

The Great Unequalizers

Six heirs to the Walmart fortune have more wealth than 41 percent of all Americans combined. That figure is from 2010, and the Waltons' wealth has grown exponentially ever since. Before Walmart came along, entrepreneurial shopkeepers in towns across America could support their families, pay their workers a living wage, pay their fair share of taxes, and pay companies that make consumer goods a fair price for their wares. Walmart, offering the promise of lower prices for consumers, changed all of this.

As Walmart got bigger and bigger, it used its power as a dominant buyer to squeeze the companies that make and wholesale goods, demanding they sell their products to Walmart for ultra-low prices. Those makers and suppliers earned less money for themselves, had less money to pay their employees, and were often forced to reduce the quality of the goods they offer consumers. Small shopkeepers went out of business when they couldn't compete against Walmart's prices, which were often below cost—amounting to illegal monopolization using predatory pricing, in my opinion. Employees who could otherwise work at those small shops became faced with few employment options, and had little choice but to accept Walmart's pay.

Walmart pays its employees so little, as we discussed in chapter 1, that Walmart employees make up the single largest group of food stamp recipients in many states. Americans pay higher taxes to make up for Walmart's exploitation of its workers and alleged tax evasion.

The end result of Walmart's extraction of wealth from taxpayers, manufacturers, shopkeepers, wholesalers, and employees? In 2019, Walmart had the highest revenue of any company in the world, according to *Fortune*'s Global 500, bringing in a cool $514 billion. (Big Tech companies have less revenue but higher valuations.) The Walton family is reportedly the world's richest, and they get $4 million richer every hour, $100 million richer every day. As a taxpayer, your hard-earned money subsidizes the richest family in the world.

Walmart gets away with monopolizing brick-and-mortar retail because of the Chicago School's twisted interpretation of antitrust law that says low prices are good for consumers, even if it destroys competition. But Walmart's low prices have enabled a host of ills that haven't been good for you at all. Even if you've never shopped at Walmart, you've paid a price.

Walmart may seem like a distant threat in the digital age, but modern monopolies, as I've explained, are following in its footsteps. Today's tech giants may be some of the most powerful extractors our world has ever seen. Amazon is most literally following Walmart's playbook of using below-cost pricing to kick out rivals, squeeze suppliers, skirt taxes, and underpay workers, and Jeff Bezos is Walton Family 2.0. He makes the annual salary of his lowest-paid employee in 11.5 seconds, according to a back-of-the-envelope calculation by Quartz in 2018. His net worth as of May 2020, according to Bloomberg, is 2,327,131 times the median U.S. household income.

I don't begrudge those who find financial success through their ingenuity, innovation, and creation. But when astronomical wealth flows mostly from extraction—illegally kicking competitors out of the game to monopolize markets, stealing the innovations of others, and leveraging monopoly power in one market to take over other markets without competing on merit—that's the American monopoly nightmare.

With monopolies controlling nearly every part of American business, we are all victims of extraction in countless ways every day. Lower wages, higher prices, and the squeezing of suppliers and creators amounts to billions of dollars in wealth transfer to monopolies, duopolies, and oligopolies. Is it really any surprise that we are experiencing economic inequality not seen since the Gilded Age?

C-suite executives and major corporate shareholders are the ones who win when monopolies reign, with the ultrarich capturing the bulk of the wealth that monopolies extract. The richest .1 percent of Americans now own more wealth than the bottom 80 percent, and 400 Americans have more wealth than 150 million Americans do.

We hear a lot about the 1 percent, but the gap between the top 1 percent and top .1 percent is enormous. People between the top 1 percent and the top .1 percent tend to earn their money through wages, and their share of national wealth has made only modest gains for forty years. The people making out like bandits in a monopolized America are the top .1 percent, the approximately 160,000 tax filers with wealth above $20 million. The top .1 percent sharing in the monopoly profits include CEOs and bankers who most benefit from gains in financial markets. They share in the profits monopolies bring in when they can charge consumers more and pay employees less.

Remember, the era of stronger antitrust enforcement spanned from 1913 to 1982, and the years since have been ruled by the Chicago School. From 1978 to 2012, the 0.1 percent of Americans with more wealth than the bottom 99.9 percent of Americans went from owning 7 percent of the country's total wealth to owning 22 percent. The richest Americans have become much richer ever since antitrust enforcement went missing. Here's yet another graph that shows the Boomers had it better than the rest of us! When they were raising their families in the 1970s and the 1980s, the ultrarich were capturing a much lower percentage of America's wealth than they are today. Boomers benefited from the robust antitrust enforcement in the decades before, which deconcentrated the economy and spread the wealth more evenly among Americans.

Although monopolies are far from the only cause of income inequality, trying to achieve equality without weakening monopoly power is a fool's errand. Monopoly is highly concentrated wealth and power in the hands of a few, making it fundamentally incompatible

TOP 0.1% WEALTH SHARE in the United States, 1913–2012

Source: Emmanuel Saez and Gabriel Zucman, 2016. "Wealth Inequality in the United States since 1913: Evidence from Capitalized Income Tax Data," *The Quarterly Journal of Economics* 131(2), pages 519–578.

with equality—the distribution of wealth, opportunity, and power among the many. The two cannot coexist.

As NYU law professor Eleanor Fox has written, the "notion of equality has run through antitrust (or competition) law since the beginning of (antitrust) time." Antitrust law, she said, "focuses particularly on equality of opportunity: keeping open pathways for outsiders to contest markets on the merits."

Inequality Causes Political Instability

Most Americans face steep barriers to financial well-being in our taking economy. That building a wall, the ultimate barrier, has garnered support from millions of Americans is no coincidence. If opportunity is not available to these Americans, they certainly don't want "others" to have it. Xenophobia and anti-immigrant sentiment are nothing new, but scarcity fuels the flames as people look for scapegoats for their suffering.

Don't be mistaken, however; apart from the systemic shock of

COVID-19, ours is not a time of scarcity. We have been living in a time of abundance, but with resources distributed inequitably. People are hopeless because the system isn't working for them, and many just want to burn it all to the ground. An authoritarian leader can pose as the solution to this despair.

Monopolistic extraction, inequality, and political instability are not limited to America's borders; today's monopolies are global. Monopolistic extraction is among the reasons we are seeing the rise of antidemocratic leaders worldwide, aided by monopoly business models that amplify disinformation and hate.

The declining dynamism in America that we discussed in chapter 3 is amplifying regional inequality, which is politically destabilizing. "The rapid retreat of dynamism from all but the largest and fastest-growing metro areas intensifies the geographic inequality being felt across the country—and the most vulnerable areas are falling the furthest behind," reports the Economic Innovation Group. During the economic expansion that occurred between 2010 and 2014, only 5 metro areas accounted for 50 percent of the growth of new companies. Compare that to the expansion from 1983 to 1987, when 50 percent of growth was spread out over 29 metro areas. These days, almost 80 percent of start-up investment goes to just three states. And only 15 percent of all venture capital in 2015 went to the states that voted for Donald Trump for president in 2016.

America the unequal is America the divided. The hyper concentration of wealth and opportunity in a few big cities has led to regional inequality. Such concentration is politically destabilizing in itself but also has rendered the Electoral College an utter disaster to democracy. A more distributed, deconcentrated economy would promote regional equality and the dispersion of wealth and opportunity throughout the country.

Mining Humanity and Knowledge Inequality

We've talked about how access to data distorts the competitive playing field between Big Tech and the companies that must compete against the tech giants on their platforms. We've talked about how data collected about us can be used to target us, manipulate us, and skew elections. We've talked about how data has value, and how massive corporations sucking up our data amounts to tremendous wealth transfer, or outright theft when done without our knowledge or consent. The race to harvest our data is perhaps best understood as a gold rush, with humans as the mines. Or, as privacy advocate Aral Balkan wrote in 2017, "These platform monopolies are factory farms for human beings; farming us for every gram of insight they can extract." Such data extraction worsens inequality.

Shoshana Zuboff, author of *The Age of Surveillance Capitalism* and Harvard Business School professor emerita, describes a new form of social inequality that she calls "epistemic inequality." "Epistemic" means relating to knowledge, so for the sake of simplicity, let's call it "knowledge inequality." Zuboff describes this inequality as "extreme asymmetries of knowledge and the power that accrues to such knowledge, as the tech giants seize control of information and learning itself." Such knowledge inequality extends even beyond the tech giants to other types of platform monopolies, like Monsanto, as it seizes control of the information and learning that used to belong to farmers.

Knowledge inequality is "not based on what we can earn but rather on what we can learn," writes Zuboff, in the form of "unequal access to learning." Knowledge inequality creates a chasm, she explains, between "what we know and what is known about us," and "what we can do and what can be done to us."

Unequal access to learning is a constant in American history, but surveillance capitalism makes it highly automated and targeted with precision, threatening to worsen existing forms of inequality—based on income, gender, race, sexual orientation, sexual identity, class, age, immigration status, disability, and any intersection of these. Using data to learn about ourselves can offer promise, like with personalized medicine, but we the people must demand that safeguards are put in place as new technologies are rolled out.

Knowledge inequality is on track to get worse as the "internet of things" turns everything from our microwave oven to our television into a data mine. This is why we must urgently check monopoly business models.

Rich White Manopoly Is Not a Fun Game

In December 2017, I wrote an article about how monopolies amplify gender inequality, knowing that antitrust lawyers—trained to think antitrust is only about corporate efficiencies and prices—would think I was crazy. I arrived at the connection between antitrust and gender inequality serendipitously.

For the three years prior, I'd been writing about antitrust issues involving the Big Tech platforms and also hosting a podcast called *Women Killing It!*, which focuses on women overcoming barriers to reaching their career potential. Both of my passions—gender equity and antitrust—became hot topics during that time. At the end of 2017, I was exhausted. I told myself, "Sally, you've got to pick just one passion," but I couldn't tear myself away from either one. And that's when it hit me. How could I not have seen it sooner? My passions for antitrust and gender equity were not only related, they were just two dimensions of the very same passion.

That passion is equal opportunity for all, or what we think of as the American dream. I immediately looked up the definition of the American dream, and found this one on Wikipedia:

The American Dream is a national ethos of the United States, the set
of ideals—democracy, rights, liberty, opportunity and equality—in
which freedom includes the opportunity for prosperity and success,
as well as an upward mobility for the family and children, achieved
through hard work in a society with few barriers.

I realized that all of these ideals are intertwined. Although the
American Dream has never been equally available to all, and the notion that our country is a meritocracy is a myth, I believe that the
more we expand opportunities to all Americans, the stronger our democracy will be.

Suddenly it made sense to me why I had been drawn to antitrust enforcement in the first place. After all, our anti-monopoly laws
are designed to promote opportunity and upward mobility, keeping
markets open so new companies and entrepreneurs can challenge established players on the merits. These laws not only make it illegal
for one powerful company to shut out competitors but also prohibit
a few powerful players from joining together to control the market
and exclude outsiders. Fighting for gender equality also has a lot to
do with equal opportunity. The whole point of the American dream
is it should apply to all of us, not just those who already have power.

On the flip side, sexism and monopolization both work against
the American dream. Sexism wrongfully excludes women and deprives them of equal opportunity to compete on a level playing field,
just like monopolies do to start-ups and smaller companies. The glass
ceiling is really just a cartel.

Concentrated economic power, unsurprisingly, is bad for women.
Discriminatory biases against women's economic participation
amount to anticompetitive regulations, writes Chris Pike, a competition expert at the Organisation for Economic Co-operation and
Development (OECD). "Competition policy may therefore have a

natural role to play in addressing those issues and in building open, fair and efficient markets, levelling the playing field for women and men alike," Pike writes with Estefania Santacreu-Vasut, a French economics professor. Competition policy could result in what they call a "double dividend." That is, "by promoting competition in certain markets, competition authorities may reduce market distortions in a particular market (*first dividend*) and contribute to reduce gender inequality (*second dividend*)."

Another OECD study, "Inequality: A Hidden Cost of Market Power," shows that market power and higher prices increase the wealth of the richest 10 percent of the population while reducing the income of the poorest 20 percent. Women and people of color, then, are particularly hurt by monopolies. Women are 35 percent more likely than men to be poor in America, and 70 percent of the nation's poor are women and children. Poverty rates in America for African Americans are more than twice that of white, non-Hispanic individuals.

And when consumers get screwed by monopolists, we're mostly talking about women, who control 70-80 percent of consumer spending. "If the consumer economy had a sex, it would be female," says a report by Bloomberg. The Chicago School of Economics' "consumer welfare standard," which has been used to justify consolidating the American economy, then, alternatively could be called the "women's welfare standard." But a monopolized America hasn't been good for women's welfare at all!

Monopolies suck for white men too, don't get me wrong, as only a select few reap monopolies' spoils. But the consequences of monopoly power we've talked about in this book are extra bad for women, people of color, and members of marginalized groups, and multiply as these identities intersect. Monopoly amplifies existing inequities in our society, like structural racism and patriarchy.

First, monopolies take even more income from women and

people of color. When concentrated labor markets deprive employees of bargaining power and depress their pay, causing wages to go down or stagnate, female employees and employees of color are even worse off. In the United States, women make 78 cents to a white man's dollar, with black women making 64 cents and Latina women making 54 cents for every dollar a white man makes. Black men earn 73 cents and Hispanic men earn 69 cents to a white man's dollar. As wages by the bottom 99 percent of earners continue to shrink, women and people of color get paid a mere percentage of fewer dollars. The top 1 percent are predominantly white men, and so are the C-suite executives whose pay has skyrocketed while employees' pay has stagnated.

In the 2016 study "Women and the 1%: How Extreme Economic Inequality and Gender Inequality Must Be Tackled Together," Oxfam said that closing gender gaps so that women participate more in paid work and move out of lower-paid sectors could add $12 trillion to the global economy by 2025. Oxfam warns, however, that "[u]nless the causes of extreme economic inequality are urgently addressed, the majority of the benefits of women-driven growth will accrue to those already at the top of the economy."

Second, we discussed in chapter 3 how concentrated markets reduce employees' ability to switch jobs. This lower mobility especially hurts employees who face on-the-job discrimination or harassment. In the wake of the #MeToo movement, the *New York Times* asked women if they've ever felt silenced at work. "Many spoke of the times they had been threatened for requesting equal pay, penalized for taking maternity leave or blacklisted for bringing suit against their attackers." The ability to switch jobs is critical for bargaining power.

Women need to be able to leave hostile work environments and to switch jobs to escape sexual harassment, which we as a society have finally admitted is ubiquitous. A study by three sociology professors found that women who are harassed are 6.5 times more likely to change jobs, and will do so even when it hurts their career and reduces opportunities for advancement. This shows a direct link between sexual harassment and the gender pay gap.

But what if the labor market is so concentrated that women who are harassed don't have anywhere to go? When women make harassment claims, their companies often retaliate against them and even can get them blacklisted from their fields. Companies can easily discredit women to an entire industry when it is ruled by only a few companies, meaning women can lose their careers for speaking up. If many companies competed in each industry for talented employees, blacklisting women would be much harder.

These same considerations apply to racial discrimination at work. Whether experiencing racial harassment or other forms of discrimination—like lower pay, lower recognition, less promotion, or marginalization—employees of color need to be able to easily switch jobs and speak up without losing their careers. Noncompete agreements are especially dangerous because they can trap people of color in hostile work environments.

Who Gets to Innovate, and for Whom?

Monopoly rule also means that women, people of color, and other marginalized groups have fewer opportunities for entrepreneurship than they would have if economic power were more distributed. "If they don't give you a seat at the table, bring a folding chair," Shirley Chisholm, the first black woman elected to Congress, famously said. But if tables today are still not welcoming diversity, entrepreneur Felecia Hatcher told me, "We're now empowered to create our own damn tables."

Hatcher cofounded Code Fever and Black Tech Week to promote inclusive innovation when she noticed Miami's start-up resources were not "crossing the tracks." Hatcher has talked about how she and her husband, Derick, would get invited to start-up events offering great entrepreneurial support and look around and say, "Why isn't there anyone else that looks like us in the room?" They started Code Fever as a way to change that, building their own ecosystem to draw resources, training, and inclusive policies into the black community.

Just as women and people of color have greater needs to be able to switch jobs, they have greater needs for entrepreneurship. Building your own table means being the captain of your own ship and lessening the harm that harassment, discrimination, and bias can cause you. "When a woman runs her own business, she has a reduced chance of being harassed or attacked," writes psychotherapist and author Stephanie Sarkis. "She is able to have more control and influence over what happens in her life."

But building your own table requires money. And the statistics for the share of start-up funding that women and people of color receive are dismal. Less than 3 percent of start-up investment goes to women, and less than 1 percent goes to African Americans and Latinos of both sexes. Since 2009, black women have raised .0006 percent of the $424.7 billion in total tech venture funding.

Now consider how four tech titans are shaping the course of innovation. "What's your exit strategy?" is one of the first questions investors ask entrepreneurs. As Ross Baird, venture capitalist and author of *The Innovation Blind Spot*, explained at the Open Markets America's Monopoly Moment conference, investors are essentially saying, "what are you building that Facebook will want or Google will want or Amazon will want, so they can acquire you one day?" To get funded, then, entrepreneurs need to develop a feature that is interesting enough for Amazon or Facebook to want to buy, said Baird. "That is the incredibly limited design constraint on our innovation economy right now." But start-ups must also avoid direct competition with giants, given their power to squash them.

When the narrow parameters for getting funded are that your creation is not in tech giants' "kill zones" but is a little feature that the tech giants will want to buy, what room does that leave for diversity in innovation? Good luck getting funded unless your innovation conforms to the vision and worldview a few white guys, and one Indian guy now that Sundar Pichai has become the CEO of Alphabet (with the influence of Google cofounders Larry Page and Sergey Brin an open question). With this start-up model, we won't benefit from maximum innovation because the next big thing won't get built. And when a few powerful companies dominate so many markets and prevent new firms and new leaders from competing, women and people of color are particularly shut out.

Baird has explained how the concentration of funding among venture capitalists (VCs) leads to investment in the wrong things. Baird writes that "the resources we're putting into new ideas are concentrated among so few people in so few places" (mostly white men in New York, California, and Massachusetts) and that blind spots prevent "great ideas around the world from having a chance to begin with." Other sources of funding for entrepreneurs have diminished in recent decades, like community banks. The number of banks with assets less than $500 million decreased by about 70 percent between 1990 and 2018, with thousands of institutions lost.

Lynn Perkins, CEO and cofounder of UrbanSitter, shared on my podcast her story of raising funding for her start-up, a popular app for hiring babysitters. Because the predominantly male VCs typically were not the ones in their families hiring babysitters, Perkins said that they did not see the customer problem that UrbanSitter was solving. Perkins got funding only *after* she acquired thousands of active users of her app. Male start-up founders frequently raise funding without any traction at all.

On top of traction, investors want to see strong revenue numbers from start-ups built by entrepreneurs from minority and marginalized groups, said Hatcher. Yet, "you open up *Inc.* magazine and see a company that has zero revenue and you wonder, 'How did they raise

$100 million?'" She noted that entrepreneurs of color face such a bigger ask to validate their start-ups.

In his book, Baird shares the story of entrepreneur Jerry Nemorin, who as a child watched his Haitian immigrant mother take out predatory loans. As an adult, Nemorin came up with a business idea that would help Americans restructure their debt, and he steadily built his business. But when it came time to raise funding to grow to the next level, he hit roadblocks. Nemorin explained that VCs "want to solve my world problems, but forget about real-world problems."

With capital concentrated in the hands of a few, we're not getting the best of the best because there's a whole group of people who are not even getting in the door. Problem-solving through innovation is less effective and impactful because solutions are limited and less diverse. And years of biases and blind spots mean the markets for innovations that serve white male needs are oversaturated, while markets that serve the needs of women and people of color are where the opportunity lies. Investors are missing out and consumers are, too, with their needs left unmet while the twelfth version of Tinder for laundry delivery gets funded.

Move Fast and Break People

When a handful of tech titans decide what innovation looks like, not only do women and people of color get shut out of entrepreneurship, but they also get hurt. The most privileged in our society have been shaping technology in ways that harm women, people of color, and other marginalized communities, without bothering to anticipate consequences. Top leadership of the tech giants is a sea of white men. While they get rich, others bear the consequences of the surveillance and discrimination they automate. Silicon Valley start-ups love to ignore rules designed to protect us, justifying their recklessness in the name of innovation.

Forget about the rules that democracies create to protect their citizens; pesky regulations just get in the way, so the techno-libertarian thinking goes. If innovations hurt people, we'll deal with those problems later, perhaps. This is an ethos that is compatible with the most privileged in society who pay the least consequences for their actions, the same kinds of guys who can be criminally prosecuted and sentenced to write a book. The "precautionary principle," in contrast, requires innovators to anticipate harms before they occur.

Uber, for example, ignored the precautionary principle when it came to protecting its riders. Uber founders probably didn't intend for their innovation to lead to women being raped and murdered, but they also didn't take significant precautionary steps to stop it from happening. After the tragic murder of a University of South Carolina student who got into a car she thought was her Uber, Uber announced it would begin sending a push notification to riders reminding them to check the driver and vehicle and providing the driver's name, photo, license plate number, and vehicle make and model. Why wasn't that feature built before Uber was even launched? Uber execs sure seem to spend a lot of effort strategizing ways to extract wages from their workers. If they had spent a fraction of that time anticipating dangers to users and taking appropriate precautions, that young woman could still be alive today.

Uber reported in 2017 that its tech leadership team was completely white and Asian, and 88.7 percent men. Failing to have women at the decision-making table was not merely a terrible business decision; it was a dangerous one. Perhaps not surprisingly, Uber's own corporate culture was reportedly toxic and hostile. Whistle-blower Susan Fowler, an engineer at Uber at the time, exposed the rampant sexual harassment and discrimination inside of the company in a viral blog post that helped fuel the #MeToo movement, and wrote about it in her book *Whistle Blower*.

While Uber's harms to women may have been accidental oversights, if I'm being generous, exploiting drivers with low pay is integral to Uber's business model. In 2015, Uber's drivers were more than 50 percent people of color. California passed a law to give Uber drivers rights, and Uber is fighting it tooth and nail. Extraction of wealth from its workers *is* Uber's business model.

We Didn't Discriminate, the Algorithm Did It

In *Race After Technology*, Princeton professor Ruha Benjamin argues that "tech fixes often hide, speed up, and even deepen discrimination, while appearing to be neutral or benevolent when compared to the racism of a previous era." She calls the set of practices with discriminatory designs "The New Jim Code." "The power of the New Jim Code," writes Benjamin, "is that it allows racist habits and logics to enter through the backdoor of tech design, in which the humans who create the algorithms are hidden from view."

We often assume that tech and data are neutral, but the data and the way technology is deployed reflects and reinforces society's biases. Cathy O'Neil, author of *Weapons of Math Destruction: How Big Data Increases Inequality and Threatens Democracy*, explains in an interview that "people like to think of algorithms as outside the landscape of morals," but an algorithmic model is a "moral projection." "A model is no more than a formal opinion embedded in code," she said, explaining that people who build algorithmic models decide matters of opinion like what success looks like, what's important, and how to get to success. But the morals projected are often "default morals" that are "thoughtlessly introduced by the ecosystem in which they're built" or "the data that's collected," says O'Neil. The result is they mirror and deepen the biases that exist in society.

That the algorithms are opaque compounds the problems of monopolies being unaccountable for their harmful business models. Each of the four tech giants has been accused of algorithmic bias.

Facebook, in an egregious example, has reportedly allowed housing, credit, and employment ads to discriminate by age and gender, which is prohibited by civil rights law. Facebook's business model, based on hypertargeting and personalization, creates huge risks of discrimination.

Discrimination through purportedly neutral tech is particularly dangerous when it comes to the criminal justice system. At every stage of the U.S. penal process, Benjamin explains, "from policing, sentencing, and imprisonment to parole—automated risk assessments are employed to determine people's likelihood of committing a crime." This predictive policing software will recommend surveillance of predominantly black neighborhoods "because the data that this software is drawing from reflect ongoing surveillance priorities that target predominantly black neighborhoods." Such predictions, then, become self-fulfilling prophecies with "the allure of accuracy." Unequal surveillance perpetuates and amplifies existing inequities, and algorithms identifying patterns from surveillance data make the problem even worse.

LGTBQ+ individuals, the disabled, and any group that does not fit the mold of those shaping new technologies also are at risk of disparate treatment. An organization called Queer in AI focuses on the impact artificial intelligence and machine-learning algorithms have on people, "and the potential for these powerful learning and classification technologies to out queer people." AI also disproportionately harms the disabled, with ableism baked into assumptions. Thinkers and advocates are highlighting the need for inclusively designed AI and rejecting forms that are discriminatory and harmful.

Not all the companies rolling out biased technologies are monopolies. But tech giants use their monopoly-power-turned-political-power to fight efforts to regulate tech and AI. Those fighting for equity in tech should work together with the anti-monopoly movement in order for their efforts to have maximum success.

Your Life, Better

The famous Monopoly board game was originally created and patented by a feminist named Lizzie Magie in 1903 to teach about the harms of monopoly. She didn't get credit for her invention (shocker) but a guy named Charles Darrow did instead. The book *The Monopolists*, by Mary Pilon, tells Magie's story, describing also how the anti-monopoly movement served as a staging ground for women's rights advocates and abolitions at the turn of the century. Today, anti-monopoly activists and advocates for gender and racial justice should join together to maximize their impact. All who advocate on behalf of marginalized groups should incorporate anti-monopoly into their policy agendas.

By overthrowing monopoly power, the New Gilded Age, like the original one, can become a thing of the history books. Polar opposite extremes of wealth and poverty begin to dissipate as the middle class is revived and broadened. People still want more, but sometimes they feel like they have enough. A more equitable distribution of America's abundance restores opportunity and hope, and lessens the despair and anger that embolden authoritarian-style politicians.

Anti-monopoly policy alone won't make this vision of America a reality, but it's an essential part of changing the status quo and sharing prosperity among all.

HOW TO STOP
MONOPOLIES

EIGHT

HOW TO TAKE BACK CONTROL

To simply know a thing is not enough. . . . We must do something about it on a large scale if we are to make headway. These are critical times, and drastic action is needed.

—Lizzie Magie, creator of the original Monopoly board game

Only by ending monopoly rule can we begin to make our lives better: lower prices, more affordable health care, lower taxes, higher pay, better benefits and working conditions, less financial stress and work overwhelm, greater opportunities for entrepreneurship, innovation that improves quality of life rather than degrades it, less corporate spying on your private life, a less agitated state of mind, reduced political polarization, reduced tech addiction, fairer elections, a stronger democracy, more accountable politicians, safer food, a healthier planet, and greater equality.

You deserve all of this.

Our problems are systemic, and we must attack them on a structural level. Keep meditating and doing yoga, or coping on a personal level in whatever way works best for you. But we also need to attack the structures of power if we are to lead better, less stressful lives. Like I said at the beginning, anti-monopoly won't magically solve everything, but we won't be able to cure America's ills if we don't first disperse monopolies' concentrated power.

I often hear the argument that antitrust enforcement isn't going to fix our problems and that a different solution is "the" answer. We don't need antitrust, we need privacy law, people say. Or the solution to tech monopolies isn't antitrust, it's blockchain. But America is in a crisis of concentrated power—no single answer is going to cut it. This isn't an either/or situation! It's a both/and situation. We need *both* antitrust enforcement *and* privacy law. We need *both* antitrust enforcement *and* new technologies that have the potential to decentralize power (as long as we don't let the giants take over these innovations, like Facebook is trying to do with its Libra digital currency). Antitrust law is the tool specifically crafted to combat corporate power, but anti-monopoly advocates like myself don't limit our toolbox and consider a range of solutions. We must attack monopoly rule from every angle.

The only reason to discard anti-monopoly weapons in our arsenal would be if they contradicted one another. For this reason, Big Tech presses the narrative that privacy and competition are incompatible, opportunistically cutting off competitors under the guise of protecting privacy. But this is a false dichotomy: competition can be promoted by giving users real control over their data, which competitors might use it, and how. Both privacy and competition are possible, and, as we've discussed, competition will open up the gates of opportunity for pro-privacy innovators.

We've Done It Before, We Can Do It Again

What monopolies have done to our world is depressing, but don't despair! We have been here before. We stood up to powerful monopolists when we broke up Standard Oil and AT&T, and when we stopped Microsoft's anticompetitive practices, among other monopolies in our history. Each time, we were better for it. We unleashed new waves of innovation. We dispersed opportunity. We restored our markets and removed gatekeepers.

The result of the golden age of antitrust enforcement from 1913 to 1982 was an economy with distributed opportunity. The Boomers benefited from this deconcentration, among other economic factors, but Generation X and Millennials are navigating their careers and raising families during a time when economic opportunity is highly concentrated. The gutting of anti-monopoly policy got us here, but life doesn't have to be this way.

As I mentioned at the start, citizens' outrage after *The History of the Standard Oil Company* was published spurred the government to break up Standard Oil. The Federal Trade Commission was established, and the Clayton Act was passed after the outcry. Standard Oil had tremendous political power and was extracting unprecedented wealth, but angered average Americans helped to break it up.

Anti-monopolists at the turn of the century used political cartoons to capture the menace of monopoly and bring their message to the American people. This rich history of art as protest inspired the cartoons in this book. In the digital age we have endless options to use creativity to inspire political action, from memes, to short videos, to documentary films, but cartoons can still bring to life the dangers of modern monopolies. Published in 1904, a famous cartoon shows Standard Oil as an octopus with its tentacles wrapped around the steel, copper, and shipping industries, the U.S. Capitol, a state legislature, and with a tentacle reaching toward the White House. Just like today's monopolies, Standard Oil had tremendous economic and political power, but the people, undaunted, decided they weren't going to take it anymore.

The fight against monopoly requires constant vigilance, to protect us from the undemocratic concentration of private power. Just like now, many saw monopolies as more powerful than government at the turn of the century. But like the Americans who came before us, we have to fight for our democracy, not just cede it to monopolists. We must hold our elected representatives accountable to the people instead of corporate overlords. The 1889 *Bosses of the Senate* cartoon portrays corporate interests as giant money bags towering over the

senators below, under the motto, "This is the Senate of the Monopolists by the Monopolists and for the Monopolists!" The popular perception of monopolies' undue influence on politics contributed to the passing of the Sherman Act the following year, in 1890.

Monopolies at the turn of the century cheated Americans out of their pay, subjected them to poor working conditions, and ripped them off with high prices. The caption to this 1901 cartoon reads, "The little boy [Common People] and the big boys [Trusts] prepare for the baseball season." Monopolies of old were called "trusts," hence the term "antitrust." The monopolies are pelting balls at "the common people" that say "low wages," "high prices," and "oppression." Sound familiar?

For at least 137 years it's been obvious that monopoly is at war with workers getting fairly compensated for the fruits of their labor, which the 1883 cartoon titled "The tournament of today—a set-to between labor and monopoly," illustrates. Shared economic prosperity and monopoly are incompatible, and we must join together to fight for the more just and equitable future we deserve.

THE TOURNAMENT OF TODAY—A SET-TO BETWEEN LABOR AND MONOPOLY.

America overcame the rule of monopoly kings before, and we can do it again. The 1904 cartoon titled "Our Uncrowned Kings" asks, "Where is the spirit of '76? This is what your forefathers did to King George." More than a century later, we again find ourselves under the rule of kings—kings of commerce, information, health care, agriculture, energy, and more. It's time we harness America's revolutionary spirit and dethrone our uncrowned kings, using democratic institutions and laws we already have.

All but one of the above cartoons were published by *Puck*, a magazine that created political satire from 1871 to 1918, which was housed in downtown New York City's famous Puck Building. In a sign of the second Gilded Age, Jared Kushner now owns the building and converted the top floors to penthouse apartments, one of which was listed for sale in March 2019 for $42.5 million.

The problems we are facing today are not new, nor are they surprising. When it comes to dominant platforms, the mystique of high tech doesn't justify monopolies' exploitative nature. At the turn of the

century, railroads were high-tech! When we broke up AT&T, it too was high-tech, as was Microsoft when the United States sued it for violating antitrust laws, and antitrust enforcement caused innovation to flourish. We have the tools to fix our monopoly problems, and we just need to use them again.

Replacing Monopoly Rule with People Rule

We know what we need to do. In our battered democracy, where members of Congress are beholden to monopoly money, voters still have the final say. With monopolies spending tens of millions of dollars per year to get their way with our elected representatives, the only way to overcome their power is through the voice of the people. We need to rise up.

It's time to start "flexing your citizenship muscle," in the words of Stacy Mitchell, codirector of the Institute for Local Self-Reliance. When it comes to fighting monopoly, you have more power as a citizen than as a consumer. If everyone who reads this book stopped using Amazon Prime tomorrow, would it make a difference? Probably not. But if everyone who reads this book becomes part of the anti-monopoly movement, which as of now consists of a small cadre of think tanks, scholars, and grassroots organizers, well, that would be a game changer.

Becoming part of the anti-monopoly movement isn't as hard as it might seem. If you start thinking about anti-monopoly, talking about anti-monopoly, supporting anti-monopoly political candidates, joining or supporting organizations that mobilize against monopoly, demanding enforcement of antitrust laws, or pressuring your political representatives to act against monopoly, you could help make your life—and indeed all Americans' lives—better.

Anti-monopoly citizen groups are in the process of forming. If you'd like to know about opportunities to get involved when they arise, sign up at monopoliessuck.com. In the meantime, organizations doing anti-monopoly policy work include the Open Markets Institute, the American Economic Liberties Project, the Institute for Local Self-Reliance, the Roosevelt Institute, and Demos, to name a few. Coalitions of organizations have already formed, like Athena mobilizing against Amazon. Social justice organizations like Demand Progress, Public Citizen, and Artist Rights Alliance frequently join together to take action on particular issues, like the Freedom from Facebook and Google Coalition. Grassroots climate and farming groups are also joining anti-monopoly efforts. Signing up for the newsletters of organizations like these, compiled at the above web address, will keep you in the know and give opportunities to play a part.

Beware false prophets, or organizations that are actually funded by monopolists. An army of supposed experts are on the payroll of corporate giants that are scared of Americans waking up and taking some of their power—including lawyers, economists, professors, and academic centers that pretend to be neutral, conservative think tanks, think tanks that pretend to be progressive, and politicians who accept monopolists' donations.

These include groups that have names designed to trick you into thinking they're on the side of the people, a well-established practice known as "astro-turfing." Money flows to those who buttress monopolists' talking points, creating a loud chorus of individuals whose livelihood depends on hiding the truth—that antitrust law has always been about fighting concentrated power.

When you hear criticism of the ideas presented in this book, ask the speaker: Does a corporation with market power fund you, your employer, or your academic center? For example, Google maintains a list of "politically-engaged trade associations, independent third-party organizations and other tax-exempt groups that receive the most substantial contributions from Google's U.S. Government Affairs and Public Policy team." At the time of writing, the most recent iteration includes more than 350 entries. Facebook has even hired "a Republican opposition-research firm to discredit activist protesters," reported the *New York Times* in an exposé of Facebook's cutthroat tactics against critics, including the Freedom from Facebook Coalition of progressive organizations.

If in addition to flexing your citizenship muscle you also want to boycott corporate giants, to the extent you have other choices, go for it. If you quit Amazon Prime, you may find you have more money and less clutter. That's what happened to me. I thought everything I was buying on Amazon was something I needed, but I was wrong. Habit experts will tell you a simple strategy—you should aim to create friction for bad habits and eliminate friction for good habits. Putting the cookie jar on the top shelf or not keeping sweets in the home are examples of creating friction to discourage a bad habit. Placing your sneakers next to your bedside is an example of reducing friction to encourage the good habit of working out in the morning. Frictionless "one-click" purchases is not what we need when we are stressed about money and drowning in stuff.

If you adopt privacy-protecting substitutes for Google like the DuckDuckGo search engine, you may feel freer like I did. If you stop using Facebook and Instagram, you may be happier and have more free time. That's what happened to me. (My accounts still technically exist, but I have been on a long, relaxing hiatus from them.) Some people can't quit these platforms because they are essential communication networks in their communities, or they need to use the networks to reach their customers, families, or more. Avoiding monopolies in things like health care and agriculture can be incredibly difficult, if not impossible, as a consumer.

Just Say No to Pro-Monopoly Excuses

If fixing our monopoly mess feels too complicated, it's understandable. But! If we give in to complication paralysis, we won't make the world—or our lives—better. "Corruption is everywhere" is another excuse, and it's true, and overwhelming. But if we throw up our hands and accept corruption, rather than trying to change the system, then we are shirking our responsibilities to do "the hard and slow" work of self-governance. With concentrated corporate power posing an existential threat with climate change and endangering democracy itself, using complication or corruption as cover for doing nothing is not an option.

Neither can we depend on monopolies to self-regulate. Corporations have fiduciary duties to maximize profits under current understandings of corporate law, which experts tell me has also been distorted by moneyed interests. For lawmakers to expect corporations to regulate in a way that risks reducing their profits is so misguided that it amounts to an abdication of their responsibility to represent the American people.

Nor can we accept the pro-monopoly talking point that America needs "national champions" to compete against China. What, is there an arms race to show citizens more creepy targeted advertising that no one told me about? In all seriousness, promoting national champions is not the American way. As we have seen through this book, competition makes companies do better. Keeping markets open so that challengers can disrupt powerful companies is what has historically made America the most innovative country in the world.

Columbia law professor Tim Wu has compared the American approach to the Japanese national champion approach in the 1970s and '80s, when Japan was seen as the biggest innovative threat. AT&T and IBM, said Wu in an interview with *Wired*'s Nicholas Thompson, asked the government to support them in their fight against Japan. Instead, the U.S. government broke up AT&T. "Out of that came a new telecom industry, a new internet industry, the ISP industry, and all the industries we're worrying about today," said Wu. Europe and Japan, however, stuck with the national champions approach. "I haven't heard from either of them in a long time in the tech markets," Wu added.

UC Berkeley professor Robert Reich has put forth another strong counterpoint against the national champions argument—America's monopoly companies are becoming less American all the time. American corporations are obligated not to Americans, but rather to their shareholders, writes Reich in the *Guardian*. "About 30% of the shareholders of large American corporations aren't even American," says Reich, and of the 500 largest corporations with U.S. headquarters, a "full 40% of their employees live and work outside the United States." American companies have also been pouring millions of dollars into research and development in China, a condition imposed by the Chinese government to gain access to China's huge market. This practice is a drain on American innovation known as "technology transfer." The ability to compete in a global economy depends, instead, says Reich, on Americans' creativity and productivity, which in turn depends on quality of education, health, and infrastructure.

The monopolization of America, however, works directly against these purposes. As we've seen, corporate behemoths drain resources from our schools by avoiding taxes, raise health care costs, and—with weak competition—reduce investment in research and development. The best way to build America's competitiveness in a global economy is to reduce concentrated corporate power and revitalize competitive markets that allow disruption and enable the American dream.

Tools to Fix Our Monopoly Mess

Policies that need citizen support fall into a few categories. Starting with Big Tech, I use the acronym PAIN to describe a set of solutions for weakening its monopoly grip: Privacy rules; Antitrust enforcement; Interoperability, which gives potential competitors access to monopoly networks; and Nondiscrimination rules, which require platforms to treat everyone equally. I use this acronym not because I'm a sadist, but because interventions that don't put the giants in pain—like the FTC's $5 billion settlement with Facebook—don't fix things.

Fines alone are not enough because they don't change destructive business models and anticompetitive practices. Google has handed over more than $9 billion to the European Commission since 2017 for antitrust violations, without skipping a beat. When it comes to fixing Big Tech, and monopolies in general, if it doesn't hurt, it doesn't work. Tech giants' pain in the short term would bring gains for competition, innovation, and democracy in the longer term.

The solutions to our problems are all possible. What makes them feel hard to achieve is that our democratically elected representatives are beholden to monopoly overlords. So there's a temptation to only propose solutions that are viewed as "realistic" because they sit well with the monopolists running our country. But such half measures are not solutions at all. They're more dangerous than doing nothing because they allow politicians to be off the hook and create the false appearance of solving problems. When we stop operating within the narrow confines of what changes will be palatable to big corporations, the solutions are simple and obvious.

Getting Antitrust Back on Track

The goals of reinvigorated antitrust enforcement should be to open the gates of competition to new and diverse innovators, decrease market concentration, and restore dynamism by halting illegal monopolization that kicks competitors out of the game. When it comes to Big Tech, antitrust enforcement should reduce choke points so that pro-democracy innovation can occur. Entrepreneurs with better business models are waiting in the wings, and antitrust enforcement should aim to enable these new start-ups to bring their innovations to users. Competition among business models is needed to help curb the massive surveillance and manipulation that today's tech monopolies allow.

Getting antitrust back on the rails requires two main approaches: 1) enforcers like DOJ, FTC, and state AGs bringing more aggressive cases under existing legal standards and 2) federal and state lawmakers passing laws that correct bad court decisions and strengthen rules. Big corporations have successfully used the Chicago School ideology to narrow the antitrust laws, throwing money at top lawyers and convincing judges time and again that their bad behavior is legal. Court victory upon victory weakened antitrust standards so that the rules created through case law bear little resemblance to the statutes

Congress enacted. "Nothing can be done," antitrust enforcers often say when faced with complaints of anticompetitive conduct, as they point to this pathetic legal precedent. The main way antitrust enforcers let the wrongheaded interpretation of antitrust statutes prevail is by not bringing enough cases they think they might lose.

Given the state of the law, being an antitrust expert these days often means being able to skillfully articulate exactly why there's no antitrust case—even when the average person plainly can see the merger or behavior is anticompetitive. I know how it happens because in some respects it happened to me when I worked at the New York Attorney General's Office. I took the complicated framework I had learned (that is, the misguided Chicago School version of antitrust law), applied it to the facts presented to me to determine whether we had a case, and in most instances—as was designed by the Chicago School—the answer was no. I did try to push the envelope with some creative case theories, and the New York AG is among the most aggressive of antitrust enforcers.

All of us AAGs were simultaneously drinking from a fire hose on a large number of merger reviews, given merger mania. There was plenty of work to go around a leanly staffed office, so I kept busy on cases that had a stronger shot at winning in court. Sherman Act Section 2 monopolization cases are much harder to win in court than are Sherman Act Section 1 cases, like price-fixing, due to legal precedent that applies a tougher standard. Potential Sherman Act Section 2 cases, then, tend to get lower priority, with the consequence that illegal monopolization runs rampant. The DOJ filed sixty-two Sherman Act Section 2 monopoly lawsuits in federal district court between 1970 and 1979, but only one such case between 2009 and 2018.

Only after I left the New York AG to become a journalist writing about antitrust did I have the luxury of stepping back from the minutiae of trying to build winnable cases and get to study the big picture. I got to see the forest, instead of just the trees. And what I saw was more like a cleared Amazon rain forest than a healthy competitive playing field.

Antitrust enforcers can no longer accept the status quo. They must be more willing to risk losing and bring the strongest cases possible, as court victories can help correct antitrust precedent. Losses can only do so much damage to already-neutered law. Even under existing law, federal antitrust enforcers are not fully using the tools available to combat illegal conduct. The FTC has a powerful law that it seldom uses for promoting competition, Section 5 of the FTC Act. Section 5 declares unfair methods of competition to be unlawful. The law is broader than the Sherman and Clayton Acts, even banning acts "that contravene the spirit of the antitrust laws," explains an FTC statement. The FTC also has the power to make rules, just like other administrative agencies do (think the Federal Communications Commission or the Environmental Protection Agency), but so far it chooses not to use that power to promulgate anti-monopoly rules.

Enforcers need to bring more monopolization cases, like *United States v. Microsoft Corp.* One remedy in monopolization cases is breaking up the corporation, like in the case of AT&T, but that's not the only fix. The Microsoft case did not ultimately result in a breakup, but it did stop Microsoft from extending its tentacles into every market that touched its operating system monopoly, allowing innovation to thrive. Breaking up Big Tech is warranted, but it doesn't solve all of the problems. Even with a breakup, privacy rules, interoperability, and nondiscrimination would be necessary to ensure fair competition.

On top of more aggressive enforcement, Congress should step in and fix bad court decisions so that the antitrust laws can work for all of us again. Legislators, until very recently, have been asleep at the wheel at best, or beholden to their corporate donors at worst. This is changing, under the leadership of lawmakers like Representative David Cicilline and Senator Elizabeth Warren, with members of Congress from both parties becoming active on antitrust issues.

Congress could fix legal precedent that imposes high bars for prevailing on monopolization and attempted monopolization cases (trying to monopolize is also illegal, by the way). Standards that particularly need fixing pertain to monopoly leveraging (using monopoly power in one market to take over other markets), predatory pricing (pricing below cost), and bundling (putting a monopoly product in a bundle with other products, often eliminating competitors in those other product markets). These are all super-effective tactics for monopolies to crush competition without competing to be the best, and they must be stopped. Congress should overrule those cases and put monopolization law back on track.

Procedural obstacles that courts have erected to limit who can sue under the antitrust laws should also be overruled. Barriers to private-class actions should be removed, including the widespread use of clauses that require people to go to arbitration instead of being able to sue in court. A real threat of class actions suing for hundreds of millions of dollars would help deter companies from monopolizing, and would supplement government enforcement.

Congress should also ban certain kinds of monopolizing practices, like the dirty tricks of Big Pharma. Enforcers' endless Whac-A-Mole could be stopped if Congress did its job. Pay-for-delay, where branded companies pay to keep generic drugs off the market, should be outright banned with an automatic fine of double the ill-gotten profits from the conduct. Wimpy fines don't work when billions of dollars of profits make breaking the law a smart business decision.

Legislators should aim to remove complexity and make antitrust cases easier, faster, and cheaper. The Chicago School's mucking up of antitrust law with misguided complexity stole from the people their weapon against concentrated power. Anyone seeking to claim their right to a competitive marketplace has to spend millions of dollars to hire economic experts, thanks to the Chicago School. In 2018, the FTC spent nearly $16 million on fees for testifying expert economists when it already employs about eighty PhD-holding economists! Monopolists' victims can rarely afford to sue them, and this enormous expense also affects enforcers' calculus of whether or not to bring cases.

State and federal legislators should allocate more resources to state antitrust enforcers, who have proven to be more aggressive in enforcement than the FTC or DOJ but are inadequately staffed. While the New York AG has a dozen or so antitrust lawyers, lots of states only have one, or even one-half of an antitrust enforcer, who spends the other half of their time doing consumer protection enforcement.

Ending Platform Privilege

I support a solution that has been advanced by Senator Elizabeth Warren and antitrust scholar Lina Khan: prohibit platforms from competing against companies that depend on them altogether. This would eliminate the problem of platform privilege—if Big Tech umpires the game, it doesn't get to play it, too.

This fix also would address a lot of the conflicts of interest that have driven Big Tech to illegally monopolize by kicking competitors out of the game. And it's not a novel concept. As Lina Khan writes in *Separations of Platforms and Commerce*, this structural solution has been done before, in industries spanning from railroads to banking to TV. Such a separation could be the remedy for a monopolization case or it could be required through new laws passed by legislators.

That platforms shouldn't be allowed to compete against businesses that depend on them is obvious when you think about it. On my *Women Killing It!* podcast I once interviewed a woman named Jillian Wright, an entrepreneur who started out as a skin care aesthetician and then developed her own skin care line. She noticed a need for a service that connects beauty entrepreneurs with buyers and consumers. She launched the Indie Beauty Expo, which provides a platform to showcase independent beauty brands and support the entrepreneurs behind them. Wright spoke to me about her decision to shut down her own beauty brand after the Indie Beauty Expo was a smashing success. She told me, "I can't compete with the brands; I have an extremely unfair advantage." She knows all the buyers and the press, she said, adding, "It's just unethical to me." Although it was not easy to bid farewell to the product she worked so hard to create, Wright said, "it was the right decision to make."

The right answer is not so complicated after all.

Putting a Stop to Harmful Mergers

Antitrust enforcers need to be more aggressive about suing to block mergers of all kinds, but particularly acquisitions of competitive threats. Tech platforms, for instance, are using their control of infrastructure to identify competitive threats when they are new and small. The deals barely even register on antitrust enforcers' radars. Enforcers also need to evaluate every merger's acquisition of data and machine learning, which can lessen competition or fortify monopoly power.

Enforcers should also unwind illegal mergers they didn't catch.

Enforcers, for example, should undo Facebook's acquisitions of WhatsApp and Instagram as violating the Clayton Act's prohibition of acquisitions where the effect "may be substantially to lessen competition, or to tend to create a monopoly." Internal Facebook documents published by the British Parliament show Facebook had identified WhatsApp as a competitive threat before the deal, as mentioned earlier. And the European Commission has already fined Facebook for telling them during the merger review that it would not merge WhatsApp's data with Facebook's data, and then doing it anyway. Since then WhatsApp cofounder Brian Acton admitted to being coached to tell European regulators that merging data would be difficult. It's likely that bad-faith representations were similarly made to the FTC, because the FTC and the European Commission coordinate with each other on global merger investigations.

Antitrust enforcers should also sue to block more mergers that involve one company buying another company that is not a direct competitor but is rather involved in a different stage of production. These types of mergers are called "vertical mergers," and an example would be Pepsi buying the company that bottles its soda. The Chicago School says such a merger is "efficient" and will help Pepsi save money and in turn reduce prices for consumers. In reality, such a merger can help Pepsi drive out competitors that depended on that bottling company by denying them access to it or raising their competitors' costs, and there's no guarantee of lower prices. To the contrary, a recent study found that such mergers drive up prices anywhere from 15 to 50 percent. The Chicago School assumption, still reflected in court decisions, that vertical mergers invariably promote competition has been proven wrong.

Enforcers also should stop putting in meaningless merger fixes that don't work, and are often violated and expire. For example, the DOJ allowed Google to buy a company called ITA, which made software that many travel booking websites depend on. But first, the DOJ filed a complaint against the deal that alleged the merger "will give Google the means and incentive" to "foreclose or disadvantage" its travel search competitors by degrading their access to ITA's software or denying them access altogether. "The proposed merger," said the DOJ's complaint, "is likely to result in reduced quality, variety, and innovation for consumers of comparative flight search services."

The DOJ then gave the deal the A-OK when Google agreed to make ITA's software available to competitors for five years. What happened about six years later? Google pulled the plug on the software, and it was no longer available to competitors, without any consequences from the DOJ. Enforcers have a bad habit of waving through deals with temporary fixes that allow monopoly power to take hold as soon as the merger conditions expire. Enforcers should more often sue to block anticompetitive deals outright, or impose fixes that are structural and permanent.

Congress should impose a moratorium on further acquisitions by mega-monopolies. Facebook, for example, already built something too big for it to control and has shown itself to be a repeat offender of consumer protection law and an FTC privacy order. If behemoths have effectively become unregulatable, lacking accountability to democratically elected governments, then putting a hold on acquisitions is entirely reasonable.

Congress should also reform the law governing mergers. It should shift the burden of proof to the merging companies—instead of the government having to prove a merger is anticompetitive, the companies have to prove a merger is good for competition. Senator Amy Klobuchar has proposed a bill that comes close, shifting the burden to the merging companies to prove their deal doesn't harm competition. Our economy is so concentrated that mergers are more likely than not to be anticompetitive, and a major course correction is needed.

From Consumer Welfare to Human Welfare

Consumers are humans, too—employees, employers, makers, entrepreneurs, creators, taxpayers, and citizens—and antitrust law should reflect this fact. When antitrust enforcers find themselves up against a defendant that insists "consumer welfare" is limited to low prices, they should push for a broader definition of what consumer welfare includes. Harm to innovation or reduced competition in the labor market, for example, should be included in what it means to harm consumers. Antitrust law should still be focused on stopping anticompetitive mergers and behavior, but prices can't be the only way to measure harm to competition.

Lawmakers could scrap the consumer welfare standard altogether as a poor indicator of whether competition itself is reduced, especially since the standard has failed to actually benefit consumers, as this book has shown. One idea that was presented by a committee of academics led by Professor Guy Rolnick was that enforcers should take "citizen welfare" into account in merger reviews that involve media and speech. In a world where the silos of different kinds of media have broken down, enforcers could evaluate "attention shares" instead of market shares to ensure that no company acquires too much control over information flow and the dissemination of news. This concept could be used not only to block mergers but also to sue tech giants when they exclude rivals from disseminating news and content and monopolize attention. Or the concept of attention shares could be used in regulation. The Federal Communications Commission has long had rules prohibiting concentrated control over television, radio, and newspapers, and the attention shares model is a creative way to apply these same types of limits in the digital age.

Because employee welfare also matters, lawmakers should outright ban noncompete clauses that trap workers in jobs and should mandate that merger reviews take into account harm to competition for employees.

Anti-Corruption Is Anti-Monopoly

You might be wondering how the heck lawmakers are going to make any of these changes when they're under the rule of monopoly overlords. Open and competitive markets protect us from highly concentrated economic and political power, so the monopolization of America means we've lost this critical check on corruption. Apple, Facebook, Amazon, and Google/Alphabet have spent more than $330 million on federal lobbying since 2008, and that doesn't include the money poured into the pro-monopoly chorus previously mentioned.

Concentrated corporate power's influence over regulators is not just dangerous to democracy, it's dangerous to human life. Boeing and Airbus together have 99 percent of the global market for large plane orders. Boeing is consistently a top spender on lobbying, greasing the wheels with $285 million in lobbying since 1998, according to the Center for Responsive Politics. Boeing used its political influence to loosen regulatory oversight of its planes, ultimately leading to a staggering loss of human life on its 737 Max. Boeing spent more than $43 billion buying back its stocks over the last decade, rather than investing the funds in research, development, and safety.

America desperately needs anti-corruption reform, including campaign finance reform to get money out of politics. We need rules to combat the "revolving door" of antitrust enforcers between jobs in government and jobs in big corporations or corporate law firms. How tough will an enforcer be on corporate abuse if they plan to later rake in cash working for the abusers? We need similar rules for lawmakers and regulators.

Your voice, and the voices of your fellow Americans, if raised loudly enough, still have the power to overcome the influence of monopoly money. Your support is needed for anti-corruption measures like campaign finance reform.

And your vote is needed for candidates who fund their campaigns with large numbers of small donations and without accepting corporate money, when you have that option. Candidates who collect cash from monopolies on the campaign trail will be beholden to them, not the people. Such candidates are unlikey to make the big structural changes that are needed to improve people's lives.

Spying Must Be Stopped

Your voice is also needed in support of privacy regulation. Strong privacy rules, not crafted by Big Tech lobbyists, would not only protect

Americans from ubiquitous surveillance, but would also level the competitive playing field.

Privacy is considered a fundamental human right in Europe, and the GDPR aims to curb the extensive tracking by Facebook, Google, and others in the digital advertising ecosystem. Although some people—including representatives from institutions funded by Facebook and Google—have argued that the GDPR is a bad idea because it will entrench the tech platforms, privacy reforms, if crafted effectively, will actually undercut Facebook's and Google's dominance. Comprehensive tracking of users is required to support the platforms' hypertargeted digital advertising business models. Unfortunately, the GDPR hasn't yet achieved its goals. As mentioned earlier, the tech giants have interpreted the law to mean what they want it to mean, and enforcement for violations has been slow.

Another step in the right direction is California's Consumer Privacy Act (CCPA), which went into effect in January 2020. Alastair Mactaggart, founder and chair of Californians for Consumer Privacy, has proposed an updated version for the November 2020 ballot. He explained two reasons why: "First, some of the world's largest companies have actively and explicitly prioritized weakening CCPA." And second, "technological tools have evolved in ways that exploit a consumer's data with potentially dangerous consequences."

Still, I worry that privacy laws based primarily on getting consent from consumers don't go far enough. People don't have time to be hypervigilant about their privacy rights, and tech platforms use this fact to their advantage. Opting in to Google's data collection takes one click, for example, while opting out takes seventeen clicks. Forty percent of people abandon a website that takes more than three seconds to load. Do we really expect a consumer to endure seventeen clicks? It's not realistic for how people use the internet.

People are under constant time pressure, in part due to monopoly rule. No one has time to individually assess every companies' tracking policies.

Cambridge Analytica whistle-blower Christopher Wylie shared this same concern in his written testimony to Congress. "Data protection is a consumer safety issue," he wrote, "and we cannot continue putting the burden on consumers by using this false narrative of choice." "We do not allow automotive companies to build unsafe cars as long as they include warning labels," Wylie added, noting that we empower regulators to create safety standards in every other sector. Concerns about regulations hampering innovation are overblown, wrote Wylie, pointing out that "car safety standards have not inhibited innovation or demand, nor have they unreasonably inhibited profit."

In my view, the most invasive forms of surveillance should be outright banned. I second journalist David Dayen, who wrote in *New Republic* that "the U.S. can take one simple, legal step to roll back this dystopian nightmare: ban targeted advertising." This could be done by the FTC through its rule-making function, without needing Congress to pass a law.

In written testimony to Congress, David Heinemeier Hansson, cofounder of Basecamp, also called for Congress to "ban the practice of targeting ads based on personal information, unless each piece of personal information used in the ads was specifically obtained with the voluntary, optional, and informed consent that it be used for marketing purposes." He gave as an example, "Yes, I give permission to Facebook to sell the fact that I'm pregnant to companies that want to advertise to pregnant women." Incidentally, voluntary, specific, and informed consent is required by the GDPR, but I have yet to see these requirements fully satisfied. And I still question whether the consent framework imposes too many burdens on busy people.

Author Shoshana Zuboff wrote in a *New York Times* op-ed that data collected about us "empty into surveillance capitalists' computational factories, called 'artificial intelligence,' where they are manufactured into behavioral predictions that are about us, but they are not *for us*." Rather, "they are sold to business customers in a new kind of market that trades exclusively in human futures," she writes. The ban Zuboff proposes is broader than just targeted advertising, but rather outlaws all human futures markets and eliminates the financial incentives to spy on us. "[S]ocieties outlaw markets that trade in human organs, babies and slaves," as morally repugnant, writes Zuboff, noting human futures markets "challenge human freedom and undermine democracy." Zuboff points out that surveillance capitalism is young but democracy is old, and "Anything made by humans can be unmade by humans."

Interoperability Promotes Competition

Interoperability is an anti-monopoly tool that has been used successfully time and again to promote innovation by reducing barriers to entering markets. Regulators and antitrust enforcers have imposed interoperability requirements against AT&T and Microsoft, opening up competition in long-distance calling, telephones, and internet browsers.

For Big Tech, interoperability would allow users to authorize networks to securely communicate with each other. It would help overcome the "network effects" barrier to entry we discussed earlier, when we talked about how a social network without your friends on it isn't much use. Interoperability could allow new platforms to communicate with Facebook's platform, for example.

Mark Zuckerberg offered up his own set of solutions that no lawmaker should listen to, and one of his proposals was data portability. This means you could take your Facebook data and port it to another platform. But data portability doesn't overcome the network effects barrier for new companies to compete with Facebook, because porting your data to a platform that doesn't allow you to communicate with your friends has little value.

Nondiscrimination and Neutrality

Dominant tech platforms should be subject to rules that prohibit discrimination in price or terms, which we have repeatedly applied to network monopolies in our history. From the post office to the telegraph to cable TV, American government has required nondiscrimination policies to protect the free press and democracy. Nondiscrimination is the principle behind net neutrality, holding that those internet service providers who control the infrastructure don't get to pick the winners and the losers of the internet.

Google being able to pick the winners and losers of internet search, for example, is the same problem we tried to address with net neutrality. We didn't want broadband companies to be able to control what content we see just because they control the pipes. We didn't want companies like Comcast to be able to prioritize their own content or let companies pay to get in fast lanes and interfere with those who don't pay, like a troll demanding a toll to cross the bridge. We have the same problem with a single search engine being the portal to the internet for the world. And with Amazon picking the winners and losers of commerce, with Facebook picking the winners and losers of internet content, and with Apple picking the winners and losers of the App Store.

Nondiscrimination and neutrality will be increasingly important as algorithms that discriminate by design continue to be rolled out, and will require algorithmic transparency to ensure compliance. The separation of platforms from commerce will partly decrease the incentives to discriminate, but not entirely, so neutrality principles would still be required in the event of such separation or a monopoly breakup of any kind. Nondiscrimination can be implemented through legislation, and it can also be a remedy in monopolization cases.

Taming the Wild, Wild West

The online and offline worlds are no longer separate, so giving carte blanche to internet actors to violate offline laws just means we live in a lawless society. Broadcasters and journalists are held to legal standards for political ads, and Facebook, too, should be held to those standards. Wiretapping and reading someone's mail is illegal, and so is recording someone without their consent in twelve states. Shouldn't spying on us through different technologies also be illegal? Fair housing laws prohibit unlawful discrimination in advertising, yet even after Facebook promised to stop this practice, a ProPublica investigation found the discrimination persisted. Discrimination by algorithm should be just as illegal as discrimination by any other means.

Fraud is illegal, but online ad fraud is estimated to cost advertisers billions of dollars per year. Yet it persists. Election tampering is illegal, but Facebook and Google are enabling voter manipulation with hypertargeted propaganda. Violating copyright law is illegal, but YouTube is rife with copyright violations. The list goes on and on.

Tristan Harris of the Center for Humane Technology has pointed out that we used to have protections for Saturday morning cartoons, but attempts at protecting kids online have fallen short. He suggests tech companies be required to report quarterly to the U.S. Department of Health and Human Services how many young users are addicted to their technology and what they are doing to stop it. Cigarettes are regulated; why shouldn't online addiction be too?

Section 230 of the Communications Decency Act has become an unruly monster, extended far beyond its intended purposes, and has allowed lawlessness as it eliminates responsibility for a wide range of illegal behavior. As the online world gobbles up the offline world and the two become one, Section 230 has helped throw our society's law and order out the window.

While the Wild West may sound fun and free, at least in the movies, laws exist for a reason. Laws protect us from abuse at the hands of private corporations that lack competitive constraint. Now there's a different set of laws, those created by the monopolists. Ask any Amazon marketplace seller and they'll tell you they're subject to an intricate web of rules and regulations; the laws are just imposed by the kingdom of Amazon.

Your Life, Better

The challenges you're dealing with in the age of monopoly are not easy. But just like those who came before you, you have the power to join with your fellow Americans and rise up in outrage against monopoly.

Anti-monopoly is one of the few issues people on both the left and the right can agree on. Attorneys general from fifty-one states and territories, for example, have joined together to investigate Google's monopoly abuses. Dethroning America's monopoly kings could begin to heal the deep divides in our country.

Now is not the time to say "it's too complicated," or "it's just the way it is," or "nothing can be done because everybody's corrupt." Now is the time to take action because, truthfully, so much is at stake that we don't have a choice. If we let a few powerful companies control each sector of our economy, then the American dream, democracy, liberty, opportunity, and equality—and worse, the future of humanity itself—are in danger. Now is our chance to build a world that's resilient, sustainable, and just, with shared power and prosperity.

The people who tell you that change is not possible are the ones who are reaping the spoils of the status quo. Don't listen to them.

Change may not be profitable for the monopolies ruling our lives, but that ain't the same thing as impossible.

Beliefs about impossibility are not facts. I learned from guests on my podcast that you can kill it in your career and create your ideal life if you don't limit yourself by false beliefs of impossibility. I talked to Christyl Johnson, the first female African American deputy center director at NASA who invented the first chromium LiSAF laser oscillator to achieve 33 millijoules. She told me, "When someone comes to me and says, 'That's really not possible,' that's when I get excited," because she thinks, "now it's my time to prove to you that that's not true."

Megan Mukuria, the founder of a nonprofit organization called ZanaAfrica, also didn't let beliefs about possibility stand in her way. She was working at a nonprofit, and she had an idea to provide sanitary pads and reproductive education for girls and women in Africa. The board of directors told her it was too big of an idea, too hard to do and not possible. Mukuria went ahead and did it on her own, without them. She recalled, "I was really interested in scale and impact, and I felt this urgency, that we can't just diddle around on the planet and not really do anything of significance. We need to do something that could affect tens of millions of girls and women." Most people on earth would think that's not possible, but Mukuria is on her way. Mukuria exposed the mirage of impossibility.

Another guest, scientist Liz Alter, didn't let beliefs about possibility stop her. She said, "I didn't think that I could be a scientist, as crazy as that might sound today, but neither of my parents were scientists. I didn't have any female role models growing up. . . . It wasn't until I was out of college that I really thought to myself, 'I need to give this a try since this is really what I'm passionate about.'" Now Alter heads up her own science lab and even discovered a new species of fish in the Congo River—the *Teleogramma obamaorum*. Can you guess who she named it after? She told me that families in the region where she discovered the fish commonly had a picture of Michelle and Barack Obama hanging on their wall.

One last example is someone we all know, Olympic swimmer Michael Phelps. No, he wasn't a guest on my *Women Killing It!* podcast, but I'll never forget a TV interview I saw of him after he had won an astonishing number of gold medals. A reporter asked him if he ever believed in his wildest dreams that it was possible for him to win that many gold medals. He looked at her like, "duh," and said that, yes, he did believe it was possible to win that many medals and that's precisely why he did it. "Nothing is impossible," Phelps said after gold medal number eight, which was just the beginning. "With so many people saying it couldn't be done, all it takes is an imagination."

Ending monopoly rule is possible. We've done it before, we can do it again, and we must.

ACKNOWLEDGMENTS

I would like to thank my brilliant editor, Stephanie Frerich, and talented assistant editor, Emily Simonson, for their hard work in bringing this book to life and for patiently shepherding me through the book process as a first-time author. Thanks also to my agent, Mollie Glick, for her unwavering advocacy and confidence in me, and Lola Bellier, for making it all happen. Deepest gratitude to Jonathan Karp, for believing in this project and for time and again publishing books on topics core to our democracy. Each member of the team at Simon & Schuster has made an invaluable contribution to this book's journey, including Cat Boyd, Stephen Bedford, Ruth Lee-Mui, Phil Metcalf, Beth Maglione, Kimberly Goldstein, Alison Forner, and Richard Rhorer.

How lucky I am to know a clever cartoonist, Christian Lowe, who helped bring levity to the heavy topic of monopoly rule and provided much-needed encouragement as the book's first reader. I'm also fortunate to count as a friend Francesca Richer, whose impeccable design sense has come to my aid in so many endeavors, including for this book's cover design.

Thank you to the wise advisors who gave me their time and thoughtful criticism, including Casey Cornelius, Phela Townsend, and Jaret Vadera.

This book is built upon the relentless efforts of the small but mighty—and growing—anti-monopoly movement. The Open Markets Institute has worked tirelessly against concentrated power for more than a decade, and contained within these pages is the expertise of Barry Lynn, Sandeep Vaheesan, Phil Longman, and Claire Kelloway, who also dedicated time to give feedback on drafts. The OMI Team, including Nidhi Hegde, Jody Brannon, Gina Salerno, Michael Bluhm, Katherine Dill, Udit Thakur, Daniel Hanley, Garphil Julien, and Jackie Filson, never ceases to impress me with creativity, energy, and dedication to the cause. Eddie Vale and Carli Kientzle play an essential communications role, as the anti-monopoly message can only have impact if it's heard.

Others whose anti-monopoly work continues to inspire me to fight for a more just economy include Sarah Miller and the team at the American Economic Liberties Project, Matt Stoller, Zephyr Teachout, Lina Khan, Stacy Mitchell, Ron Knox, the full Institute for Local Self-Reliance team, Frank Pasquale, Marshall Steinbaum, Felicia Wong and the thinkers at the Roosevelt Institute, Sanjukta Paul, David Dayen, Tim Wu, Maurice Stucke, and many more who challenge the antitrust establishment. This book includes the ideas of countless smart people whose thinking has informed my own, especially Jason Kint, Roger McNamee, Zeynep Tufecki, Shoshana Zuboff, Lillian Salerno, and Ross Baird. Warm welcome to the young guard of the anti-monopoly movement, who give me hope for the future. I remain in awe of the progressive activists who fight every day for social, economic, and environmental justice, as well as the journalists who give sunlight to monopoly abuses, with extra thanks to those whose work is cited in this book.

Teddy Downey at *The Capitol Forum* gave me the opportunity to see a broader competition picture as a journalist than I had known as an antitrust litigator. Trevor Baine, Jake Williams, and the bright minds at the one-of-a-kind startup publication taught me how to uncover the truth (or rather threw me in and gave me the choice to sink or swim—and learn a ton in the process). Special thanks to Macrui Dostourian, for being my partner in tech monopoly reporting, and Anne MacGregor, for jump-starting my international speaking tour.

The Antitrust Bureau of the New York Attorney General's Office is a rare, noble place with dedicated civil servants fighting for a fair economy for New York citizens and businesses. My former colleagues each taught me so much not only about antitrust law but also about keeping at the hard and slow, but not often glamorous, work of ensuring a just society.

I am thankful for the local, federal, and international lawmakers and antitrust enforcers who bravely hold monopoly to account, like many state AGs and FTC Commissioners Rohit Chopra and Rebecca Slaughter. The list of members of Congress serving their constituents in the fight against monopoly is thankfully getting longer every day, but Representative David Cicilline, the members of the House Antitrust Caucus, and their dedicated staff and counsel, particularly Slade Bond, deserve recognition for their leadership. Senator Elizabeth Warren has long played a lead role in the Senate, and Senator Amy Klobuchar has proposed numerous antitrust reforms, both supported by their hard-working staff.

The guests on my *Women Killing It!* podcast inspired me to look beyond limiting beliefs about what is and isn't possible, and I am indebted to them for sharing their life lessons with me. My dear friends who have provided boundless support over the years and encouraged me to keep going—you know who you are, and I couldn't have made it here without you. Jill Richburg has also provided integral guidance on my path.

Thank you to Ben, Madhu, Sarita, Samar, Sunil, Leena, Aden, Amita, and Rajesh Khurana, and Jill Robinson, for their love and support.

I would never have written this book if not for my mother, a lifelong activist who doesn't accept injustice or buy the lie of "that's just the way it is," who fearlessly speaks truth to power, and feels the pain of others as if it were her own. My father has been a willing wingman in protest, who taught me, in his midwestern, Eagle Scout way, just to do my best, for that's all I can do. My brother gave me the thick skin to handle attacks by monopolists and their shills. I may not have appreciated it as a child, but it comes in handy now! My husband gives his absolute all as a father to our children and an equal partner, and for that I will be forever grateful. I love you all.

NOTES

Introduction

1   *unemployed Americans face hunger and homelessness*: Clodagh McGowan, "Hundreds Line Up for Blocks in Queens for Free Food Distribution," *Spectrum News*, May 4, 2020, https://www.ny1.com/nyc/all-boroughs/news/2020/05/02/hundreds-line-up-for-blocks-in-queens-for-free-food-distribution.

1   *the wealthiest profiteer*: "The Rich Are Having Themselves a Fine Coronavirus," *HuffPost*, April 17, 2020, https://www.huffpost.com/entry/rich-coronavirus-bailout-stimulus-banks_n_5e9762acc5b686ec1570cb44?, and "What You Need to Know about the CARES Act Bailouts," American Economic Liberties Project, April 2020, https://static1.squarespace.com/static/5df44e0792ff6a63789b5c02/t/5e973cdcb00b992d1ceb9b50/1586969820773/Corporate+Power+Quick+Takes_1_CARES+Act+Explainer.pdf.

2   *75 billionaires coexist with thousands of homeless people*: Katelyn Newman, "San Francisco Is Home to the Highest Density of Billionaires," *U.S. News & World Report*, May 10, 2019, https://www.usnews.com/news/cities/articles/2019-05-10/san-francisco-is-home-to-the-worlds-most-billionaires-per-capita, and Kevin Fagan, "Bay Area Homelessness: 89 Answers to Your Questions," *San Francisco Chronicle*, July 28, 2019, https://projects.sfchronicle.com/sf-homeless/homeless-questions/, and "Homeless Population," *City of San Francisco*, https://sfgov.org/scorecards/safety-net/homeless-population.

5   *"about what can be achieved"*: "Transcript: President Obama's Democratic National Convention speech," *Los Angeles Times*, July 27, 2016.

5   *"Power concedes nothing without a demand"*: Frederick Douglass, "West India Emancipation" speech, August 3, 1857, available at https://www.blackpast.org/african-american-history/1857-frederick-douglass-if-there-no-struggle-there-no-progress/.

6   *Ida Tarbell exposed*: Ida Tarbell, *The History of the Standard Oil Company* (New York: McClure, Phillips, 1904).

6   *sparked a citizen outcry that spurred*: U.S. Capitol Visitor Center, "Ida M. Tarbell: Exposing Standard Oil" ("Journalist Ida M. Tarbell brought the company's shady dealings to light, and the federal government sued Standard Oil. The Supreme Court ordered Standard Oil's breakup in 1911. . . . Congress strengthened antitrust laws with the Federal Trade Commission Act and the Clayton Act"), https://www.visitthecapitol.gov/exhibitions/artifact/senate-amendment-hr-15613-act-create-federal-trade-commission-federal-trade.

6   *as Teddy Roosevelt was called*: Tim Wu, *The Curse of Bigness* (New York: Columbia Global Reports, 2018).

7   *"Justice Brandeis declared"*: Peter Scott Campbell, "Democracy v. Concentrated Wealth: In Search of a Louis D. Brandeis Quote," 16 Green Bag 2D 251, Spring 2013, http://www.greenbag.org/v16n3/v16n3_articles_campbell.pdf.

Mini-Lesson: Antitrust Is Not Just for Nerds

8   *"If we will not endure"*: 21 Cong. Rec. 2461 (1890) (statement of Senator Sherman).

8   *Section 1 of the Sherman Act*: 15 U.S.C. § 1.

9   *"Every person who shall monopolize"*: 15 U.S.C. § 2

9   *"may be substantially to lessen competition, or to tend to create a monopoly"*: Clayton Antitrust Act of 1914, Section 7, 15 U.S. Code § 18.

10   *Antitrust class actions lawsuits*: Rathod, Jason and Vaheesan, Sandeep, "The Arc and Architecture of Private Enforcement Regimes in the United States and Europe: A View Across the Atlantic," 14 University of New Hampshire Law Review 303, October 31, 2015, https://ssrn.com/abstract=2684559.

11   *increased in 80 percent of industries*: Gustavo Grullon, Yelena Larkin, and Roni Michaely, "Are US Industries Becoming More Concentrated?" *Review of Finance*, 23, no. 4 (July 2019): 697–743, https://academic.oup.com/rof/article/23/4/697/5477414, and David Autor et al., "The Fall of the Labor Share and the Rise of Superstar Firms," NBER Working Paper, 1981–2012, average industry concentration across all economic sectors increased.

11   *crisis pervades our economy*: "America's Concentration Crisis: An Open Markets Institute Report," Open Markets, https://concentrationcrisis.openmarketsinstitute.org.

11   *textbook prices increased 88 percent between 2006 and 2016*: "Textbooks Are Pricey. So Students Are Getting Creative," *Washington Post*, https://www.washingtonpost.com/local/education/textbooks-keep-getting-pricier-so-students-are-getting-creative/2020/01/17/4e1306b8-30b9-11ea-91fd-82d4e04a3fac_story.html, and "College Tuition and Fees Increase 63 Percent since

January 2006," *U.S. Bureau of Labor Statistics: The Economics Daily*, Aug. 30, 2016, https://www.bls.gov/opub/ted/2016/college-tuition-and-fees-increase-63 -percent-since-january-2006.htm.

12   *Robert Bork:* Robert H. Bork, *The Antitrust Paradox: A Policy at War with Itself* (1978), 405. ("The only goal that should guide interpretation of the antitrust laws is the welfare of consumers. . . . In judging consumer welfare, productive efficiency, the single most important factor contributing to that welfare, must be given due weight along with allocative efficiency.")

12   *could rarely win monopolization cases in court:* Michael A. Carrier, "The Four-Step Rule of Reason," *Antitrust* 33, no. 2 (Spring 2019): 50–55, https://www .antitrustinstitute.org/wp-content/uploads/2019/04/ANTITRUST-4-step -RoR.pdf. Ninety-seven percent dismissal rate in rule of reason cases brought between 1999 and 2009.

13   *mergers and acquisitions have climbed:* "M&A in the United States," IMAA, https://imaa-institute.org/m-and-a-us-united-states/#m-and-a-history.

13   *In 2018 alone, there were 19,757 mergers and acquisitions:* M. Szmigiera, "Number of M&A Deals in the U.S. 2005–2018," *Statista*, June 24, 2019, https:// www.statista.com/statistics/914665/number-of-ma-deals-usa/.

13   *decades of robust antitrust enforcement:* Barry C. Lynn and Phillip Longman, "Who Broke America's Jobs Machine?" *Washington Monthly*, March/April 2010, https://washingtonmonthly.com/magazine/marchapril-2010/who-broke -americas-jobs-machine-3/.

14   *money and power fought the people, and money and power won:* See Matt Stoller, *Goliath: The 100-Year War Between Monopoly Power and Populism* (New York: Simon & Schuster, 2019).

7 WAYS MONOPOLIES RULE YOUR LIFE

One: Monopolies Take Your Money

19   *"Increases in the price of airline tickets":* "Remarks Prepared for Delivery by Assistant Attorney General Bill Baer at the Conference Call Regarding the Justice Department's Lawsuit Challenging US Airways' Proposed Merger with American Airlines," United States Department of Justice, *Justice News*, Aug. 13, 2013, https://www.justice.gov/opa/speech/remarks-prepared-delivery-as sistant-attorney-general-bill-baer-conference-call-regarding.

19   *On a press call, Baer said:* "US Airways/American Airlines: DOJ Sues to Block Airlines Deal; Mitigation Agreement Very Unlikely," *Capitol Forum*, Aug. 13, 2013.

19   *The DOJ's complaint:* "Justice Department Files Antitrust Lawsuit Challenging Proposed Merger between US Airways and American Airlines," United States Department of Justice, *Justice News*, Aug. 13, 2013, https://www.justice

.gov/opa/pr/justice-department-files-antitrust-lawsuit-challenging-proposed
-merger-between-us-airways-and.

20   *Some commentators*: "US Airways/American Airlines: With Settlement, DOJ
      Abandons Vision of Competitive Harm Outlined in Complaint; Did PR, Lob-
      bying Influence DOJ Front Office?" *Capitol Forum*, Nov. 15, 2013.

20   *Economists studied*: "Economists Identify an Unseen Force Holding Back Af-
      fordable Housing," *Washington Post*, Oct. 17, 2019, https://www.washington
      post.com/business/2019/10/17/economists-identify-an-unseen-force-hold
      ing-back-affordable-housing/.

21   *fewer than 20 percent of U.S. census blocks*: "But according to Federal Commu-
      nications Commission data, at a download speed of 100 Mbps, 11% of U.S.
      census blocks had no access to broadband, more than one-third had only one
      choice of a fixed broadband provider, and 37% had access to only two." "Three
      Important Points on Broadband Competition," Benton Institute for Broadband
      & Society, March 20, 2019, https://www.benton.org/blog/three-important
      -points-broadband-competition.

21   *Comcast offers 25 percent higher discounts*: Inti Pacheco, and Shalini Rama-
      chandran, "Do You Pay Too Much for Internet Service? See How Your Bill
      Compares," *Wall Street Journal*, Dec. 24, 2019,https://www.wsj.com/articles
      /do-you-pay-too-much-for-internet-service-see-how-your-bill-compares-11
      577199600.

21   *Consider this typical practice*: Christopher Mitchell, "Fleeced by the Telecoms
      and Your State Is Blessing It," *American Conservative*, Oct. 21, 2019, https://
      www.theamericanconservative.com/articles/is-your-state-allowing-the-cable
      -company-to-rook-you/.

21   *nineteen states have laws discouraging such networks*: Katie Kienbaum, "19 States
      Restrict Local Broadband Solutions," Institute for Local Self-Reliance, Aug. 8,
      2019,https://ilsr.org/preemption-detente-municipal-broadband-networks-face
      -barriers-in-19-states/.

21   *HB 129*: Katie Kienbaum, "How Telecom Monopolies Killed Competition in
      North Carolina with HB 129," *Community Broadband Bits*, Episode 412, May
      26, 2020, https://muninetworks.org/content/how-telecom-monopolies-killed
      -competition-north-carolina-hb-129-community-broadband-bits.

22   *In 2019, the DOJ approved a merger between Sprint and T-Mobile*: "Justice De-
      partment Settles with T-Mobile and Sprint in Their Proposed Merger by
      Requiring a Package of Divestitures to Dish," *The United States Department
      of Justice*, July 26, 2019, https://www.justice.gov/opa/pr/justice-department
      -settles-t-mobile-and-sprint-their-proposed-merger-requiring-package.

22   *Several state attorneys general sued to block the deal*: "State Attorneys General
      Sue to Block Merger between Sprint and T-Mobile," *Washington Post*, June 11,

2019, https://www.washingtonpost.com/technology/2019/06/11/state-attorneys -general-sue-block-merger-between-sprint-t-mobile/.

22   *Roger Solé*: David McLaughlin, and Scott Moritz. "Sprint Executive Saw Future Price Hike from T-Mobile Deal," Bloomberg, Dec. 9, 2019, https://www .bloomberg.com/news/articles/2019-12-09/top-sprint-executive-saw-future -price-hike-from-t-mobile-deal.

22   *"The text messages show"*: "How a Top Antitrust Official Helped T-Mobile and Sprint Merge," *New York Times*, Dec. 19, 2019, https://www.nytimes .com/2019/12/19/technology/sprint-t-mobile-merger-antitrust-official.html, and "Open Markets Respond to Report That DOJ Antitrust Chief Helped T-Mobile and Sprint Merge," *Open Markets*, Dec. 20, 2019, https://openmarket sinstitute.org/releases/open-markets-responds-report-doj-antitrust-chief -helped-t-mobile-sprint-merge/.

22   *filing a brief arguing that the deal should be cleared*: "Justice Department Welcomes Decision in New York v. Deutsche Telecom, the T-Mobile/Sprint Merger," United States Department of Justice, *Justice News*, Feb. 11, 2020, https://www.justice.gov/opa/pr/justice-department-welcomes-decision-new -york-v-deutsche-telecom-t-mobilesprint-merger.

22   *The judge bizarrely credited "the demeanor"*: Steve Goldstein, "The Judge Who Cleared the T-Mobile-Sprint Merger Says He Relied on Witness Demeanor and Not Numbers to Make His Decision," *MarketWatch*, Feb. 11, 2020, https:// www.marketwatch.com/story/the-judge-who-cleared-the-t-mobile-sprint -merger-says-he-relied-on-witness-demeanor-and-not-numbers-to-make -his-decision-2020-02-11.

23   *A recent lawsuit alleges*: Ben Popken, "You're Getting Skinned on Chicken Prices, Suit Says," NBC News, Feb. 17, 2017, https://www.nbcnews.com/busi ness/consumer/you-re-getting-skinned-chicken-prices-suit-says-n721821.

23   *Your monthly overhead creeps higher and higher*: See study by Manhattan Institute about rising cost of living: Oren Cass, "The Cost-of-Thriving Index: Reevaluating the Prosperity of the American Family," Manhattan Institute, Feb. 20, 2020, https://www.manhattan-institute.org/reevaluating-prosperity-of-ameri can-family.

23   *Eleven rental car brands are really a mere three companies*: "Car Rental Industry," Open Markets, https://concentrationcrisis.openmarketsinstitute.org/industry /car-rental/.

23   *If Au Bon Pain*: Leah Douglas, "Private Equity Firms Are Buying Up Your Favorite Food Brands," *Fern's AG Insider*, June 18, 2018, https://thefern.org /ag_insider/private-equity-firms-are-buying-up-your-favorite-food-brands/.

23   *Burger King and Popeyes have the same owner!*: Sarah Whitten, "Restaurant Brands in Deal to Acquire Popeyes Louisiana Kitchen for $1.8 Billion,"

CNBC, Feb. 21, 2017, https://www.cnbc.com/2017/02/21/restaurant-brands
-in-deal-to-acquire-popeyes-louisiana-kitchen.html.

24 *which owns 107 brands of*: Molson Coors Beverage Company, http://www.mol
soncoors.com/en/brands.

24 *with over 500 brands and 42 percent of the beer industry as of 2017*: "Beer Industry
Revenue 2017," Open Markets, https://concentrationcrisis.openmarketsinsti
tute.org/industry/beer/, and https://www.ab-inbev.com/our-brands.html.

24 *In the recent case* Apple v. Pepper: *Apple, Inc. v. Pepper et al.*, Certiorari to the
United States Court of Appeals for the Ninth Circuit, 587 U.S. __ (2019),
https://www.supremecourt.gov/opinions/18pdf/17-204_bq7d.pdf.

25 *the Android app store doesn't meaningfully constrain*: European Commission, "Antitrust: Commission Fines Google €4.34 Billion for Illegal Practices Regarding Android Mobile Devices to Strengthen Dominance of Google's Search
Engine," July 18, 2018, https://ec.europa.eu/commission/presscorner/detail/en
/IP_18_4581.

25 *Federal Communications Commission ruled in 1968*: *Carterfone* (13 F.C.C. 2d
420), 1968.

25 *Only by tracking us*: J. Clement, "Facebook: Annual Revenue 2009–2019,"
Statista, Feb. 3, 2020, https://www.statista.com/statistics/268604/annual
-revenue-of-facebook/, and Davey Alba, "Google and Facebook Still Reign
over Digital Advertising," *Wired*, July 29, 2017, https://www.wired.com/story
/google-facebook-online-ad-kings/.

25 *it has tremendous value*: Andrea M. Matwyshyn, "Privacy, the Hacker Way,"
Southern California Law Review 87, no. 1 (August 1, 2013), available at SSRN:
https://ssrn.com/abstract=3004803.

25 *"I worry that if all of the data"*: Aarti Shahani, "Microsoft President: Democracy Is at Stake. Regulate Big Tech," NPR, Sept. 13, 2019, https://www.npr
org/2019/09/13/760478177/microsoft-president-democracy-is-at-stake-regu
late-big-tech 11/9/19.

26 *economists say the platforms should be paying you*: "Stigler Committee on Digital
Platforms: Final Report," Stigler Center for the Study of the Economy and
the State, https://research.chicagobooth.edu/stigler/media/news/committee
-on-digital-platforms-final-report. "([T]he information is more valuable than
the cost of the services. The economics literature has modeled this setting and
is able to define a data markup. . . . While the low price can be a blessing for
consumers, it has drawbacks for competition and market structure in a world
where institutions have not arisen to manage negative prices . . . platforms are
able to mark up the competitive price all the way to zero.")

26 *The concept is called "digital labor"*: "What Is Digital Labor?" *I'MTech: IMT*

Science and Technology News, July 25, 2017, https://blogrecherche.wp.imt.fr /en/2017/07/25/what-is-digital-labor/.

26 *"Companies have turned"*: "Joe Toscano," Tedx Lincoln, https://www.tedxlin coln.com/speakers/2019/joe-toscano.html.

27 *Ninety-one corporations paid zero federal income tax in 2018*: "Corporate Tax Avoidance in the First Year of the Trump Tax Law," Institute on Taxation & Economic Policy, December 2019, https://itep.org/wp-content/up loads/121619-ITEP-Corporate-Tax-Avoidance-in-the-First-Year-of-the -Trump-Tax-Law.pdf.

27 *Facebook is currently fighting*: Paul Kiel, "Who's Afraid of the IRS? Not Facebook," ProPublica, https://www.propublica.org/article/whos-afraid-of-the -irs-not-facebook, and Colleen Murphy, "Facebook, IRS Summer Tax Trial Canceled Due to Pandemic," *Bloomberg Tax*, March 27, 2020, https://news bloombergtax.com/daily-tax-report/facebook-irs-summer-tax-trial-canceled -due-to-pandemic.

27 *donating $25 million for therapeutics research*: Theodore Schleifer, "Mark Zuckerberg Is Teaming Up with Bill Gates to Try to Find a Drug to Treat Coronavirus," *Vox*, March 27, 2020, https://www.vox.com/recode/2020/3/27/21196421 /coronavirus-mark-zuckerberg-priscilla-chan-drug-treatment-bill-gates-zuck erberg-initiative.

27 *2010 U.S. Supreme Court case* Citizens United: Tim Lau, "Citizens United Explained," Brennan Center for Justice, Dec. 12, 2019, https://www.brennancen ter.org/our-work/research-reports/citizens-united-explained.

28 *third-party sellers on Amazon's marketplace failed*: "Amazon: Data Analysis Reveals an Estimated $1.9B in Unpaid State Sales Tax from FBA Sales in 2016 Alone; States Targeting Amazon and Sellers in Mounting Legislative and Enforcement Efforts," *Capitol Forum* 5, no. 96 (March 21, 2017), http://create send.com/t/j-2649D429940A23FE.

29 *Under political and legal pressure in 2018, Amazon*: Tae Kim, "Here's the Controversial Tax Practice by Amazon That's Got Trump So Upset," CNBC, March 29, 2018, https://www.cnbc.com/2018/03/29/heres-the-controversial -tax-practice-by-amazon-thats-got-trump-so-upset.html.

29 *Amazon didn't pay taxes in Virginia until 2013*: Graham Moomaw, "Virginia Got Amazon. But Small Bookstores Aren't Cheering," *Richmond Times-Dispatch*, Nov. 30, 2018, https://www.richmond.com/news/virginia/virginia -got-amazon-but-small-bookstores-aren-t-cheering/article_bba9e4cf -778f-5102-9073-dec7e1fe3e13.html.

29 *told the* Richmond Times-Dispatch: Ibid.

30 *an opportunity for Amazon to gather data about cities and their citizens*: Nick Tabor,

"Amazon Is an Infrastructure Company. The HQ2 Bids Were Reconnaissance," *Intelligencer*, Dec. 3, 2018, https://nymag.com/intelligencer/2018/12/amazons -hq2-bids-gave-it-a-blueprint-for-expansion.html.

30   *$3 billion of incentives*: Jimmy Vielkind, "New York Dangled Extra Incentives in Initial Bid to Lure Amazon HQ2," *Wall Street Journal*, Jan. 5, 2020, https:// www.wsj.com/articles/new-york-dangled-extra-incentives-in-initial-bid-to -lure-amazon-hq2-11578153600.

30   *taxpayers were not pleased with the notion of funding a helipad*: Peter Page, "New York Is Giving Amazon a Helipad and New Yorkers Are Furious," *Entrepreneur*, Nov. 14, 2018, https://www.entrepreneur.com/article/323281.

30   *coming to New York City regardless*: Keiko Morris, "Amazon Leases New Manhattan Office Space, Less Than a Year after HQ2 Pullout," *Wall Street Journal*, Dec. 6, 2019, https://www.wsj.com/articles/amazon-leases-new-manhattan -office-space-less-than-a-year-after-hq2-pullout-11575671243?mod=article _inline.

30   *Amazon has reportedly received close to $3 billion*: "Tracking Amazon's Rapidly Expanding Footprint," *Business Journals*, Oct. 19, 2017, https://www.bizjour nals.com/bizjournals/maps/the-amazon-effect, and Good Jobs First, "Amazon Tracker," https://www.goodjobsfirst.org/amazon-tracker, updated June 2020.

30   *company is nearly four times more likely to receive an economic incentive package*: Daniel Aobdia, Allison Koester, and Reining Petacchi, "Who Benefits When State Governments Award Incentives to Politically-Connected Companies?" Chicago Booth Stigler Center, Jan. 7, 2020, https://promarket.org/who-benefits -when-state-governments-award-incentives-to-politically-connected-companies/.

31   *tacking on a monthly fee to Virginians' utility bills*: Mya Frazier, "Amazon Isn't Paying Its Electric Bills. You Might Be," *Bloomberg Businessweek*, Aug. 20, 2018, https://www.bloomberg.com/news/articles/2018-08-20/amazon-isn-t -paying-its-electric-bills-you-might-be.

31   *data centers industry-wide*: Quentin Hardy, "Cloud Computing Brings Sprawling Centers, but Few Jobs, to Small Towns," *New York Times*, Aug. 26, 2016, https://www.nytimes.com/2016/08/27/technology/cloud-computing-brings -sprawling-centers-but-few-jobs-to-small-towns.html.

31   *In 2017, Walmart had sixty-two lobbyists*: "Wal-Mart Says It's 'Neutral' on a Minimum Wage Hike. Lobbying Disclosures Suggest Otherwise," *Washington Post*, Feb. 21, 2014, https://www.washingtonpost.com/news/wonk/wp/2014/02/21 /wal-mart-says-its-neutral-on-a-minimum-wage-hike-lobbying-disclosures -suggest-otherwise/.

31   *the single largest group of food stamp recipients*: Peter Van Buren, "Walmart Wages Are the Main Reason People Depend on Food Stamps," *Nation*,

Feb. 16, 2016, https://www.thenation.com/article/walmart-wages-are-the
-main-reason-people-depend-on-food-stamps/.

31   *an estimated 18 percent of all food stamps are redeemed at Walmart*: H. Claire Brown,
"Amazon Gets Tax Breaks While Its Employees Rely on Food Stamps, New
Data Shows," *Intercept*, April 19, 2018, https://theintercept.com/2018/04/19
/amazon-snap-subsidies-warehousing-wages/.

31   *participating in a pilot program*: "Attention, Walmart Executives: Amazon's
Coming after Your Low-Income Shoppers," *Washington Post*, June 18, 2019,
https://www.washingtonpost.com/technology/2019/06/18/amazons-growing
-prime-focus-americas-poor/.

31   *one-third of its employees in Arizona*: Chavie Lieber, "Amazon and Walmart Are
Testing a Program to Accept Food Stamps Online," *Vox*, April 19, 2019, https://
www.vox.com/the-goods/2019/4/19/18507813/amazon-walmart-snap-usda-pi
lot-food-stamps, and H. Claire Brown, "Amazon Gets Tax Breaks While Its Employees Rely on Food Stamps, New Data Shows," *Intercept*, April 19, 2018, https://
theintercept.com/2018/04/19/amazon-snap-subsidies-warehousing-wages/.

31   *skimped on $2.6 billion tax dollars using a purportedly fake Chinese joint venture*:
Max de Haldevang, "Walmart Dodged Up to $2.6 Billion in US Tax through
a 'Fictitious' Chinese Entity, Former Executive Says," *Quartz*, Sept. 5, 2019,
https://qz.com/1701404/walmart-allegedly-created-fictitious-chinese-jv-to
-avoid-us-tax/.

31   *sheltered $76 billion in tax havens*: Jesse Drucker and Renee Dudley, "Wal-Mart
Has $76 Billion in Undisclosed Overseas Tax Havens," Bloomberg, June 16,
2015, https://www.bloomberg.com/news/articles/2015-06-17/wal-mart-has-76
-billion-in-overseas-tax-havens-report-says.

31   *the Centers for Disease Control's public*: Katelyn Newman, "Chronic Underfund-
ing Crippled America's COVID-19 Response," *U.S. News & World Report*,
April 16, 2020, https://www.usnews.com/news/healthiest-communities/ar
ticles/2020-04-16/crippled-coronavirus-response-tied-to-chronic-underfund
ing-report-says.

32   *record levels of companies buying back their own stocks*: Ben Popken, "What Did
Corporate America Do with That Tax Break? Buy Record Amounts of Its
Own Stock," NBC News, June 26, 2018, https://www.nbcnews.com/business
/economy/what-did-corporate-america-do-tax-break-buy-record-amounts
-n886621.

32   *Major airlines spent 96 percent*: David Slotnick, "Airlines Will Get the $60
Billion Bailout They Asked for in the $2 Trillion Coronavirus Stimu-
lus Bill That Trump Signed into Law. It Also Prohibits Layoffs, Stock
Buybacks, and Dividends," *Business Insider*, March 27, 2020, https://www

.businessinsider.com/airlines-coronavirus-bailout-senate-stock-buybacks
2020-3?op=1, and "U.S. Airlines Spent 96% of Free Cash Flow on Buybacks:
Chart," Bloomberg, March 16, 2020, https://www.bloomberg.com/news
/articles/2020-03-16/u-s-airlines-spent-96-of-free-cash-flow-on-buybacks
-chart, and Phillip van Doorn, "Airlines and Boeing Want a Bailout—but Look
How Much They've Spent on Stock Buybacks," *MarketWatch*, March 22, 2020,
https://www.marketwatch.com/story/airlines-and-boeing-want-a-bailout
-but-look-how-much-theyve-spent-on-stock-buybacks-2020-03-18,andhttps://
www.nytimes.com/interactive/2020/03/27/opinion/coronavirus-bailout.html.

Two: *Monopolies Gouge You When You're Sick*

34   *two companies make the swabs used for coronavirus testing*: Dina Shanker,
     "Swabs, Stat! Inside the Maine Factory Racing to Supply America with
     Virus Test Swabs," Bloomberg, March 25, 2020, https://www.bloomberg.com
     /features/2020-coronavirus-puritan-medical-test-swab/

35   *Corporate concentration in health care put*: Barry Lynn, *End of the Line*, (New
     York: Doubleday, 2005). In a 2005 *Financial Times* op-ed, Open Markets In-
     stitute president Barry Lynn wrote that the production of medical masks was
     particularly at risk of collapse, building on the argument in his book *End of the
     Line* about how corporate concentration put critical supply chains at risk of
     catastrophic collapse in the event of a pandemic or other systemic shock.

35   *created a legal safe harbor for these kickbacks*: "AAPS News April 2018: Safe Kick-
     backs," AAPS, April 1, 2018, https://aapsonline.org/aaps-news-april-2018-safe
     -kickbacks/; Brian Klepper, "Connecting the Dots: How Anticompetitive Con-
     tracting Practices, Kickbacks, and Self-dealing by Hospital Group Purchasing
     Organizations (GPOs) Caused the U.S. Drug Shortage," *Care and Cost*, Feb. 14,
     2012, https://careandcost.com/2012/02/14/connecting-the-dots-how-anticom
     petitive-contracting-practices-kickbacks-and-self-dealing-by-hospital-group
     -purchasing-organizations-gpos-caused-the-u-s-drug-shortage/.

35   *GPOs designate the biggest corporations*: Diana L. Moss, "Healthcare Interme-
     diaries: Competition and Healthcare Policy at Loggerheads?" AAI, May 7,
     2012, https://www.antitrustinstitute.org/wp-content/uploads/2012/05/AAI
     -White-Paper-Healthcare-Intermediaries.pdf; Mary William Walsh, "Health-
     care Intermediaries: Competition and Healthcare Policy at Loggerheads?"
     New York Times, Aug. 13, 2009, https://www.nytimes.com/2009/08/14/health
     /policy/14purchasing.html; "What the Experts Say About GPOs," *Puncture*,
     http://www.puncturemovie.com/what-the-experts-say-about-gpos/.

35   *GPOs don't even get hospitals lower prices than they would get if they did their own
     negotiating*: "Purchasing Organizations (GPOs) Often Fail to Deliver Best
     Prices for Hospitals," *Business Wire*, Oct. 6, 2010, https://www.businesswire

.com/news/home/20101006005130/en/Empirical-Study-Competitive
-Bidding-Data-Shows-Group.

36 *spend huge sums to lobby Washington*: Mariah Blake, "Dirty Medicine," *Wash-ington Monthly*, July/Aug. 2010, https://washingtonmonthly.com/magazine
/julyaugust-2010/dirty-medicine-2/.

36 *"Government officials"*: Nicholas Kulish, Sarah Kliff, and Jessica Silver-Greenberg, "The U.S. Tried to Build a New Fleet of Ventilators. The Mission Failed," *New York Times*, updated April 20, 2020, https://www.nytimes
.com/2020/03/29/business/coronavirus-us-ventilator-shortage.html; Diana L.
Moss, "Can Competition Save Lives? The Intersection of COVID-19, Ventilators, and Antitrust Enforcement," AAI, March 31, 2020, https://www
.antitrustinstitute.org/can-competition-save-lives-the-intersection-of-covid
-19-ventilators-and-antitrust-enforcement/.

36 *The FTC cleared the merger quickly*: "Medtronic, Inc. and Covidien plc, In the Matter of," FTC, Jan. 21, 2015, https://www.ftc.gov/enforcement/cases-pro
ceedings/141-0187/medtronic-inc-covidien-plc-matter.

36 *Philips hadn't yet supplied*: Nicholas Kulish, Sarah Kliff and Jessica Silver-Greenberg, "The U.S. Tried to Build a New Fleet of Ventilators. The Mission Failed," *New York Times*, updated April 20, 2020, https://www.nytimes
.com/2020/03/29/business/coronavirus-us-ventilator-shortage.html, and Pa-tricia Callahan, Sebastian Rotella and Tim Golden, "Taxpayers Paid Millions to Design a Low-Cost Ventilator for a Pandemic. Instead, the Company Is Selling Versions of It Oversees," *ProPublica*, March 30, 2020, https://www.pro
publica.org/article/taxpayers-paid-millions-to-design-a-low-cost-ventilator
-for-a-pandemic-instead-the-company-is-selling-versions-of-it-overseas-.

37 *Newport was only one of 17 companies that Covidien bought*: Diana L. Moss, "Can Competition Save Lives? The Intersection of COVID-19, Ventilators, and Antitrust Enforcement," AAI, March 31, 2020, https://www.antitrustinsti
tute.org/can-competition-save-lives-the-intersection-of-covid-19-ventilators
-and-antitrust-enforcement/.

37 *the FTC let the Covidien deal go through*: "Medtronic, Inc. and Covidien plc, In the Matter of," FTC, Jan. 21, 2015, https://www.ftc.gov/enforcement/cases
-proceedings/141-0187/medtronic-inc-covidien-plc-matter.

37 *Buying Covidien made Medtronic's stock value instantly jump*: Joe Carlson, "5 Years Later, a Lawsuit Challenging a $49.9B Medtronic Acquisition Churns On," *Star Tribune*, Feb. 15, 2020, https://www.startribune.com/5-years-later
-a-lawsuit-challenging-a-49-9b-medtronic-acquisition-churns-on/56788
5432/.

38 *you're still paying a price for them through your insurance premiums*: Orphan drug monopolies: For example, one patient's annual bill for the drug Strensiq, which

treats a debilitating genetic disorder, totaled close to $2 million last year. The impact on the patient's health plan, available through her husband's labor union, is sobering. As described in one account, 35 cents of every hour of pay for each of the union's 16,000 workers went to pay for that single patient's prescriptions for this one drug. See Katie Thomas and Reed Abelson, "The $6 Million Drug Claim," *New York Times*, Aug. 25, 2019, https://www.nytimes.com/2019/08/25 /health/drug-prices-rare-diseases.html.

38   *in 2018, the average cost of health care*: Christopher S. Girod, Susan K. Hart, David M. Liner, Thomas D. Snook, and Scott A. Weltz, "2019 Milliman Medical Index," Milliman, July 25, 2019, https://www.milliman.com/en/insight /~/media/Milliman/importedfiles/ektron/2019-milliman-medical-index.ashx.

38   *median household income in 2018 of $63,179*: https://www.census.gov/content /dam/Census/library/publications/2019/demo/p60-266.pdf.

39   *insurance premiums rose by a whopping 242 percent*: Martin Gayor, "Examining the Impact of Health Care Consolidation, Statement before the Committee on Energy and Commerce Oversight and Investigation Subcommittee, U.S. House of Representatives," docs.house.gov, Feb. 14, 2018, https://docs.house.gov /meetings/IF/IF02/20180214/106855/HHRG-115-IF02-Wstate-GaynorM -20180214.pdf.

39   *deductibles have increased eight times as fast as wages*: "Average Annual Real Wages in the United States from 2000 to 2018 (in 2018 U.S. dollars)," Statista, https://www.statista.com/statistics/612519/average-annual-real-wages-united -states/; Phillip Longman, "How to End the Democrats' Health Care Demolition Derby," *Washington Monthly*, January/February/March 2020, https:// washingtonmonthly.com/magazine/january-february-march-2020/how-to -end-the-democrats-health-care-demolition-derby/; "Premiums for Employer-Sponsored Family Health Coverage Rise 5% to Average $19,616; Single Premiums Rise 3% to $6,896," KFF, https://www.kff.org/health-costs/press-release /employer-sponsored-family-coverage-premiums-rise-5-percent-in-2018/.

39   *a full one-third of total health care spending*: Caitlin Owens, "Health Care's Big Spending Mismatch," *Axios*, May 6, 2019, https://www.axios.com/health -cares-spending-out-of-pocket-most-expensive-83ace437-b84e-4379-b348 -dd2edf6a50fc.html; Martin Gayor, "Examining the Impact of Health Care Consolidation, Statement before the Committee on Energy and Commerce Oversight and Investigation Subcommittee, U.S. House of Representatives," docs.house.gov, Feb. 14, 2018, https://docs.house.gov/meetings/IF /IF02/20180214/106855/HHRG-115-IF02-Wstate-GaynorM-201802 14.pdf.

39   *hospital inpatient prices grew 42 percent*: "Paper 2: Hospital Prices Grew Substantially Faster than Physician Prices for Hospital-Based Care in 2007–14,"

Health Care Pricing Project, Feb. 2019, https://healthcarepricingproject.org
/paper/paper-2-hospital-prices-grew-substantially-faster-physician-prices
-hospital-based-care-2007,Äi14.

39   *more than 100 per* year: Stefano Feltri, "Hospital Mergers: The Forgotten Problem of American Health Care," ProMarket, Sept. 23, 2019, https://promarket
.org/hospital-mergers-the-forgotten-problem-of-american-health-care/.

39   *to approximately 900,000 in 2017*: Andrea Flynn and Ron Knox, "We're Short on Hospital Beds Because Washington Let Too Many Hospitals Merge," *Washington Post*, April 8, 2020, https://www.washingtonpost.com/outlook/2020/04/08
/were-short-hospital-beds-because-washington-let-too-many-hospitals-merge.

39   *Cerberus had financially weakened the hospital*: Eileen Applebaum, "How Private Equity Makes You Sicker," *Prospect*, Oct. 7, 2019, https://prospect.org
/health/how-private-equity-makes-you-sicker/; Rosemary Batt and Eileen Appelbaum, "Profiteers Plunder Hospitals, Then Line Up for Federal Subsidies," *Waco Tribune*, April 7, 2020, https://www.wacotrib.com/opinion/columns
/rosemary-batt-eileen-appelbaum-profiteers-plunder-hospitals-then-line-up
-for-federal-subsidies/article_d848ffcc-f5fe-5d9b-8b0b-db26eb40c011.html.

40   *They dictate high prices*: See, for example, Catherine Ho, "Major Antitrust Case Against Sutter Over Health Prices Nears Trial," *San Francisco Chronicle*, Aug. 24, 2019, https://www.sfchronicle.com/business/article/Landmark-anti
trust-case-against-Sutter-over-14374893.php?psid=l0yeZ.

40   *will cost you 12 percent more*: "Paper 1: The Price Ain't Right? Hospital Prices and Health Spending on the Privately Insured," Health Care Pricing Project, May 2015, https://healthcarepricingproject.org/papers/paper-1.

40   *Inpatient prices were 70 percent higher in Northern California*: Catherine Ho, "Health Care Costs 30% More in Northern California Than in the Rest of the State," *San Francisco Chronicle*, March 26, 2018, www.sfchronicle.com/business
/article/Healthcare-costs-30-more-in-Northern-than-in-12782446.php.

40   *Not patients*: Melanie Evans, "Hospitals Merged. Quality Didn't Improve," *Wall Street Journal*, Jan. 1, 2020, https://www.wsj.com/articles/hospitals-merged
-quality-didnt-improve-11577916000?mod=hp_lista_pos3.

40   *a more than 3 percent increase in the mortality rate*: Stefano Feltri, "Hospital Mergers: The Forgotten Problem of American Health Care," ProMarket, Sept. 23, 2019, https://promarket.org/hospital-mergers-the-forgotten-problem
-of-american-health-care/.

40   *their wages rose only 8 percent*: "Average Annual Real Wages in the United States from 2000 to 2018 (in 2018 U.S. dollars)," *Statista*, https://www.statista.com
/statistics/612519/average-annual-real-wages-united-states/.

40   *the price of hospital-based outpatient care*: "Paper 2: Hospital Prices Grew Substantially Faster than Physician Prices for Hospital-Based Care in 2007–14,"

Health Care Pricing Project, Feb. 2019, https://healthcarepricingproject.org /paper/paper-2-hospital-prices-grew-substantially-faster-physician-prices -hospital-based-care-2007–14.

40 *CEOs' pay has risen by 93 percent*: Jerry Y. Du, MD, Alexander S. Rascoe, MD, MBA, and Randall E. Marcus, "The Growing Executive-Physician Wage Gap in Major US Nonprofit Hospitals and Burden of Nonclinical Workers on the US Healthcare System," *Clinical Orthopaedics and Related Research*, October 2018, https://journals.lww.com/clinorthop/Fulltext/2018/10000/The_Growing _Executive_Physician_Wage_Gap_in_Major.4.aspx.

41 *more than 8,000 between 2016 and 2018*: Andrea Flynn and Ron Knox, "We're Short on Hospital Beds Because Washington Let Too Many Hospitals Merge," *Washington Post*, Apr. 8, 2020, https://www.washingtonpost.com /outlook/2020/04/08/were-short-hospital-beds-because-washington-let-too -many-hospitals-merge.

41 *quality of care doesn't*: Lawrence C. Baker, M. Kate Bundorf, and Daniel P. Kessler, "Vertical Integration: Hospital Ownership of Physician Practices Is Associated with Higher Prices and Spending," *HealthAffairs*, May 2014, https:// www.healthaffairs.org/doi/full/10.1377/hlthaff.2013.1279; Martin Gayor, "Examining the Impact of Health Care Consolidation, Statement before the Committee on Energy and Commerce Oversight and Investigation Subcommittee, U.S. House of Representatives," docs.house.gov, Feb. 14, 2018, https://docs .house.gov/meetings/IF/IF02/20180214/106855/HHRG-115-IF02-Wstate -GaynorM-20180214.pdf.

41 *charge an average of 14 percent more*: Cory Capps, David Dranove, and Christopher Ody, "The Effect of Hospital Acquisitions of Physician Practices on Prices and Spending," MIT, Jan 12, 2017, http://economics.mit.edu/files/12747.

42 *control a 92 percent market share*: "Dialysis Center," Open Markets Institute, 2018, https://concentrationcrisis.openmarketsinstitute.org/industry/dialysis -centers/.

42 *misclassified as out of network*: Jenny Gold, "They May Owe Nothing—Half-Million-Dollar Dialysis Bill Canceled," *Kaiser Health News*, July 26, 2019, https://khn.org/news/bill-of-the-month-half-million-dollar-kidney-dialysis -bill-fresenius-now-zero/.

42 *hurt patient health*: James Ives, "Acquisitions by Large, For-profit Dialysis Chains Hurt Patient Health," *News-Medical*, Oct. 24, 2019, https://www .news-medical.net/news/20191024/Acquisitions-by-large-for-profit-dialysis -chains-hurt-patient-health.aspx.

42 *19 and 24 percent higher risk of death*: Yi Zhang, Dennis J. Cotter, and Mae Thamer, "The Effect of Dialysis Chains on Mortality Among Patients

Receiving Hemodialysis," *Wiley Online Library*, Dec. 9, 2010, https://online
library.wiley.com/doi/full/10.1111/j.1475-6773.2010.01219.x.

42 *from medical device makers to syringe manufacturers*: Angie Stewart, "5 Major
Developments in the US Medical Device Industry," beckersasc, June 15, 2018,
http://www.beckersasc.com/supply-chain/5-major-developments-in-the-u-s
-medical-device-industry.html; "America's Concentration Crisis," Open Markets Institute, https://concentrationcrisis.openmarketsinstitute.org.

42 *Health insurance companies, too, have merged*: "Health Insurance and Monopoly," Open Markets Institute, http://www.openmarketsinstitute.org/explainer
/health-insurance-and-monopoly/.

43 *increased its price by more than 4,000 percent*: "Case 1:20-cv-00706-DLC Document 86 Filed 04/14/20," FTC, April 14, 2020, https://www.ftc.gov/system
/files/documents/cases/161_0001_vyera_amended_complaint.pdf.

43 *on Shkreli working in pharma*: Ibid.; "Attorney General James Sues 'Pharma Bro'
Martin Shkreli and Vyera Pharmaceuticals for Illegally Monopolizing Life-
Saving Drug," ag.ny.gov, Jan. 27, 2020, https://ag.ny.gov/press-release/2020
/attorney-general-james-sues-pharma-bro-martin-shkreli-and-vyera-pharma
ceuticals.

43 *convicted of securities fraud*: Adam Smith and Julia Horowitz, "Martin Shkreli
Convicted of Securities Fraud, Conspiracy," *Money*, Aug. 4, 2017, https://
money.cnn.com/2017/08/04/news/martin-shkreli-verdict/index.html.

43 *making threats against Hillary Clinton*: "Case 1:20-cv-00706-DLC Document
86 Filed 04/14/20," FTC, April 14, 2020, https://www.ftc.gov/system/files
/documents/cases/161_0001_vyera_amended_complaint.pdf.

43 *allegedly runs Phoenixus from prison*: Rod Copeland and Bradley Hope, "Martin Shkreli Steers His Old Company from Prison—with Contraband Cellphone," *Wall Street Journal*, March 7, 2019, https://www.wsj.com/articles
/martin-shkreli-steers-his-company-from-prisonwith-contraband-cellphone
-11551973574.

43 *"plans to emerge from jail richer than he entered"*: Ibid.

44 *"From 1995–2015, 60 pharma companies"*: Rohit Chopra, "Dissenting Statement
of Commissioner Rohit Chopra," Twitter, Nov. 18, 2019, https://twitter.com
/chopraftc/status/1196514076400214018?s=20.

44 *both dissented*: "Dissenting Statement of Commissioner Rebecca Kelly Slaughter," FTC, Nov. 15, 2019, https://www.ftc.gov/system/files/documents/pub
lic_statements/1554283/17_-_final_rks_bms-celgene_statement.pdf.

44 *fewer drug companies are left to compete*: Justus Haucap and Joel Stiebale, *How
Mergers Affect Innovation: Theory and Evidence from the Pharmaceutical Industry* (Düsseldorf Inst. for Competition Economics, Discussion Paper No. 218,

2016), http://www.dice hhu.de/fileadmin/redaktion/Fakultaeten/Wirtschafts wissenschaftliche Fakultaet/DICE/Discussion Paper/218 Hauca p Stiebale .pdf.; Justus Haucap and Joel Stiebale, "Research: Innovation Suffers When Drug Companies Merge," *Harvard Business Review* (Aug. 3, 2016).

45   *"protected nearly $2 billion . . . and often life-saving medications"*: "FTC Charges Bristol-Myers Squibb with Pattern of Abusing Government Processes to Stifle Generic Drug Competition," FTC, March 7, 2003, https://www.ftc.gov /news-events/press-releases/2003/03/ftc-charges-bristol-myers-squibb-pattern -abusing-government.

46   *"The prosecutions of BMS"*: "Former Bristol-Myers Squibb Senior Executive Pleads Guilty for Role in Dishonest Dealings with the Federal Government," Justice.gov, April 6, 2009, https://www.justice.gov/sites/default/files/atr/legacy /2009/04/09/244479.pdf.

46   *a book called* The First Question: Ed Silverman, "Writing with Conviction: BMS Fraudster Pens His Penalty," Contract Pharma, May 30, 2012, https:// www.contractpharma.com/issues/2012-06/view_pharma-beat/writing-with -conviction/.

46   *"The financial crisis"*: "Dissenting Statement of Commissioner Rebecca Kelly Slaughter," FTC, Nov. 15, 2019, https://www.ftc.gov/system/files/documents /public_statements/1554283/17_-_final_rks_bms-celgene_statement.pdf.

47   *by 85,000 percent*: "Case 1:17-cv-00120 Document 10-1 Filed 01/25/17," FTC, Jan. 25, 2017, https://www.ftc.gov/system/files/documents/cases/170118 mallinckrodt_complaint_public.pdf

48   *acquiring the rights to EpiPen when it was priced at $100*: Carolyn Y. Johnson and Catherine Ho, "How Mylan, the Maker of EpiPen, Became a Virtual Monopoly," *Washington Post*, Aug. 25, 2016, https://www.washingtonpost.com /business/economy/2016/08/25/7f83728a-6aee-11e6-ba32-5a4bf5aad4fa _story.html.

48   *refused to cover Epi-Pen's competitor, Auvi-Q*: Robert B. Barnett Jr., "EpiPen An- titrust Suit Against Mylan for Sherman Act Violations Mostly Survives Dis- missal," Wolters Kluwer, Dec. 28, 2017, https://lrus.wolterskluwer.com/news /antitrust-law-daily/epipen-antitrust-suit-against-mylan-for-sherman-act -violations-mostly-survives-dismissal/43716; "Case 2:17-md-02785-DDC -TJJ Document 98 Filed 12/21/17," business.cch, Dec. 21, 2017, http://business .cch.com/ald/inreepipen12282017.pdf.

48   *adding lobbyists in thirty-six states between 2010 and 2014*: Yue Qiu, Ben Wie- der, and Chris Zubak-Skees, "Here Are the Interests Lobbying in Every State- house," Center for Public Integrity, Feb. 11, 2016, https://publicintegrity.org /federal-politics/state-politics/here-are-the-interests-lobbying-in-every-state house/.

48 *Multiple senators and antitrust enforcers*: Ed Silverman, "Lawmakers call for FTC probe into potential antitrust violations in EpiPen school program," *Stat-News*, November 8, 2016, https://www.statnews.com/pharmalot/2016/11/08 /ftc-mylan-epipen-antitrust/, and "Blumenthal and Klobuchar Call for Immediate Federal Investigation into Possible Antitrust Violations by EpiPen Manufacturer," Press Release, September 6, 2016, https://www.blumenthal.senate .gov/newsroom/press/release/blumenthal-and-klobuchar-call-for-immediate -federal-investigation-into-possible-antitrust-violations-by-epipen-manufac trurer, and "A.G. Schneiderman Launches Antitrust Investigation into Mylan Pharmaceuticals Inc., Maker of Epipen," September 6, 2016: https://ag.ny.gov /press-release/2016/ag-schneiderman-launches-antitrust-investigation -mylan-pharmaceuticals-inc-maker.

49 *more than one hundred and twenty-five entries*: "Current and Resolved Drug Shortages and Discontinuations Reported to FDA, US Food & Drug Administration," FDA, https://www.accessdata.fda.gov/scripts/drugshortages/default .cfm.

49 *costs $16,000 or more in the United States*: Paul S. Hewitt and Phillip Longman, "The Case for Single Price Health Care," *Washington Monthly*, April/May/June 2018, https://washingtonmonthly.com/magazine/april-may-june-2018/the -case-for-single-price-health-care/

49 *more than $18,000*: Ibid.

50 *a hospital stay in the U.S. costs more than double that*: Dana Sarnak, "Multinational Comparisons of Health Systems Data, 2016," The Commonwealth Fund, https://www.commonwealthfund.org/sites/default/files/documents/___media _files_publications_chartbook_2016_att_fsarnak2016_oecd_data_chartpack _final_pdf.pdf.

50 *hospital stays in America are shorter*: "Length of Hospital Stay," OECD, https:// data.oecd.org/healthcare/length-of-hospital-stay.htm.

50 *Our life expectancy is lower*: "Life Expectancy at Birth," OECD, https://data .oecd.org/healthstat/life-expectancy-at-birth.htm#indicator-chart.

50 *"It's not that we're getting more"*: Gerard F. Anderson, "U.S. Health Care Spending Highest Among Developed Countries," Johns Hopkins, Jan. 7, 2019, https://www.jhsph.edu/news/news-releases/2019/us-health-care-spending -highest-among-developed-countries.html.

50 *50 percent more for the same drugs*: IHS Markit, "US Price Gouging in the Pharmaceutical Industry," International Drug Price Database, https://ihsmarkit .com/solutions/us-price-gouging-pharmaceutical-industry.html.

51 *$102 million on lobbying in the 2018 election cycle alone*: "Hospitals & Nursing Homes: Long-Term Contribution Trends," OpenSecrets, https://www.open secrets.org/industries/totals.php?cycle=2020&ind=H02, Visited May 14, 2020.

51 *laws could prohibit the conduct in the first place*: For example, the California state legislature passed a law in October 2019 that makes pay-for-delay arrangements between branded drugmakers and generic drugmakers automatically illegal. See "AB-824 Business: Preserving Access to Affordable Drugs," California Legislative Information, https://leginfo.legislature.ca.gov/faces/billNav Client.xhtml?bill_id=201920200AB824

51 *$167 million last year on lobbying, and 573*: "Industry Profile: Pharmaceutical Manufacturing," Open Secrets, https://www.opensecrets.org/federal-lobbying /industries/summary?cycle=2019&id=h4300, Visited May 14, 2020.

51 *for Medicare Part D drug prices*: Ibid.

51 *"Medicare Prices for All"*: Phillip Longman, "How to End the Democrats' Health Care Demolition Derby," *Washington Monthly*, January/February/March 2020, https://washingtonmonthly.com/magazine/january-february-march-2020 /how-to-end-the-democrats-health-care-demolition-derby/.

52 *drags down our economy*: "Does Employer-Based Health Insurance Discourage Entrepreneurship and New Business Creation?" Rand Corporation, https://www .rand.org/pubs/research_briefs/RB9579/index1.html; Noah Smith, "National Health Insurance Might Be Good for Capitalism," Bloomberg, Sept. 23, 2019, https://www.bloomberg.com/opinion/articles/2019-09-23/employer-based -health-insurance-holds-back-u-s-economy.

52 *the study concludes*: Ibid.

53 *know what your medical procedure would cost*: Austin Frakt, "Medical Mystery: Something Happened to U.S. Health Spending After 1980," *New York Times*, May 14, 2018, https://www.nytimes.com/2018/05/14/upshot/medical-mystery -health-spending-1980.html.

53 *27.5 million Americans not being covered at all*: "Health Insurance Coverage Eight Years After the ACA," Commonwealth Fund, https://www.commonwealth fund.org/sites/default/files/2019-02/Collins_hlt_ins_coverage_8_years_after _ACA_2018_biennial_survey_tables.pdf#page=1.

Mini Lesson: People V. Giant Tech Monopolies

55 *"Pitting browser against browser"*: U.S. District Court Findings of Fact, "U.S. v. Microsoft," paragraph 166, justice.gov, Nov. 5, 1999, https://www.justice.gov /atr/us-v-microsoft-courts-findings-fact#iva.

56 *"never gets a chance on these systems"*: Ibid.

56 *the ability to control prices or exclude competition*: United States v. E. I. du Pont de Nemours & Co. (*Cellophane*), 351 U.S. 377, 391 (1956).

57 *lesser market shares can be enough, too*: Image Technical Services, 125 F.3d at 1207 ("50% [market share] . . . would suffice to support a jury finding of market

power for the purposes of ISO's attempted monopolization claim)"; *Weyerhauser*, 411 F.3d at 1044-45 (65 percent monopsony power was enough).

57 *market defined as "Intel-compatible PC operating systems"*: "Microsoft Conclusions of Law: *U.S. v. Microsoft Corporation; State of New York, et al. v. Microsoft Corporation; Microsoft Corporation v. Eliot Spitzer*," justice.gov., https://www.justice.gov/atr/microsoft-conclusions-law-us-v-microsoft-corporation-state-new-york-et-al-v-microsoft.

59 *long past time to bring back Sherman Act Section 2*: "The State of Antitrust Enforcement and Competition Policy in the U.S., Antitrust Institute, April 14, 2020, https://www.antitrustinstitute.org/wp-content/uploads/2020/04/AAI_StateofAntitrust2019_FINAL.pdf (stating "[S]ince the [*U.S. v. Microsoft*] case some 20 years ago and the handful of other cases litigated at that same time, the DOJ has actually brought only one comparatively insignificant Section 2 case").

60 *bought over 150 companies just since 2013*: Rani Molla, "Amazon's Ring Buy Gives It the Same Number of Acquisitions This Year as Facebook and Google," *ReCode*, March 4, 2018, https://www.vox.com/2018/3/4/17062538/amazon-ring-acquisitions-2018-apple-google-cbinsights.

60 *nearly 250 companies since 2006*: "Infographic: Google's Biggest Acquisitions," CB Insights, Nov. 1, 2019, https://www.cbinsights.com/research/google-biggest-acquisitions-infographic/.

60 *over 100 companies*: "Infographic: Apple's Biggest Acquisitions," CB Insights, May 29, 2019, https://www.cbinsights.com/research/apple-biggest-acquisitions-infographic/.

60 *Amazon nearly 90*: "Amazon Acquisitions," *Crunchbase*, retrieved February 1, 2020, https://www.crunchbase.com/organization/amazon/acquisitions/acquisitions_list#section-acquisitions.

60 *Facebook bought it*: "Facebook Buys Instagram for $1 Billion; Turns Budding Rival Into Its Standalone Photo App," techcrunch, April 2012, https://techcrunch.com/2012/04/09/facebook-to-acquire-instagram-for-1-billion/.

60 *buy them or build its own versions*: Elizabeth Dwoskin, "Facebook's Willingness to Copy Rivals' Apps Seen as Hurting Innovation," *Washington Post*, August 10, 2017, https://www.washingtonpost.com/business/economy/facebooks-willingness-to-copy-rivals-apps-seen-as-hurting-innovation/2017/08/10/ea7188ea-7df6-11e7-a669-b400c5c7e1cc_story.html; Betsy Morris and Deepa Seetharaman, "The New Copycats: How Facebook Squashes Competition from Startups," *Wall Street Journal*, Aug. 9, 2017, https://www.wsj.com/articles/the-new-copycats-how-facebook-squashes-competition-from-startups-1502293444.

61 *"Facebook used Onavo"*: Damian Collins MP, Chair of the UK Parliament Digital, Culture, Media and Sport Committee, "Summary of Key Issues from

Six4Three Files," December 2018, British Parliament, www.parliament.uk /documents/commons-committees/culture-media-and-sport/Note-by-Chair -and-selected-documents-ordered-from-Six4Three.pdf.

61   *identified WhatsApp as the top contender*: Charlie Warzel and Ryan Mac, "These Confidential Charts Show Why Facebook Bought WhatsApp," *BuzzFeed News*, Dec. 5, 2018, https://www.buzzfeednews.com/article/charliewarzel /why-facebook-bought-whatsapp; Parmy Olson, "Exclusive: WhatsApp Co- founder Brian Acton Gives the Inside Story on #DeleteFacebook and Why He Left $850 Million Behind," *Forbes*, Sept. 26, 2018, https://www.forbes .com/sites/parmyolson/2018/09/26/exclusive-whatsapp-cofounder-brian-ac ton-gives-the-inside-story-on-deletefacebook-and-why-he-left-850-million -behind/#2165dc6d3f20.

61   *surveilled them and analyzed their usage*: Lily Hay Newman, "Don't Trust the VPN Facebook Wants You to Use," *Wired*, Feb. 14, 2017, http://www.wired .com/story/facebook-onavo-protect-vpn-privacy/; Josh Constine, "Facebook Will Shut Down Its Spyware VPN App Onavo," Feb. 21, 2019, techcrunch, https://techcrunch.com/2019/02/21/facebook-removes-onavo/.

62   *Certainly not all retail*: Renee Dudley, "The Amazon Lockdown: How an Un- forgiving Algorithm Drives Suppliers to Favor the E-Commerce Giant Over Other Retailers," ProPublica, April 26, 2020, https://www.propublica.org/ar ticle/the-amazon-lockdown-how-an-unforgiving-algorithm-drives-suppliers -to-favor-the-e-commerce-giant-over-other-retailers.

62   *urging it to investigate Amazon*: Richard Blumenthal, "Letter to Joseph Simons," Blumenthal.senate.gov, Dec. 19, 2018, https://www.blumenthal.senate.gov /imo/media/doc/12.19.18%20-%20FTC%20-%20Price%20Parity.pdf.

62   *drop the contractual terms in the United States*: Makena Kelly, "Amazon Silently Ends Controversial Pricing Agreements with Sellers," *Verge*, March 11, 2019, https://www.theverge.com/2019/3/11/18260700/amazon-anti-competitive -pricing-agreements-3rd-party-sellers-end.

62   *"Absent Amazon's"*: Western District of Washington at Seattle, *Frame-Wilson v. Amazon*, Case 2:20-cv-00424-RAJ, para. 63, March 19, 2020.

Three: Monopolies Lower Your Pay and Crush the American Dream

65   *from around 20 percent in the 1980s to around 40 percent in 2017*: Tommaso Valletti, "Concentration Trends," European Commission, June 18-20, 2018, https://www.ecb.europa.eu/pub/conferences/shared/pdf/20180618_ecb _forum_on_central_banking/Valletti_Tommaso_Presentation.pdf.

65   *stagnating for forty years*: Nathan Wilmers, "Wage Stagnation and Buyer Power: How Buyer-Supplier Relations Affect U.S. Workers' Wages, 1978–2014,"

Sage Journals, March 27, 2018, journals.sagepub.com/doi/full/10.1177 /0003122418762441; Drew Desilver, "For Most U.S. Workers, Real Wages Have Barely Budged in Decades," Pew Research Center, Aug. 7, 2018, https:// www.pewresearch.org/fact-tank/2018/08/07/for-most-us-workers-real -wages-have-barely-budged-for-decades/.

65   *productivity . . . rose 72 percent, a rate of 1.33 percent*: Josh Bivens and Lawrence Mishel, "Understanding the Historic Divergence Between Productivity and a Typical Worker's Pay," Economic Policy Institute, Sept. 2, 2015, https://www .epi.org/publication/understanding-the-historic-divergence-between-produc tivity-and-a-typical-workers-pay-why-it-matters-and-why-its-real/.

66   *58 times employees' pay*: Lawrence Mishel and Julia Wolfe, "CEO Compensation Has Grown 940% Since 1978," Economic Policy Institute, Aug. 14, 2019, https://www.epi.org/publication/ceo-compensation-2018.

66   *What changed since the 1980s*: David Autor, David Dorn, Lawrence F. Katz, Christina Patterson, and John Van Reenen, "The Fall of the Labor Share and the Rise of Superstar Firms," Harvard University, May 1, 2017, https://scholar .harvard.edu/files/lkatz/files/labshare-superstars-may1-2017.pdf.

67   *each industry included dozens of potential employers*: See, for example, "Defense Contracting Chart," Myth of Capitalism, https://www.mythofcapitalism.com /merger-chart (100 to 6 potential employers in defense contracting from 1980 until now).

67   *17 percent decline in wages*: J. Azar, I. Marinescu, and M. I. Steinbaum, "Labor Market Concentration," NBER Working Paper No. 24147, NBER, 2017, https://www.nber.org/papers/w24147.pdf.

67   *"impairs the transmission"*: E. Benmelech, N. Bergman, and H. Kim, "Strong Employers and Weak Employees: How Does Employer Concentration Affect Wages?" NBER Working Paper No. 24307, NBER, 2018. https://www.nber .org/papers/w24307.

68   *nurses have seen their wages depressed*: Elena Prager and Matt Schmitt, "When an Industry Consolidates, What Happens to Wages?" *Kellogg Insight*, April 4, 2019, insight.kellogg.northwestern.edu/article/merger-consolidation-wages -effect.

68   *"a true competitive wage"*: Suresh Naidu, Eric Posner, and Glen Weyl, "More and More Companies Have Monopoly Power Over Workers' Wages. That's Killing the Economy," *Vox*, April 6, 2018, https://www.vox.com/the-big -idea/2018/4/6/17204808/wages-employers-workers-monopsony-growth -stagnation-inequality.

68   *"labor markets where mobility has decreased"*: Michael Konczal and Marshall Steinbaum, "Declining Entrepreneurship, Labor Mobility, and Business

Dynamism: A Demand-Side Approach," Roosevelt Institute, July 21, 2016, https://rooseveltinstitute.org/declining-entrepreneurship-labor-mobility-and -business-dynamism/.

69   *"appear to be increasing in magnitude over time"*: Kevin Rinz, "Did Timing Mat- ter? Life Cycle Differences in Effects of Exposure to the Great Recession," Center for Economic Studies, US Census Bureau, Sept. 8, 2019, https://kevin rinz.github.io/recession.pdf.

69   *cut costs by reducing employees' pay*: Nelson Lichtenstein, "The Return of Merchant Capitalism," *International Labor and Working-Class History* 81 (2012): 8–27.

69   *"Concentration can also affect"*: Sandeep Vaheesan, "Antitrust Law: A Current Foe, but Potential Friend, of Workers," Harvard University, https://lwp.law.harvard .edu/files/lwp/files/webpage_materials_papers_vaheesan_june_13_2018.pdf; Nathan Wilmers, "Wage Stagnation and Buyer Power: How Buyer-Supplier Relations Affect U.S. Workers' Wages, 1978 to 2014," *Sage Journals*, March 27, 2018, https://journals.sagepub.com/doi/full/10.1177/0003122418762441.

70   *10,000 workers being laid off*: Leah Douglas, "Private Equity Firms Are Buying up Your Favorite Food Brands," *Fern*, June 18, 2018, https://thefern.org/ag_in sider/private-equity-firms-are-buying-up-your-favorite-food-brands/.

70   *estimated to result in 6,000 job losses*: "Boy Meets Girl: Gillette and P&G Hook Up Their Brands," Wharton School, March 20, 2005, https://knowledge.whar ton.upenn.edu/article/boy-meets-girl-gillette-and-pg-hook-up-their-brands/.

70   *several rounds of ongoing layoffs*: Nellie Andreeva, "ViacomCBS Layoffs Un- derway As Re-Merged Company Continues to Cut Costs," *Deadline*, Feb. 27, 2020, https://deadline.com/2020/02/viacomcbs-layoffs-underway-re-merged -company-continues-to-cut-costs-1202870391/; Lisette Voytko, "Coronavirus Layoffs: Lyft, Boeing Latest to Cut Workers Amid Pandemic," *Forbes*, April 29, 2020, https://www.forbes.com/sites/lisettevoytko/2020/04/29/coronavirus -layoffs-boeing-cuts-10-of-workforce-amid-pandemic/#6d09d2c33487.

70   *made people lose their jobs*: Leslie Josephs, "American Airlines Plans Manager Layoffs, Buyouts to Slim Down 5 Years after US Airways Merger," CNBC, June 29, 2018, https://www.cnbc.com/2018/06/19/american-airlines-plans-for -layoffs-buyouts-due-to-us-airways-merger.html.

70   *leads to loss of institutional knowledge*: "The Human Side of Mergers: Those Laid Off and Those Left Aboard," Wharton School, March 30, 2005, https://knowl edge.wharton.upenn.edu/article/the-human-side-of-mergers-those-laid-off -and-those-left-aboard/.

70   *ranges from 70 to 90 percent*: Clayton M. Christensen, Richard Alton, Curtis Rising, and Andrew Waldeck, "The Big Idea: The New M&A Playbook," *Har- vard Business Review*, March 2011, https://hbr.org/2011/03/the-big-idea-the -new-ma-playbook; see also Bruce Blonigen and Justin R. Pierce, "Evidence for

the Effects of Mergers on Market Power and Efficiency," NBER, Oct. 2016, https://www.nber.org/papers/w22750.

71 *should scrutinize whether the merger would reduce competition for employees*: J. Azar, I. Marinescu and M. I. Steinbaum, "Labor market concentration. NBER Working Paper No. 24147," *NBER*, 2017, https://www.nber.org/papers/w24147.pdf.

71 *because the deals would decrease the prices paid to suppliers of goods*: "Justice Department and State Attorneys General Sue to Block Anthem's Acquisition of Cigna, Aetna's Acquisition of Humana," justice.gov, July 21, 2016, https://www.justice.gov/opa/pr/justice-department-and-state-attorneys-general-sue-block-anthem-s-acquisition-cigna-aetna-s; "Department of Justice Statement on the Abandonment of the JBS/National Beef Transaction," justice.gov, Feb. 20, 2009, https://www.justice.gov/opa/pr/department-justice-statement-abandonment-jbsnational-beef-transaction.

71 *"commands the price of labor"*: Senator Sherman (Congressional Record 2457, 1890).

72 *labor union membership . . . the lowest it's been since 1964*: Doug Henwood, "Unions Still Haven't Rebounded," *Jacobin*, Jan. 25, 2019, https://www.jacobinmag.com/2019/01/union-density-united-states-2018-bls.

72 *"only a small percentage of workers"*: Sandeep Vaheesan, "How Contemporary Antitrust Robs Workers of Power," *Law and Political Economy*, July 18, 2018, https://lpeblog.org/2018/07/19/how-contemporary-antitrust-robs-workers-of-power/.

72 *actively fight unionization*: Verne Kopytoff, "How Amazon Crushed the Union Movement," *Time*, Jan. 16, 2014, https://time.com/956/how-amazon-crushed-the-union-movement/.

72 *"While Amazon has"*: Michael Sainato, "Exploited Amazon Workers Need a Union. When Will They Get One?" *Guardian*, July 8, 2018, https://www.theguardian.com/commentisfree/2018/jul/08/amazon-jeff-bezos-unionize-working-conditions.

72 *an investigation from the New York attorney general*: Alina Selyukh, "Amazon Warehouse Safety 'Inadequate,' N.Y. Attorney General's Office Says," NPR, April 28, 2020, https://www.npr.org/2020/04/27/846438983/amazon-warehouse-safety-inadequate-n-y-attorney-general-s-office-says.

73 *"the face of the entire union/organizing movement"*: Paul Blest, "Leaked Amazon Memo Details Plan to Smear Fired Warehouse Organizer: 'He's Not Smart or Articulate,' " *Vice*, April 2, 2020, https://www.vice.com/en_us/article/5dm8bx/leaked-amazon-memo-details-plan-to-smear-fired-warehouse-organizer-hes-not-smart-or-articulate.

73 *Amazon workers continued to protest unsafe conditions*: https://jewishcurrents.org/amazon-workers-say-warehouse-health-precautions-are-insufficient/;

Karen Weise and Kate Conger, "Gaps in Amazon's Response as Virus Spreads to More Than 50 Warehouses," *New York Times*, updated April 6, 2020, https://www.nytimes.com/2020/04/05/technology/coronavirus-amazon-workers.html; "athenaforall," Twitter, April 29, 2020, https://twitter.com/athenaforall/status/1255571329912320000?s=20.

73 *Jeff Bezos grew an estimated $6.4 billion richer*: Sergei Klebnikov, "Jeff Bezos Gets $6.4 Billion Richer as Amazon Stock Hits a New Record High," *Forbes*, April 14, 2020, https://www.forbes.com/sites/sergeiklebnikov/2020/04/14/jeff-bezos-gets-63-billion-richer-as-amazon-stock-hits-a-new-record-high/#4fc4bb6e53b0.

73 *accusing Google of illegally firing them*: "Another Fired Google Engineer Alleges Retaliation for Union Activity," *Washington Post*, Dec. 17, 2019, https://www.washingtonpost.com/technology/2019/12/17/google-fires-fifth-engineer-who-alleges-retaliation-union-activity/.

73 *Google had urged the NLRB*: Josh Eidelson, Hassan Kanu, and Mark Bergen, "Google Urged the U.S. to Limit Protection for Activist Workers," Bloomberg, Jan. 24, 2019, ttps://www.bloomberg.com/news/articles/2019-01-24/google-urged-the-u-s-to-limit-protection-for-activist-workers.

73 *At least 35 million employees*: Alexander J.S. Colvin and Heidi Shierholz, "Non-compete Agreements," Economic Policy Institute, December 10, 2019, https://www.epi.org/publication/noncompete-agreements/, and FTC, "Re: Petition for Rulemaking to Prohibit Worker Non-Compete Clauses," Open Markets Institute, https://openmarketsinstitute.org/wp-content/uploads/2019/03/Petition-for-Rulemaking-to-Prohibit-Worker-Non-Compete-Clauses.pdf.

74 *like fast-food workers*: "Why Aren't Paychecks Growing? A Burger-Joint Clause Offers a Clue," *New York Times*, Sept. 27, 2017, https://www.nytimes.com/2017/09/27/business/pay-growth-fast-food-hiring.html.

74 *"dries up opportunities for employees"*: FTC, Letter to the Honorable Makan Delrahim "RE: Department of Justice Initiative on Competition in Labor Markets," FTC, Sept. 18, 2019, https://www.ftc.gov/system/files/documents/public_statements/1544564/chopra_-_letter_to_doj_on_labor_market_competition.pdf.

74 *has petitioned the FTC*: FTC, "Re: Petition for Rulemaking to Prohibit Worker Non-Compete Clauses," Open Markets Institute, https://openmarketsinstitute.org/wp-content/uploads/2019/03/Petition-for-Rulemaking-to-Prohibit-Worker-Non-Compete-Clauses.pdf.

74 *"Please extend my apologies as appropriate to Steve Jobs"*: Dan Levine, "High-Tech Employee Antitrust Litigation: Apple's Steve Jobs to Google's Eric Schmidt to Stop Poaching Workers," *Huffington Post*, Jan. 27, 2012, https://www.huffpost.com/entry/high-tech-employee-antitrust-litigation_n_1237692.

75 *for conspiring to depress their wages*: FTC, "How the Federal Trade Commission Can Help—Instead of Hurt—Workers," FTC, https://www.ftc.gov/system /files/documents/public_comments/2018/08/ftc-2018-0054-d-0014-154953 .pdf; "No. 17-1113 in The United States Court of Appeals for the Tenth Circuit," Open Market Institute, https://openmarketsinstitute.org/wp-content /uploads/2019/09/OMI-Brief-in-Llacua-v.-WRA-FINAL.pdf.

75 *"interfered with"*: "Justice Department Requires Six High Tech Companies to Stop Entering into Anticompetitive Employee Solicitation Agreements," justice.gov, Sept. 24, 2010, https://www.justice.gov/opa/pr/justice-department -requires-six-high-tech-companies-stop-entering-anticompetitive-employee.

75 *this most serious*: Sandeep Vaheesan and Matt Buck, "Antitrust's Monopsony Problem," *ProMarket*, February 3, 2020, https://promarket.org/2020/02/03 /antitrusts-monopsony-problem/.

75 *"Let me clarify"*: Dan Levine, "Steve Jobs Told Google to Stop Poaching Workers," *Reuters*, January 27, 2012, https://www.reuters.com/article/us-apple-law suit-idUSTRE80Q27420120127, and *In Re: High-Tech Employee Antitrust Litigation*, No. 11 CV 2509 (N.D. Cal.).

76 *private class actions settled for $435 million*: "In re High Tech Employees Antitrust Litigation," Berger Montague, https://bergermontague.com/cases/re-high -tech-employee-antitrust-litigation/.

76 *"artists would need their music to be streamed 2.4 million times"*: Ron Knox, "The Copyright Killer," *Global Competition Review*, Jan. 11, 2019, https://globalcom petitionreview.com/insight/gcr-q1-2019/1179029/the-copyright-killer.

77 *have appealed the decision*: Dani Deahl, "Here's Why Apple Is Saying Spotify Is Suing Songwriters," *Verge*, March 15, 2019, https://www.theverge .com/2019/3/15/18267288/apple-music-spotify-suing-songwriters-eu-anti trust.

78 *Google has fought copyright laws worldwide*: Richard Smirke, "Music Chiefs Slam Google Lobbying Spend Ahead of EU Copyright Vote," *Billboard*, July 3, 2018, https://www.billboard.com/articles/business/8463917/google -lobbying-dollars-eu-copyright-vote-uk-music; Tom Hamburger and Matea Gold, "Google, Once Disdainful of Lobbying, Is Now a Master of Washington," *Washington Post*, April 12, 2014, https://www.washingtonpost.com /politics/how-google-is-transforming-power-and-politicsgoogle-once-dis dainful-of-lobbying-now-a-master-of-washington-influence/2014/04/12/516 48b92-b4d3-11e3-8cb6-284052554d74_story.html; Julia Horowitz, "Google Will Remove News Previews Rather Than Pay Publishers in Europe," CNN, Sept. 25, 2019, https://www.cnn.com/2019/09/25/tech/google-france-copy right-news/index.html.

78   *songs often just go right up again*: "New Survey Documents Independent Labels'
     Experience with Notice & Takedown," *Future of Music*, Jan. 8, 2019, https://
     futureofmusic.org/filing/new-survey-documents-independent-labels-experi
     ence-notice-takedown (68 percent of the respondents reported that an in-
     fringing copy of their music reappeared on the same service even after that
     music had previously been taken down—the so-called "whack-a-mole" prob-
     lem); Todd C. Frankel, "Why Musicians Are So Angry at the World's Most
     Popular Music Streaming Service," *Washington Post*, July 14, 2017, https://www
     .washingtonpost.com/business/economy/why-musicians-are-so-angry-at-the
     -worlds-most-popular-music-streaming-service/2017/07/14/bf1a6db0-67ee
     -11e7-8eb5-cbccc2e7bfbf_story.html.

78   *96.5 percent of all YouTubers*: Chris Stokel-Walker, "'Success' on YouTube Still
     Means a Life of Poverty," Bloomberg, Feb. 26, 2018, https://www.bloomberg
     .com/news/articles/2018-02-27/-success-on-youtube-still-means-a-life-of
     -poverty.

78   *$15.1 billion in 2019I*:"Worldwide Advertising Revenues of YouTube from
     2017 to 2019," *Statista*, https://www.statista.com/statistics/289658/youtube
     -global-net-advertising-revenues/.

79   *"fresh thinking and revitalized anti-trust enforcement"*: "Policy Priorities for
     2018," Future of Music Coalition, Jan. 8, 2019, https://www.futureofmusic.org
     /blog/2019/01/08/policy-priorities-2019.

80   *"You know"*: Panel, "Innovation and Entrepreneurship in an Age of Concentrated
     Power," Open Markets Institute, Dec. 6, 2017, https://www.youtube.com/watch
     ?list=PL17VSnPfVKIjDjjK9yw6bQK4964lbJ_Go&time_continue=8&v=bmY
     Bv4Zbn2Y&feature=emb_logo, and author's interview of Lillian Salerno.

81   *Becton settled the case for $100 million in 2004*: Mary Williams Walsh and Salt
     Bogdanich, "Business Syringe Manufacturer Settles Claim of Market Manipu-
     lation," *New York Times*, July 3, 2004, https://www.nytimes.com/2004/07/03
     /business/syringe-manufacturer-settles-claim-of-market-manipulation.html.

81   *an untruthful claim that Becton's syringes*: "District Court Issues Final Judgment—
     Retractable Technologies, Inc., et. al. v. Becton, Dickinson and Co.," Retractable
     Technologies, https://retractable.com/profiles/investor/ResLibraryView.asp?Res
     LibraryID=74829&GoTopage=6&Category=35&BzID=577&G=984.

81   *to preserve the "10–30% price premium" that Becton enjoyed*: "Retractable Tech-
     nologies, Inc. v. Becton Dickinson and Company," *Pacer Monitor*, https://www
     .pacermonitor.com/public/case/5539052/Retractable_Technologies,_Inc_v
     _Becton_Dickinson_and_Company.

82   *"We've been denied every time"*: Panel, "Innovation and Entrepreneurship in an
     Age of Concentrated Power," Open Markets Institute, Dec. 6, 2017.

83   *charging customers monthly rental fees for cable boxes*: Herb Weisbaum, "Consumers

Have Scant Choices When It Comes to Set-Top Pay TV Boxes," NBC News, June 11, 2015, https://www.nbcnews.com/business/consumer/consumers -have-scant-choices-when-it-comes-set-top-pay-n407261.

83 *entrepreneurship has plummeted*: Economic Innovation Group, "Dynamism in Retreat: Consequences for Regions, Markets, and Workers," EIG, February 2017, https://eig.org/wp-content/uploads/2017/07/Dynamism-in-Retreat -A.pdf.

83 *all four have dominated their respective arenas*: Mark A. Lemley and Andrew McCreary, "Exit Strategy," Stanford Law and Economics Working Paper #542, SSRN, Dec. 19, 2019, https://ssrn.com/abstract=3506919.

83 *entrepreneurship is suffering across the economy*: Ben Casselman, "A Start-Up Slump Is a Drag on the Economy. Big Business May Be to Blame," *New York Times*, Sept. 20, 2017, https://www.nytimes.com/2017/09/20/business /economy/startup-business.html; Jason Furman and Peter Orszag, "Slower Productivity and Higher Inequality: Are They Related?" Working Paper, Peterson Institute for International Economics, 2018, https://piie.com/system/files /documents/wp18-4.pdf.

83 *hurts both job creation and innovation*: Ryan Decker, John Haltiwanger, Ron Jarmin, and Javier Miranda, "The Role of Entrepreneurship in US Job Creation and Economic Dynamism," *Journal of Economic Perspectives* 28, no. 3 (2014): 3–24, https://www.aeaweb.org/articles?id=10.1257/jep.28.3.3.

83 *"[T]he great burst of business activity"*: Barry C. Lynn and Phillip Longman, "Who Broke America's Jobs Machine?" *Washington Monthly*, March/April 2010, https://washingtonmonthly.com/magazine/marchapril-2010/who-broke -americas-jobs-machine-3/.

84 *"are as important to the preservation of economic freedom"*: "United States v. Topco Associates, Inc., 405 U.S. 596, 610," Justia, 1972, https://supreme.justia.com /cases/federal/us/405/596/.

86 *92 percent of internet search*: "Search Engine Market Share Worldwide Feb. 2019–Feb. 2020," Statcounter, retrieved March 1, 2020, https://gs.statcounter .com/search-engine-market-share.

86 *more than 85 percent of the world's smartphones*: "Smartphone Market Share," IDC, retrieved March 1, 2020, https://www.idc.com/promo/smartphone -market-share/os.

86 *was nearly $135 billion*: "Advertising Revenue of Google from 2001 to 2019," *Statista*, retrieved March 7, 2020, https://www.statista.com/statistics/266249 /advertising-revenue-of-google/.

86 *fined Google $5 billion*: "Statement by Commissioner Vestager on Commission Decision to Fine Google €4.34 Billion for Illegal Practices Regarding Android Mobile Devices to Strengthen Dominance of Google's Search Engine,"

European Commission, July 18, 2018, https://ec.europa.eu/commission/press
corner/detail/en/STATEMENT_18_4584.

87   *didn't have a shot at getting pre-installed:* "Google EC Antitrust Enforcement:
Expected Android EC Remedies Likely to Make Google Vulnerable to Competitive Threats in Mobile Advertising," *Capitol Forum,* Sept. 30, 2016, http://
createsend.com/t/j-189AEA75109E1FA5.

87   *Google paid Apple more than $12 billion in 2019:* Kif Leswing, "Apple Quietly
Makes Billions from Google Search Each Year, and It's a Bigger Business than
Apple Music," *Business Insider,* February 13, 2019, https://www.businessin
sider.com/aapl-share-price-google-pays-apple-9-billion-annually-tac-goldman
-2018-9.

87   *requested a "yes or no" answer:* Letter to Kent Walker, Chief Legal Officer of
Google, from Representative David N. Cicilline, Chairman of the Subcommittee on Antitrust, Commercial and Administrative Law, Committee on the
Judiciary, cicilline.house.gov, July 23, 2019, https://cicilline.house.gov/sites
/cicilline.house.gov/files/7.23.2019_ACAL%20Company%20Clarification
%20Requests.pdf.

87   *"long sent large amounts of traffic to other sites":* Letter to Chairman Cicilline
from Kent Walker, Google Chief Legal Officer, cicilline.house.gov, July 26,
2019, https://judiciary.house.gov/sites/democrats.judiciary.house.gov/files/doc
uments/07.26.19%20-%20google%20response.pdf.

88   *met this exact fate:* Tom Fairless, "The British Couple Who Began Google's
Antitrust Battle," *Wall Street Journal,* April 15, 2015, https://www.wsj.com
/articles/foundem-the-unlikely-instigator-of-googles-antitrust-battle-with-the
-eu-1429094448.

88   *fined Google $2.7 billion for abuse of dominance:* "Antitrust: Commission Fines
Google €2.42 Billion for Abusing Dominance as Search Engine by Giving
Illegal Advantage to Own Comparison Shopping Service," European Com-
mission, June 27, 2017, https://ec.europa.eu/commission/presscorner/detail/en
/IP_17_1784.

88   *the Raffs say Google is still not complying:* "Google's CSS Auction: Different
Name, Same Illegal Conduct," Search Neutrality, Nov. 2, 2019, http://www
.searchneutrality.org/google/google-css-auction-different-name-same-illegal
-conduct; "Google's Blatantly Non-Compliant 'Remedy' Part III," Foundem,
April 18, 2018, http://www.foundem.co.uk/fmedia/Foundem_Apr_2018_Final
_Debunking_of_Google_Auction_Remedy/.

88   *"The Commission is concerned":* "Antitrust: Commission Sends Statement of
Objections to Google on Comparison Shopping Service," European Commis-
sion, April 15, 2015, https://ec.europa.eu/commission/presscorner/detail/en
/MEMO_15_4781.

88   *degraded its search quality results*: See Luca, Wu, Couvidat, Frank, and Seltzer, "Does Google Content Degrade Google Search? Experimental Evidence," Harvard Business School Working Paper, No. 16-035, September 2015 (revised August 2016); Jack Nicas, "Google Has Picked an Answer for You—Too Bad It's Often Wrong," *Wall Street Journal*, Nov. 16, 2017, https://www.wsj.com /articles/googles-featured-answers-aim-to-distill-truthbut-often-get-it -wrong-1510847867.

88   *pays upwards of $72,000 a year*: "Written Testimony of David Heinemeier Hansson CTO & Cofounder, Basecamp," house.gov, Jan. 17, 2020, https:// docs.house.gov/meetings/JU/JU05/20200117/110386/HHRG-116-JU05 -Wstate-HanssonD-20200117.pdf.

89   *but it did not take action*: "Statement of the Federal Trade Commission Regarding Google's Search Practices in the Matter of Google Inc. FTC File Number 111-0163," FTC, Jan. 3, 2013, https://www.ftc.gov/system/files/documents /public_statements/295971/130103googlesearchstmtofcomm.pdf.

89   *"conduct has resulted"*: Brody Mullins et al., "Inside the U.S. Antitrust Probe of Google," *Wall Street Journal*, March 19, 2015, https://www.wsj.com/articles /inside-the-u-s-antitrust-probe-of-google-1426793274.

89   *"Google representatives"*: David Dayen, "The Android Administration, *Intercept*, April 22, 2016, https://theintercept.com/2016/04/22/googles-remarkably -close-relationship-with-the-obama-white-house-in-two-charts/.

90   *fifty-one states and territories*: Tony Romm, "50 U.S. States and Territories Announce Broad Antitrust Investigation of Google," *Washington Post*, Sept. 9, 2019, https://www.washingtonpost.com/technology/2019/09/09/states-usterri tories-announce-broad-antitrust-investigation-google/.

90   *"It's not a supply-and-demand"*: Lucas Shaw and Mark Bergen, "YouTube's Trampled Foes Plot Antitrust Revenge," *Bloomberg*, July 15, 2019, https://www .bloomberg.com/news/articles/2019-07-15/youtube-s-trampled-foes-plot -antitrust-revenge.

90   *fined Google*: "Antitrust: Commission fines Google €1,49 billion for abusive practices in online advertising," European Commission, March 20, 2019, https://ec.europa.eu/commission/presscorner/detail/en/IP_19_1770

90   *acquired every spoke*: "Infographic: Google's Biggest Acquisitions," CB Insights, May 2019, https://www.cbinsights.com/research/google-biggest-acquisitions -infographic/

91   *"By closing its investigation"*: Dissenting Statement of Commissioner Pamela Jones Harbour, *In the matter of Google/DoubleClick, F.T.C. File No. 071-0170*, Dec. 20, 2007, https://www.ftc.gov/sites/default/files/documents/public_state ments/statement-matter-google/doubleclick/071220harbour_0.pdf

91   *one out of every two dollars spent online*: Jay Greene, "Attention Walmart

Executives: Amazon's Coming After Your Low-Income Shoppers," *Washington Post*, June 18, 2019, https://www.washingtonpost.com/technology/2019/06/18 /amazons-growing-prime-focus-americas-poor/.

91   *112 million Prime customers*: "Number of Amazon Prime Members in the United States as of December 2019," *Statista*, https://www.statista.com/statis tics/546894/number-of-amazon-prime-paying-members/.

91   *129 million households in 2019*: "US World and Population Clock," US Census Bureau, https://www.census.gov/popclock/.

91   *an estimated 12 percent of the U.S. population living in poverty*: "Number of Households in the U.S. from 1960 to 2019," *Statista*, https://www.statista.com /statistics/183635/number-of-households-in-the-us/.

91   *spent on average $1,400*: J. Clement, "Projected Retail E-Commerce GMV Share of Amazon in the United States from 2016 to 2021," *Statista*, Aug. 9, 2019, https://www.statista.com/statistics/788109/amazon-retail-market-share -usa/.

92   *"We believe there is"*: Antoine Gara, "Why One Amazon Bull Thinks Jeff Bezos Is Building a $3 Trillion Company," *Forbes*, May 4, 2016, https://www.forbes .com/sites/antoinegara/2016/05/04/why-one-amazon-bull-thinks-jeff-bezos -can-build-a-3-trillion-company/#4c3983315d27.

92   *more than 400 Amazon house labels*: "Share of Amazon's Private-Label Products, by Product Category, March 2019," eMarketer, March 18, 2019, https://www .emarketer.com/chart/227300/share-of-amazons-private-label-products-by -product-category-march-2019-of-total-number-of-brands.

92   *dominate, markets*: Amy Gresenhues, "Amazon Owns More Than 90% Market Share Across 5 Different Product Categories [Report]," Marketing Land, May 31, 2018, https://marketingland.com/amazon-owns-more-than-90-mar ket-share-across-5-different-product-categories-report-241135.

92   *"constantly looking to cut you out"*: "Amazon Ousted Marketplace Sellers in Order to Be Only Seller of Certain Products; A Closer Look at Monopolization Enforcement Risk," *Capitol Forum*, June 14, 2018, http://thecapitolforum.cmail19 .com/t/ViewEmail/j/96AD55196B0C02DE2540EF23F30FEDED/690A88 7987F4ABF13FEC1D8A50AFD3BD.

93   *"on multiple occasions"*: "Statement of David Barnett, CEO and Founder of PopSockets LLC, Online Platforms and Market Power, Part 5: Competitors in the Digital Economy," house.gov, Jan. 15, 2020, https://docs.house.gov /meetings/JU/JU05/20200117/110386/HHRG-116-JU05-Wstate-BarnettD -20200117.pdf. "It was not until December of 2017, in exchange for our commitment to spend nearly two million dollars on retail marketing programs (which our team expected to be ineffective and would otherwise not have pledged), that Amazon Retail agreed to work with Brand Registry to require

sellers of alleged PopGrips to provide evidence, in the form of an invoice, of authenticity. As a result, in early 2018, our problem of counterfeits largely dissolved. (Soon thereafter Brand Registry agreed to enforce our utility patent, resulting in the disappearance of most knockoffs.)"

93 *prohibiting marketplace sellers from listing*: "Amazon Ousted Marketplace Sellers in Order to Be Only Seller of Certain Products; a Closer Look at Monopolization Enforcement Risk," *Capitol Forum*, June 14, 2018, http://thecapitolforum.cmail19.com/t/ViewEmail/j/96AD55196B0C02DE2540EF23F30F EDED/690A887987F4ABF13FEC1D8A50AFD3BD; Stacy Mitchell and Olivia Lavecchia, "Report: Amazon's Monopoly," Institute for Local Self-Reliance, November 29, 2016, https://ilsr.org/amazons-monopoly/; "Standards for Brands Selling in the Amazon Store," Amazon, https://sellercentral.amazon.com/gp/help/external/G201797950; Jason Del Rey, "An Amazon Revolt Could Be Brewing as the Tech Giant Exerts More Control over Brands," *Vox*, Nov. 29 2018, https://www.vox.com/2018/11/29/18023132/amazon-brand-policy-changes-marketplace-control-one-vendor.

93 *elevating its own products to the top*: Julie Creswell, "How Amazon Steers Shoppers to Its Own Products," *New York Times*, June 23, 2018, https://www.nytimes.com/2018/06/23/business/amazon-the-brand-buster.html; "Amazon: EC Investigation to Focus on Whether Amazon Uses Data to Develop and Favor Private Label Products; Former Employees Say Data Key to Private Label Strategy," *Capitol Forum*, Nov. 5, 2018, https://thecapitolforum.com/wp-content/uploads/2018/11/Amazon-2018.11.05.pdf.

94 *"You basically have to liquidate your inventory"*: "Amazon: Amazon at Risk of Antitrust Investigation for Working with Manufacturers to Control Prices, Foreclose Competing Sellers, and Ultimately Monopolize Direct Sales of their Products on its Platform," *Capitol Forum*, March 7, 2017, http://createsend.com/t/j-60990BCFC736F15D.

94 *do not consider other online marketplaces to be viable alternatives*: Spencer Soper, "Amazon Squeezes Sellers That Offer Better Prices on Walmart," Bloomberg, updated Aug. 5, 2019, https://www.bloomberg.com/news/articles/2019-08-05/amazon-is-squeezing-sellers-that-offer-better-prices-on-walmart.

94 *marketplace sellers lack bargaining power*: Karen Weise, "Prime Power: How Amazon Squeezes the Businesses Behind Its Store," *New York Times*, Dec. 19, 2019, https://www.nytimes.com/2019/12/19/technology/amazon-sellers.html.

95 *knocking off their ideas*: Spencer Soper, "Got a Hot Seller on Amazon? Prepare for E-Tailer to Make One Too," Bloomberg, April 20, 2016, https://www.bloomberg.com/news/articles/2016-04-20/got-a-hot-seller-on-amazon-prepare-for-e-tailer-to-make-one-too; Ben Fox Rubin, "Amazon 'Probably Copied Us' on Echo Show, Start Up CEO Says," CNET, May 10, 2017, https://

www.cnet.com/news/amazon-echo-show-alexa-probably-copied-us-nucleus
-intercom-startup-ceo-says/.

95   *"It has given an edge"*: Daisuke Wakabayashi, "Prime Leverage: How Amazon Wields Power in the Technology World," *New York Times*, Dec. 15, 2019,
https://www.nytimes.com/2019/12/15/technology/amazon-aws-cloud-com
petition.html.

96   *I spoke to former Amazon employees*: "Amazon: EC Investigation to Focus on
Whether Amazon Uses Data to Develop and Favor Private Label Products;
Former Employees Say Data Key to Private Label Strategy," *Capitol Forum*,
Nov. 5. 2018, https://thecapitolforum.com/wp-content/uploads/2018/11/Am
azon-2018.11.05.pdf

97   *handing over their proprietary business information*: See also Dana Mattioli,
"Amazon Scooped Up Data from Its Own Sellers to Launch Competing Products," *Wall Street Journal*, updated April 23, 2020, https://www.wsj.com/articles
/amazon-scooped-up-data-from-its-own-sellers-to-launch-competing-prod
ucts-11587650015.

97   *Walmart's path of monopolization through a low pricing strategy*: Stacy Mitchell,
"Wal-Mart Charged with Predatory Pricing," ILSR, Nov. 1, 2000, https://ilsr
.org/walmart-charged-predatory-pricing/

97   *original robber barons*: Justice Louis Brandeis, "Competition That Kills," *Harper's
Weekly*, November 15, 1913. Neither Amazon nor Walmart invented predatory
pricing. Late Justice Brandeis wrote about monopolies using low-pricing to
eliminate rivals, noting that the consumer unwittingly cooperates in the anti-
competitve scheme. He wrote, "Thoughtless or weak, he yields to the temptation of trifling immediate gain, and, selling his birthright for a mess of pottage,
becomes himself an instrument of monopoly."

97   *Amazon was able to evade antitrust laws*: Lina M. Khan, "Amazon's Antitrust
Paradox," *Yale Law Journal* 126 (2017): 710, 754, https://www.yalelawjournal
.org/pdf/e.710.Khan.805_zuvfyyeh.pdf.

97   *"We are going to cut off their air supply"*: "U.S. v. Microsoft complaint" (par ¶¶
16-17), https://www.justice.gov/atr/complaint-us-v-microsoft-corp; Steve
Lohr with John Marshall, "Why Microsoft Is Taking a Hard Line with the
Government," *New York Times*, Jan. 12, 1998, https://www.nytimes.com/1998
/01/12/business/why-microsoft-is-taking-a-hard-line-with-the-government
.html.

98   *well-documented track record of pricing below cost*: Eric Savitz, "Amazon Selling
Kindle Fire Below Cost, Analyst Contends," *Forbes*, Sept. 30, 2011, https://
www.forbes.com/sites/ericsavitz/2011/09/30/amazon-selling-kindle-fire-be
low-cost-analyst-contends/#3521f2326534.

98   *lose $100 million in three months on diapers alone*: Will Oremus, "The Time Jeff

Bezos Went Thermonuclear on Diapers.com," *Slate*, Oct. 10, 2013, https://slate.com/technology/2013/10/amazon-book-how-jeff-bezos-went-thermonuclear-on-diapers-com.html; Jason Del Rey, "Amazon Is Shutting Down Diapers.com—Whose Founder Is Now at War with Amazon," *Vox*, March 29, 2017, https://www.vox.com/2017/3/29/15112314/amazon-shutting-down-diapers-com-quidsi-soap-com.

99   *accused of discriminating against Spotify*: Daniel Ek, "Consumers and Innovators Win on a Level Playing Field," Newsroom, March 13, 2019, https://newsroom.spotify.com/2019-03-13/consumers-and-innovators-win-on-a-level-playing-field/.

99   *general counsel of Tile*: "Testimony of Kirsten Daru, Chief Privacy Officer and General Counsel for Tile, Inc, on Online Platforms and Market Power Part 5: Competitors in the Digital Economy, Before the House Committee on the Judiciary, Subcommittee on Antitrust, Commercial and Administrative Law," house.gov, Jan. 17, 2020, https://docs.house.gov/meetings/JU/JU05/20200117/110386/HHRG-116-JU05-Wstate-DaruK-20200117.pdf.

99   *incorporates the features of the most popular apps*: Buster Hein, "8 Apps Apple Killed Today at WWDC," Cult of Mac, June 10, 2013, https://www.cultofmac.com/231121/seven-apps-apple-killed/.

99   *killing its rival Watson*: Mikey Campbell, "F.lux Says It Is 'Original Innovator' of Nighttime Display Colortech, Asks Apple to Open Night Shift API," *Apple Insider*, Jan. 14, 2016, https://appleinsider.com/articles/16/01/14/flux-says-it-is-original-innovator-of-nighttime-display-color-tech-asks-apple-to-open-night-shift-api.

100   *"Apple used us for market research"*: William Gallagher, "Developers Talk About Being 'Sherlocked' as Apple Uses Them 'for Market Research,'" *Apple Insider*, June 6, 2019, https://appleinsider.com/articles/19/06/06/developers-talk-about-being-sherlocked-as-apple-uses-them-for-market-research.

100   *is the dominant revenue source*: Killian Bell, "App Store Made Almost Twice as Much as Google Play in 2018," *Cult of Mac*, January 18, 2019, https://www.cultofmac.com/601492/app-store-google-play-revenue-2018/.

101   *copied Snapchat and Foursquare's popular features*: Georgia Wells and Deepa Seetharaman, "Snap Detailed Facebook's Aggressive Tactics in 'Project Voldemort' Dossier," *Wall Street Journal*, Sept. 24, 2019, https://www.wsj.com/articles/snap-detailed-facebooks-aggressive-tactics-in-project-voldemort-dossier-11569236404.

101   *210 million users*: "Number of Daily Active Snapchat Users from 1st Quarter 2014 to 1st Quarter 2020," *Statista*, https://www.statista.com/statistics/545967/snapchat-app-dau/

101   *Project Voldemort*: Georgia Wells and Deepa Seetharaman, "Snap Detailed

Facebook's Aggressive Tactics in 'Project Voldemort' Dossier," *Wall Street Journal*, Sept. 24, 2019, https://www.wsj.com/articles/snap-detailed-facebooks-aggressive-tactics-in-project-voldemort-dossier-11569236404.

102 *businesses would have to pay for their fans to see their content*: Cotton Delo, "Facebook Admits Organic Reach Is Falling Short, Urges Marketers to Buy Ads," *AdAge*, Dec. 5, 2013, https://adage.com/article/digital/facebook-admits-organic-reach-brand-posts-dipping/245530?; Julia Campbell, "Facebook Finally Admits That You Do Have to Pay for Ads to Reach Your Fans," business2 community, Dec. 11, 2013, https://www.business2community.com/facebook/facebook-finally-admits-pay-ads-reach-fans-0711525.

103 *by about $1.25 trillion*: Thomas Philippon, Twitter, Oct. 29, 2019, https://twitter.com/thomasphi2/status/1189172544718462976?s=11; "Innovation and Entrepreneurship in an Age of Concentrated Power," Open Markets Institute, Dec. 12, 2017, https://www.youtube.com/watch?list=PLl7VSnPfVKIjDjjK9yw6bQK4964lbJ_Go&time_continue=8&v=bmYBv4Zbn2Y&feature=emb_logo.

Four: Monopolies Spy on and Manipulate You

105 *employees listen to recordings*: Matt Day, Giles Turner, and Natalia Drozdiak, "Amazon Workers Are Listening to What You Tell Alexa," Bloomberg, April 10, 2019, https://www.bloomberg.com/news/articles/2019-04-10/is-anyone-listening-to-you-on-alexa-a-global-team-reviews-audio, and Joshua Bote, "Google Workers Are Eavesdropping on Your Private Conversations via Its Smart Speakers," *USA Today*, July 11, 2019, https://www.usatoday.com/story/tech/2019/07/11/google-home-smart-speakers-employees-listen-conversations/1702205001/.

106 *gathered millions of Americans' health records*: Rob Copeland, "Google's 'Project Nightingale' Gathers Personal Health Data on Millions of Americans," *Wall Street Journal*, Nov. 11, 2019, https://www.wsj.com/articles/google-s-secret-project-nightingale-gathers-personal-health-data-on-millions-of-americans-11573496790.

106 *an all-encompassing view*: Michael Nunez, "All of the Creepy Things Facebook Knows about You," *Gizmodo*, Aug. 19, 2016, https://gizmodo.com/all-of-the-creepy-things-facebook-knows-about-you-1785510980, and "What Google and Facebook Know about You," Al Jazeera, March 29, 2018, https://www.aljazeera.com/news/2018/03/google-facebook-180329092252320.html.

107 *340 times in twenty-four hours*: Douglas C. Schmidt, "Google Data Collection," DigitalContentNext.org, Aug. 2018, https://www.ftc.gov/system/files/documents/public_comments/2018/08/ftc-2018-0074-d-0018-155525.pdf.

107 *trackers on 74 percent of pornography sites*: Elena Maris, Timothy Libert, and

Jennifer Henrichsen, "Tracking Sex: The Implications of Widespread Sexual Data Leakage and Tracking on Porn Websites," arXiv Cornell University, July 15, 2019, https://arxiv.org/abs/1907.06520.

107 *8.4 million websites with the Facebook "like" button and 16.4 million*: David Baser, "Hard Questions: What Data Does Facebook Collect when I'm Not Using Facebook, and Why?" Facebook, April 16, 2018, https://about.fb.com /news/2018/04/data-off-facebook/, and Rebecca Stimson, "Letter to Damian Collins," Facebook, June 8, 2018, https://www.parliament.uk/documents /commons-committees/culture-media-and-sport/180608-Rebecca-Stimson -Facebook-to-Chair-re-oral-ev-follow-up.pdf.

107 *"shadow profiles"*: Kurt Wagner, "This Is How Facebook Collects Data on You Even If You Don't Have an Account," *Vox*, April 20, 2018, https://www.vox .com/2018/4/20/17254312/facebook-shadow-profiles-data-collection-non -users-mark-zuckerberg, and Salvador Rodriguez and Mike Isaac, "New York Attorney General to Investigate Facebook Email Collection," *New York Times*, April 25, 2019, https://www.nytimes.com/2019/04/25/technology/facebook -new-york-attorney-general-investigation.html.

107 *through its Facebook Audience Network*: David Baser, "Hard Questions: What Data Does Facebook Collect when I'm Not Using Facebook, and Why?" Facebook, April 16, 2018, https://about.fb.com/news/2018/04/data-off-face book/, and Kurt Wagner, "This Is How Facebook Collects Data on You Even If You Don't Have an Account," *Vox*, April 20, 2018, https://www.vox .com/2018/4/20/17254312/facebook-shadow-profiles-data-collection-non -users-mark-zuckerberg, and https://www.facebook.com/business/marketing /audience-networkm.

107 *uses facial recognition technology to identify you in pictures*: David Nield, "You Probably Don't Know All the Ways Facebook Tracks You," *Gizmodo*, June 8, 2017, https://gizmodo.com/all-the-ways-facebook-tracks-you-that-you-might -not-kno-1795604150.

108 *"I'm in an arms race I'm not going to win"*: Marian Berelowitz, "Everybody Has Information about Everybody,"Wunderman Thompson, Feb. 26, 2014, https:// www.jwtintelligence.com/2014/02/qa-with-julia-angwin-wall-street-journal -reporter-and-author-of-dragnet-nation/.

109 *"even when you think you're alone, the birds and mice can hear you whisper"*: Tom Huddleston Jr., "This Woman Escaped North Korea at 13—These Are Her Lessons on Perseverance," Make It, Aug. 20, 2018, https://www.cnbc .com/2018/08/20/north-korean-defector-yeonmi-parks-lessons-on-persever ance.html.

109 *shows Chinese police interrogating a man*: Gerry Shih (tweet), https://twitter .com/gerryshih/status/1199525930156216320.

109   *"Truthfully confess and your whole body will feel at ease"*: Gary Feuerberg, "China's Systemic Use of Torture Put under Congressional Scrutiny," *Epoch Times*, April 18, 2016, https://www.theepochtimes.com/chinas-systemic-use-of-torture-put -under-congressional-scrutiny_2026675.html.

110   *building an architecture of surveillance*: Zeynep Tufecki, "We're Building a Dys- topia Just to Make People Click on Ads," TedTalks, https://www.ted.com/talks /zeynep_tufekci_we_re_building_a_dystopia_just_to_make_people_click_on _ads/transcript.

110   *"deeply optimistic" about what Alexa can do*: Jason Del Rey, "Land of the Giants," VoxMedia Podcast Network, https://podcasts.voxmedia.com/show/land-of -the-giants.

110   *"automated and ubiquitous monitoring"*: "Ban Facial Recognition," BanFacialRec- ognition.com, https://www.banfacialrecognition.com.

110   *protests about Amazon's government contracts*: Caroline O'Donovan, "Amazon Employees Demand It Stop Working with ICE. The Company Said It's Up to the Government," *BuzzFeed News*, July 12, 2019, https://www.buzzfeednews .com/article/carolineodonovan/amazon-says-the-government-should-decide -whether-it-can, and Kari Paul, "Protesters Demand Amazon Break Ties with ICE and Homeland Security," *Guardian*, July 11, 2019, https://www.theguard ian.com/us-news/2019/jul/11/amazon-ice-protest-immigrant-tech.

110   *against the most vulnerable*: Nick Statt, "Amazon Told Employees It Would Continue to Sell Facial Recognition Software to Law Enforcement," *Verge*, Nov. 8, 2018, https://www.theverge.com/2018/11/8/18077292/amazon-rekog nition-jeff-bezos-andrew-jassy-facial-recognition-ice-rights-violations, https://mijente.net/notechforice/, and Kate Conger, "Amazon Workers Demand Jeff Bezos Cancel Face Recognition Contracts with Law Enforcement," *Giz- modo*, June 21, 2018, https://gizmodo.com/amazon-workers-demand-jeff-bezos -cancel-face-recognitio-1827037509.

110   *nearly 8,500 government requests*: "United States of America: Transparency Report," *Apple.com*, January–June 2019, https://www.apple.com/legal/transpar ency/us.html.

111   *Google received 26,964 government requests*: "Global Requests for User Infor- mation," Google Transparency Report, https://transparencyreport.google.com/ user-data/overview?hl=en&user_requests_report_period=series:requests,accou nts;authority:US;time:&lu=user_requests_report_period.

111   *even labeled Martin Luther King Jr. a communist*: "In the Latest JFK Files: The FBI's Ugly Analysis on Martin Luther King Jr., Filled with Falsehoods," *Wash- ington Post*, Nov. 4, 2017, https://www.washingtonpost.com/news/retropolis /wp/2017/11/04/in-the-latest-jfk-files-the-fbis-ugly-analysis-on-martin-lu ther-king-jr-filled-with-falsehoods/.

112   *monitored members of the Black Lives Matter movement*: George Joseph, "Exclusive: Feds Regularly Monitored Black Lives Matter since Ferguson," *Intercept*, July 24, 2015, https://theintercept.com/2015/07/24/documents-show-department-homeland-security-monitoring-black-lives-matter-since-ferguson/.

113   *a live feed into your home*: "If These Walls Could Talk: The Smart Home and the Fourth Amendment Limits of the Third Party Doctrine," *Harvard Law Review*, 130, 7 (May 9, 2017), https://harvardlawreview.org/2017/05/if-these-walls-could-talk-the-smart-home-and-the-fourth-amendment-limits-of-the-third-party-doctrine/.

113   *"It's like having thousands of eyes and ears on the street"*: Sam Biddle, "Amazon's Home Surveillance Chief Declared War on 'Dirtbag Criminals' as Company Got Closer to Police," *Intercept*, Feb. 14, 2019,https://theintercept.com/2019/02/14/amazon-ring-police-surveillance/.

113   *identified by Google data as being in the area of a crime*: Jennifer Valentino-DeVries, "Tracking Phones, Google Is a Dragnet for the Police," *New York Times*, April 13, 2019, https://www.nytimes.com/interactive/2019/04/13/us/google-location-tracking-police.html.

115   *"companies gonna company"*: *The Daily Show with Trevor Noah*, April 28, 2020 (broadcast).

115   *competing against MySpace as the more privacy-protecting alternative*: Dina Srinivasan, "The Antitrust Case against Facebook: A Monopolist's Journey towards Pervasive Surveillance in Spite of Consumers' Preference for Privacy," *Berkeley Business Law Journal* 16, 1 (Feb. 9, 2019).

117   *tell you about all the spying the platforms have already done on you*: Nicole Nguyen and Ryan Mac, "You Can Finally See All of the Info Facebook Collected about You from Other Websites," *BuzzFeed News*, Aug. 20, 2019, https://www.buzzfeednews.com/article/nicolenguyen/off-facebook-activity-feature-clear-history.

118   *"privacy-friendly smart home of the future"*: "About Candle," Candle Smarthome, https://www.candlesmarthome.com/about.

118   *"data that's been collected through a monopoly"*: "The Commissioners: The European Commission's Political Leadership," Commissioners, speech delivered September 9, 2016, https://ec.europa.eu/commission/commissioners/2014-2019/vestager/announcements/making-data-work-us_en.

118   *allows two applications to talk to each other*: Shana Pearlman, "What Are APIs and How Do APIs Work?" MuleSoft, Sept. 7, 2016,https://blogs.mulesoft.com/biz/tech-ramblings-biz/what-are-apis-how-do-apis-work/.

119   *"the primary way to get data into and out of the Facebook platform"*: "Overview," Facebook for Developers, https://developers.facebook.com/docs/graph-api/overview.

119   *competing with a Facebook "core functionality"*: House of Commons Digital,

Culture, Media and Sport Committee, UK Parliament, "Disinformation and 'Fake News': Final Report," Feb. 14, 2019, https://publications.parliament.uk /pa/cm201719/cmselect/cmcumeds/1791/1791.pdf, and Donie O'Sullivan and Hadas Gold, "Facebook Internal Emails Show Zuckerberg Targeting Competitor Vine," CNN Business, https://www.cnn.com/2018/12/05/media/face book-six4three-internal-documents-emails/index.html.

119 *"discriminatory refusal to deal"*: "Refusal to Deal," Federal Trade Commission, https://www.ftc.gov/tips-advice/competition-guidance/guide-antitrust-laws /single-firm-conduct/refusal-deal.

119 *use privacy as a pretense for monopolization*: House of Commons Digital, Culture, Media and Sport Committee, UK Parliament, "Disinformation and 'Fake News': Final Report," Feb. 14, 2019, https://publications.parliament.uk/pa /cm201719/cmselect/cmcumeds/1791/1791.pdf, and Katie Paul and Mark Hosenball, "Newly Released Court Documents Reveal Facebook Executives Quietly Planned a Data Policy 'Switcharoo,'" *Business Insider*, Nov. 6, 2019, https://www.businessinsider.com/facebook-executives-planned-switcharoo-on -data-policy-change-court-filings-2019-11?op=1.

121 *still struggling to get Facebook and Google to comply*: Johnny Ryan, "New Data on GDPR Enforcement Agencies Reveal Why the GDPR Is Failing," Brave Insights, April 27, 2020, https://brave.com/dpa-report-2020/.

121 *inquiries into the two companies ongoing*: Data Protection Commission, "Annual Report, 1 January—31 December 2019," https://www.dataprotection.ie/sites /default/files/uploads/2020-02/DPC%20Annual%20Report%202019.pdf

121 *The law puts forth a different*: "California Consumer Privacy Act (CCPA) Fact Sheet," California Department of Justice, https://www.oag.ca.gov/sys tem/files/attachments/press_releases/CCPA%20Fact%20Sheet%20%280 0000002%29.pdf.

122 *FTC fined Facebook $5 billion*: "FTC Imposes $5 Billion Penalty and Sweeping New Privacy Restrictions on Facebook," Federal Trade Commission, July 24, 2019, https://www.ftc.gov/news-events/press-releases/2019/07/ftc-imposes -5-billion-penalty-sweeping-new-privacy-restrictions, and Rohit Chopra, "Dissenting Statement of Commissioner Rohit Chopra Regarding the Matter of Facebook, Inc.," Federal Trade Commission, July 24, 2019, https://www .ftc.gov/public-statements/2019/07/dissenting-statement-commissioner-rohit -chopra-regarding-matter-facebook, and Rebecca Kelly Slaughter, "Dissenting Statement of Commissioner Rebecca Kelly Slaughter Regarding the Matter of FTC vs. Facebook," Federal Trade Commission, July 24, 2019, https://www.ftc .gov/public-statements/2019/07/dissenting-statement-commissioner-rebecca -kelly-slaughter-regarding-matter.

122 *consider that Facebook made over $70 billion in 2019 alone*: J. Clement, "Facebook:

Annual Revenue 2009–2019," *Statista*, Feb. 3, 2020, https://www.statista.com /statistics/268604/annual-revenue-of-facebook/.

122 *"not misrepresent"*: "Agreement Containing Consent Order," *In the Matter of Facebook, Inc., a corporation*, https://www.ftc.gov/sites/default/files/documents /cases/2011/11/111129facebookagree.pdf.

123 *Facebook's stock surged*: Jon Swartz, "Facebook Stock Hits Highest Price in Nearly a Year after Reports of $5 Billion FTC Fine," *MarketWatch*, July 14, 2019, https://www.marketwatch.com/story/facebook-stock-hits-highest-price-in -nearly-a-year-after-reports-of-5-billion-ftc-fine-2019-07-12.

123 *personal information can be used to screw you over*: Arwa Mahdawi, "Cookie Monsters: Why Your Browsing History Could Mean Rip-Off Prices," *Guardian*, Dec. 6, 2016, https://www.theguardian.com/commentisfree/2016/dec/06 /cookie-monsters-why-your-browsing-history-could-mean-rip-off-prices.

124 *"engages" humans the most*: Tobias Rose-Stockwell, "This Is How Your Fear and Outrage Are Being Sold for Profit," *Quartz*, July 28, 2017, https:// qz.com/1039910/how-facebooks-news-feed-algorithm-sells-our-fear-and -outrage-for-profit/, and Marcia Stepanek, "The Algorithms of Fear," *Stanford Social Innovation Review*, June 14, 2016, https://ssir.org/articles/entry/the_al gorithms_of_fear.

124 *up ten minutes from the number reported in 2014*: James B. Stewart, "Facebook Has 50 Minutes of Your Time Each Day. It Wants More," *New York Times*, May 5, 2016, https://www.nytimes.com/2016/05/06/business/facebook-bends-the -rules-of-audience-engagement-to-its-advantage.html.

124 *84 percent of Google's revenue and 98 percent of Facebook's revenue*: "Advertising Revenue of Google from 2001 to 2019," *Statista*, retrieved March 7, 2020, https://www.statista.com/statistics/266249/advertising-revenue-of-google/; J. Clement, "Facebook's Advertising Revenue Worldwide from 2009 to 2019," *Statista*, Feb. 28, 2020; https://www.statista.com/statistics/271258/facebooks -advertising-revenue-worldwide/.

124 *"We're not talking about the realm of the possible here"*: "Transcript of Tech Conference with Scott Galloway," http://thecapitolforum.cmail20.com/t/View Email/j/A39DA2A85002EAE22540EF23F30FEDED/647939D224BDE7F 5C06B463AA70A4F2C.

125 *getting our cortisol pumping*: Nina Godlewski, "Deleting Facebook Could Lower Stress Hormone Levels, Study Finds," *Newsweek*, April 4, 2018, https://www .newsweek.com/facebook-stress-cortisol-social-media-health-break-quit -871521.

126 *some of the tricks tech companies employ to addict users*: Tristan Harris, "Unregulated Tech Mediation, Inevitable Online Deception, Societal Harm," Center for Humane Technology, Jan. 8, 2020, https://energycommerce.house.gov/sites

/democrats.energycommerce.house.gov/files/documents/010820%20CPC%20 Hearing%20Testimony_Harris.pdf.

126 *psychologist B. F. Skinner:* "Variable Rewards: Want to Hook Users? Drive Them Crazy," Nir & Far, https://www.nirandfar.com/want-to-hook-your-users -drive-them-crazy/.

126 *"It's a social-validation feedback loop":* Olivia Solon, "Ex-Facebook President Sean Parker: Site Made to Exploit Human 'Vulnerability,'" *Guardian,* Nov. 9, 2017, https://www.theguardian.com/technology/2017/nov/09/facebook-sean -parker-vulnerability-brain-psychology.

126 *"aren't allowed to use that shit":* James Vincent, "Former Facebook Exec Says Social Media Is Ripping Apart Society," *Verge,* Dec. 11, 2017, https://www .theverge.com/2017/12/11/16761016/former-facebook-exec-ripping-apart -society.

127 *put tight controls on their own kids' use of technology:* Nellie Bowles, "A Dark Consensus about Screens and Kids Begins to Emerge," *New York Times,* Oct. 26, 2018, https://www.nytimes.com/2018/10/26/style/phones-children-silicon-valley .html.

127 *"God only knows what it's doing to our children's brains":* Olivia Solon, "Ex-Facebook President Sean Parker: Site Made to Exploit Human 'Vulnerability,'" *Guardian,* Nov. 9, 2017, https://www.theguardian.com/technology/2017 /nov/09/facebook-sean-parker-vulnerability-brain-psychology.

127 *170 percent increase in high-depressive symptoms:* Tristan Harris, "Unregulated Tech Mediation, Inevitable Online Deception, Societal Harm," Center for Humane Technology, January 8, 2020, https://energycommerce.house.gov/sites /democrats.energycommerce.house.gov/files/documents/010820%20CPC% 20Hearing%20Testimony_Harris.pdf.

127 *NYU researchers link to social media usage:* J. M. Twenge, T. E. Joiner, M. L. Rogers, and G. N. Martin, "Corrigendum: Increases in Depressive Symptoms, Suicide-Related Outcomes, and Suicide Rates among U.S. Adolescents after 2010 and Links to Increased New Media Screen Time," Association for Psychological Science, https://journals.sagepub.com/doi/pdf/10.1177/2167702617723376.

127 *doubling for girls aged 15 to 19 between 2007 and 2015:* Susan Scutti, "Suicide Rate Hit 40-Year Peak among Older Teen Girls in 2015," CNN Health, Aug. 3, 2017, https://www.cnn.com/2017/08/03/health/teen-suicide-cdc-study-bn/index.html.

128 *determined by recommendation algorithms:* "23 YouTube Statistics That Matter to Marketers in 2020," Hootsuite, Dec. 17, 2019, https://blog.hootsuite.com /youtube-stats-marketers/.

128 *Emily Gadek tweeted in September 2019:* "Emily Gadek" (tweet), https://twitter .com/emilygadabout/status/1176517141400440834?s=11.

129 *Among the stories collected were*: "01: A Deadly Fall," Mozilla, https://foundation
.mozilla.org/en/campaigns/youtube-regrets/.

129 *target you based on your particular vulnerability*: Zeynep Tufekci, "#78–
Persuasion and Control," Sam Harris, samharris.org/podcasts/persuasion-and
-control/, and Jeremy B. Merrill and Olivia Goldhill, "These Are the Political Ads Cambridge Analytica Designed for You," Quartz Daily Brief, https://
qz.com/1782348/cambridge-analytica-used-these-5-political-ads-to-target
-voters/.

129 *their algorithms draw inferences about you*: Sandra Wachter and Brent Mittel-
stadt, "A Right to Reasonable Inferences: Re-Thinking Data Protection Law
in the Age of Big Data and AI," *Columbia Business Law Review* 2 (April 2019),
https://ssrn.com/abstract=3248829.

131 *rolled back long-standing rules*: Cecilia Kang, Eric Lipton, and Sydney Ember,
"How a Conservative TV Giant Is Ridding Itself of Regulation," *New York
Times*, Aug. 14, 2017, https://www.nytimes.com/2017/08/14/us/politics/how-a
-conservative-tv-giant-is-ridding-itself-of-regulation.html, and Cecilia Kang,
"F.C.C. Watchdog Looks into Changes That Benefited Sinclair," *New York
Times*, Feb. 15, 2018, https://www.nytimes.com/2018/02/15/technology/fcc
-sinclair-ajit-pai.html?partner=IFTTT.

131 *has appealed*: Michael Balderston, "FCC Eyes Supreme Court for Media Ownership Dereg Case," TV Technology, https://www.tvtechnology.com/news/fcc
-eyes-supreme-court-for-media-ownership-dereg-case.

131 *he and his staff had several meetings with executives*: Cecilia Kang, Eric Lipton,
and Sydney Ember, "How a Conservative TV Giant Is Ridding Itself of Regulation," *New York Times*, Aug. 14, 2017, https://www.nytimes.com/2017/08/14
/us/politics/how-a-conservative-tv-giant-is-ridding-itself-of-regulation.html,
and Cecilia Kang, "F.C.C. Watchdog Looks into Changes That Benefited Sinclair," *New York Times*, Feb. 15, 2018, https://www.nytimes.com/2018/02/15
/technology/fcc-sinclair-ajit-pai.html?partner=IFTTT.

131 *used shell corporations to evade broadcast ownership limits*: https://www.fcc
.gov/document/broadcast-radio-ownership-47-cfr-section-733555 47 C.F.R.
§ 73.3555(e), and Timothy Karr, "Sinclair's Defense Is as Bogus as the Shell
Companies It Uses to Evade the FCC Rules," *Free Press*, Oct. 24, 2013, https://
www.freepress.net/news/press-releases/sinclairs-defense-bogus-shell-compa
nies-it-uses-evade-fcc-rules.

131 *racist and anti-Muslim propaganda*: Dana Floberg, "Free Press to FCC: Viral
Vid Shows We Must Stop Sinclair," *Free Press*, April 19, 2018, https://www
.freepress.net/news/updates/free-press-fcc-viral-vid-shows-we-must-stop
-sinclair.

131 *reportedly ordered its stations to air a video segment*: Sydney Ember, "Sinclair Requires TV Stations to Air Segments That Tilt to the Right," *New York Times*, May 14, 2017, https://www.nytimes.com/2017/05/12/business/media/sinclair -broadcast-komo-conservative-media.html?_r=0.

131 *has a strong grip on the dissemination of information*: "Who Controls the Votes?" Columbia Business School, Ideas and Insights, https://www8.gsb.columbia .edu/articles/ideas-work/who-controls-votes.

131 *"Rupert Murdoch is the most powerful"*: Patrick Kennedy and Andrea Prat, "Information Inequality" *Vox CEPR Policy Portal*, November 25, 2017, https:// voxeu.org/article/information-inequality.

131 *referring to it as a hoax*: Bryan Sullivan, "Fox News Faces Lawsuit for Calling COVID-19 a 'Hoax,'" *Forbes*, April 10, 2020, https://www.forbes .com/sites/legalentertainment/2020/04/10/covid-19-lawsuit-against-fox -news/#586e45885739, and Luke Darby, "Fox News Staffers Got Coronavirus after Anchors Downplayed the Pandemic," *GQ*, March 23, 2020, https:// www.gq.com/story/fox-news-coronavirus, and Ken Stone, "Washington State Group Is 1st to Sue Fox News for Calling Coronavirus a 'Hoax,'" *Times of San Diego*, April 2, 2020, https://timesofsandiego.com/business/2020/04/02 /washington-state-group-is-1st-to-sue-fox-news-for-calling-coronavirus -a-hoax/, and "A Beloved Bar Owner Was Skeptical about the Virus. Then He Took a Cruise," *New York Times*, April 18, 2020, https://www.nytimes .com/2020/04/18/nyregion/coronavirus-jjbubbles-joe-joyce.html.

132 *"help protect the lives of all Americans"*: James Walker, "Journalism Professors Call for an End to Fox News Coronavirus 'Misinformation' in Open Letter to Rupert Murdoch," *Newsweek*, April 2, 2020, https://www.newsweek.com/journalism -professors-fox-news-end-coronavirus-misinformation-open-letter-1495688.

Five: Monopolies Threaten Democracy and Your Freedom

135 *Cambridge Analytica had developed psychological profiles*: See Karim Amer and Jehane Noujaim (producers and directors), *The Great Hack*, Netflix, 2019.

135 *targeted "persuadable" American voters*: Sabrina Siddiqui, "Cambridge Analytica's US Election Work May Violate Law, Legal Complaint Argues," *Guardian*, March 26, 2018, https://www.theguardian.com/uk-news/2018/mar/26/cam bridge-analytica-trump-campaign-us-election-laws; Eric Auchard and David Ingram, "Cambridge Analytica CEO Claims Influence on U.S. Election, Facebook Questioned," Reuters, March 20, 2018, https://www.reuters.com/article /us-facebook-cambridge-analytica-idUSKBN1GW1SG; Alex Hern, "Cambridge Analytica: How Did it Turn Clicks into Votes?" *Guardian*, May 6, 2018, https://www.theguardian.com/news/2018/may/06/cambridge-analytica-how -turn-clicks-into-votes-christopher-wylie.

135 *"It doesn't have to be true, it just has to be believed"*: Ben Popken and Anna Schecter, "Hidden Camera Shows Cambridge Analytica Pitching Deceptive Tactics," NBC News, March 18, 2018, https://www.nbcnews.com/news/all/hidden-camera-shows-cambridge-analytica-pitching-tricky-tactics-n857936.

135 *helping to elect far-right leaders*: Larry Madowo, "How Cambridge Analytica Poisoned Kenya's Democracy," *Washington Post*, March 20, 2018, https://www.washingtonpost.com/news/global-opinions/wp/2018/03/20/how-cambridge-analytica-poisoned-kenyas-democracy/.

135 *to suppress African American voting*: "Part," *Listen Notes*, April 29, 2019, https://www.listennotes.com/podcasts/deepak-chopras/part-two-minds-and-machines-Li02qCOt81l/.

136 *"was in 'psychological operations'"*: Carole Cadwalladr, "'I Made Steve Bannon's Psychological Warfare Tool': Meet the Data War Whistleblower," *The Guardian*, March 18, 2018, https://www.theguardian.com/news/2018/mar/17/data-war-whistleblower-christopher-wylie-faceook-nix-bannon-trump.

136 *"insurgency that was catalyzed by targeted disinformation"*: Ibid.

137 *"This was targeted at narrow segments of the population"*: Chris Wylie, "Written Statement to the United States Senate Committee on the Judiciary In the Matter of Cambridge Analytica and Other Related Issues," para. 42, https://www.judiciary.senate.gov/imo/media/doc/05-16-18%20Wylie%20Testimony.pdf.

137 *breaking a rule*: UK Information Commissioner's Office, "Investigation Into the Use of Data Analytics in Political Campaigns, Investigation Update," July 11, 2018, https://ico.org.uk/media/action-weve-taken/2259371/investigation-into-data-analytics-for-political-purposes-update.pdf, "Facebook's policies permitted third-party apps to obtain personal data about users who installed the app. . . . Facebook's default settings also allowed user's friends' data to be collected by the app unless the friends themselves had specifically changed their privacy settings to prevent this from occurring. There were, however, limitations in what this data could be used for . . ."

137 *classified as being interested in "pseudoscience"*: Aaron Sankin, "Want to Find a Misinformed Public? Facebook's Already Done it," Markup, April 23, 2020, https://themarkup.org/coronavirus/2020/04/23/want-to-find-a-misinformed-public-facebooks-already-done-it.

137 *"By monitoring"*: Darren Davidson, "Facebook Targets 'Insecure' Young People," *Australian*, May 1, 2017, https://www.theaustralian.com.au/business/media/digital/facebook-targets-insecure-young-people-to-sell-ads/news-story/a89949ad016eee7d7a61c3c30c909fa6.

138 *"does not offer tools to target people"*: Facebook, "Comments on Research and

Ad Targeting," April 30, 2017, https://about.fb.com/news/h/comments-on
-research-and-ad-targeting/.

138 *using Facebook data and Facebook micro-targeting*: Sophia Porotsky, "Cambridge
Analytica: The Darker Side of Big Data," *Global Security Review*, June 10, 2019,
https://globalsecurityreview.com/cambridge-analytica-darker-side-big-data/.

138 *"determining user personality characteristics,"* Patent #9,740,752, June 3, 2016,
available at https://patents.justia.com/patent/9740752.

138 *U.S. political ads with rubles*: Harper Neidig, "Franken Blasts Facebook for
Accepting Rubles for U.S. Election Ads," *Hill*, October 31, 2017, https://the
hill.com/policy/technology/358102-franken-blasts-facebook-for-accepting
-rubles-for-us-election-ads.

138 *ad revenue jumped*: J. Clement, "Facebook: Annual Revenue 2009–2019,"
Statista, Feb. 3, 2020, https://www.statista.com/statistics/268604/annual-reve
nue-of-facebook/.

138 *Facebook threatened to sue them*: Justin Carissimo, "Facebook Knew of Illicit User
Profile Harvesting for 2 Years, Never Acted," CBS News, March 17, 2018,
https://www.cbsnews.com/news/cambridge-analytica-facebook-knew-for
-two-years-no-action-taken/, and Jamie Grierson, "Facebook Says Warning
to Guardian Group 'Not Our Wisest Move,'" *The Guardian*, March 23, 2018,
https://www.theguardian.com/news/2018/mar/23/facebook-says-warning-to
-guardian-group-not-our-wisest-move.

138 *"What happens"*: Chris Wylie, "Written Statement to the United States Senate
Committee on the Judiciary In the Matter of Cambridge Analytica and Other
Related Issues," para. 48, https://www.judiciary.senate.gov/imo/media/doc/05
-16-18%20Wylie%20Testimony.pdf.

139 *"I would bet"*: Casey Newton, "Read the Full Transcript of Mark Zuckerberg's
Leaked Internal Facebook Meetings," *Verge*, October 1, 2019, https://www
.theverge.com/2019/10/1/20892354/mark-zuckerberg-full-transcript-leaked
-facebook-meetings.

139 *two unannounced meetings*: Dylan Byers and Ben Collins, "Trump Hosted
Zuckerberg for Undisclosed Dinner at the White House in October," NBC
News, November 20, 2019, https://www.nbcnews.com/tech/tech-news/trump
-hosted-zuckerberg-undisclosed-dinner-white-house-october-n1087986.

139 *"We don't fact-check political ads"*: Salvador Rodriguez, "Mark Zuckerberg:
I thought about banning political ads from Facebook, but decided not to,"
CNBC, October 17, 2019, https://www.cnbc.com/2019/10/17/mark-zucker
berg-says-he-wont-ban-political-ads-on-facebook.html.

139 *grounded in free expression*: Ben Gilbert, "Facebook refuses to fact-check political ads and it's infuriating employees and lawmakers. Here's why the issue

continues to dog the company," *Business Insider*, December 14, 2019, https://
www.businessinsider.com/facebook-political-ads-fact-check-policy-explained
-2019-11?op=1#so-what-is-it-about-according-to-zuckerberg-its-about-free
-speech-3.

140 *"As a public"*: Zeynep Tufekci, "We're Building a Dystopia Just to Make People Click on Ads," Ted, September 2017, https://www.ted.com/talks/zeynep
_tufekci_we_re_building_a_dystopia_just_to_make_people_click_on_ads.

140 *"If there be"*: "Whitney v. California, 274 U.S. 357 (1927)," Justia, https://su
preme.justia.com/cases/federal/us/274/357/.

141 *"Our assessment"*: Renee DiResta et al., "The Tactics and Tropes of the Internet Research Agency," int.nyt, https://int.nyt.com/data/documenthelper/533
-read-report-internet-research-agency/7871ea6d5b7bedafbf19/optimized/full
.pdf#page=1.

142 *"in Bolsonaro's rise"*: Max Fisher and Amanda Taub, "What Is YouTube Pushing You to Watch Next?" *New York Times, The Weekly*, August 9, 2019, https://www
.nytimes.com/2019/08/09/the-weekly/youtube-brazil-far-right.html.

142 *own employees have called for restrictions*: "Read the Letter Facebook Employees Sent to Mark Zuckerberg About Political Ads," *New York Times*, October 28, 2019, https://www.nytimes.com/2019/10/28/technology/facebook-mark
-zuckerberg-letter.html.

143 *proposed limits to micro-targeting as a solution*: Peter Kafka, "Facebook's Political Ad Problem, Explained by an Expert," *Vox*, December 10, 2019, https://
www.vox.com/recode/2019/12/10/20996869/facebook-political-ads-targeting
-alex-stamos-interview-open-sourced.

143 *Ellen L. Weintraub, a Democratic commissioner*: Ellen L. Weintraub, "Don't Abolish Political Ads on Social Media. Stop Microtargeting," *Washington Post*, Nov. 1, 2019, https://www.washingtonpost.com/opinions/2019/11/01/dont
-abolish-political-ads-social-media-stop-microtargeting/.

143 *target their devices with text messages or app alerts*: Thomas Edsall, "Opinion: Trump's Digital Advantage Is Freaking Out Democratic Strategists," *New York Times*, January 29, 2020, https://www.nytimes.com/2020/01/29/opinion
/trump-digital-campaign-2020.html.

143 *more than 80 percent of America's voting machines*: Penn Wharton Public Policy Initiative Report, "The Business of Voting," March 2017, https://trustthevote
.org/wp-content/uploads/2017/03/2017-whartonoset_industryreport.pdf; Jordan Wilkie, " 'They Think They Are above the Law': The Firms That Own America's Voting System," *Guardian*, April 23, 2019, https://www.theguard
ian.com/us-news/2019/apr/22/us-voting-machine-private-companies-voter
-registration; Sue Halpern, "How Voting-Machine Lobbyists Undermine the

Democratic Process," *New Yorker*, January 22, 2019, https://www.newyorker
.com/tech/annals-of-technology/how-voting-machine-lobbyists-undermine
-the-democratic-process?.

143   *lobbyists reportedly made contributions to Mitch McConnell's campaign*: Donald Shaw, "As He Blocks Election Security Bills, McConnell Takes Checks
from Voting Machine Lobbyists," Sludge, June 10, 2019, https://readsludge
.com/2019/06/10/as-he-blocks-election-security-bills-mcconnell-takes
-checks-from-voting-machine-lobbyists/, and Nicole Goodkind, "Mitch
McConnell Received Donations from Voting Machine Lobbyists Before
Blocking Election Security Bills," *Newsweek*, July 26, 2019, https://www.news
week.com/mitch-mcconnell-robert-mueller-election-security-russia-1451361.

144   *they're decimating journalism*: See *Online Platforms and Market Power, Part 1: The
Free and Diverse Press: Before the Subcomm. on Regulatory Reform, Commercial
and Antitrust Law of the H. Comm. on the Judiciary*, 116th Cong. (2019) (submitted testimony of Sally Hubbard, Director of Enforcement Strategy, Open Markets Institute), https://docs.house.gov/meetings/JU/JU05/20190611/109616
/HHRG-116-JU05-Wstate-HubbardS-20190611.pdf.

144   *newspaper employment fell about 47 percent*: Jonathan O'Connell and Rachel
Siegel, "America's Two Largest Newspaper Chains Are Joining Forces. Will
It Save Either?" *Washington Post*, August 5, 2019 https://www.washingtonpost
.com/business/2019/08/05/gannett-merge-with-gatehouse-media/.

145   *thirty-three thousand employees*: Victor Pickard, "Coronavirus Is Hammering the
News Industry. Here's How to Save It," Jacobin, April 20, 2020, https://jacobin
mag.com/2020/04/coronavirus-news-industry-newspapers-journalists-layoffs.

145   *85 to 90 percent of the growth of the more than $150 billion*: Testimony of Jason
Kint, CEO of Digital Content Next, House of Commons Standing Com-
mittee on Access to Information, Privacy and Ethics, May 27, 2019, https://
www.ourcommons.ca/DocumentViewer/en/42-1/ETHI/meeting-151
/evidence#Int-10649964.

145   *More than 68 percent of American adults*: Media Subcommittee, Digital Platforms
Project, "How to Protect the News Media in the Age of Digital Platforms,"
Pro Market, May 10, 2019, https://promarket.org/how-to-protect-the-news
-media-in-the-age-of-digital-platforms/.

145   *share of Americans' attention*: Ibid.

145   *has long maintained it is a neutral platform and not a publisher*: Sam Levin, "Is
Facebook a Publisher? In Public It Says No, but in Court It Says Yes," *Guardian*, July 2, 2018, https://www.theguardian.com/technology/2018/jul/02/face
book-mark-zuckerberg-platform-publisher-lawsuit.

145   *wide-reaching legal immunity*: "Artist Rights Alliance Opposes Exporting Safe
Harbors in Trade Deals," medium, Oct. 29, 2019, https://medium.com/@art

istrightsnow/artist-rights-alliance-opposes-exporting-safe-harbors-in-trade
-deals-befc5fa3976d.

146 *More than 70 percent of Google's revenue*: J. Clement, "Distribution of Google's
Revenues From 2001 to 2018, By Source," *Statista*, Feb. 5, 2020, https://www
.statista.com/statistics/266471/distribution-of-googles-revenues-by-source/.

146 *depriving publishers of the ad revenue that funds journalism*: Sally Hubbard, "Fake
News Is a Real Antitrust Problem," *Competition Policy International Antitrust
Chronicle*, December 2017, https://www.competitionpolicyinternational.com
/wp-content/uploads/2017/12/CPI-Hubbard.pdf.

147 *from friends and family*: Mark Zuckerberg's Facebook page, January 11, 2018.

147 *like* Mother Jones, Vox, *and* Slate: Monika Bauerlein and Clara Jeffery, "How
Facebook Screwed Us All," *Mother Jones*, March 2019, https://www.mother
jones.com/politics/2019/02/how-facebook-screwed-us-all/; Jeremy Barr. "Post-
Facebook News Feed Tweaks, Vox Media Lays off 50 Employees," *Holly-
wood Reporter*, February 21, 2018, https://www.hollywoodreporter.com/news
/vox-media-laying-around-50-people-1086869; Will Oremus, "The Great
Facebook Crash," *Slate*, June 27, 2018, https://slate.com/technology/2018/06
/facebooks-retreat-from-the-news-has-painful-for-publishers-including-slate
.html.

149 *"At times, the AJC's reporters"*: Congressional testimony of Kevin Riley, editor,
Atlanta Journal-Constitution, *Online Platforms and Market Power, Part 1: The
Free and Diverse Press*, June 11, 2019, https://www.congress.gov/event/116th
-congress/house-event/109616

149 *reporting of coronavirus case numbers*: Alan Judd and Carrie Teegardin, "Faulty
Data Obscures Virus' Impact on Georgia," *AJC*, April 14, 2020, https://www
.ajc.com/news/faulty-data-obscures-virus-impact-georgia/LhCiI0bVKXO
QW9VuEF9OrN/.

149 *publicly apologized*: Willoughby Mariano and J. Scott Trubey, "'It's Just Cuckoo':
State's Latest Data Mishap Causes Critics to Cry Foul," *AJC*, May 13, 2020,
https://www.ajc.com/news/state—regional-govt—politics/just-cuckoo
-state-latest-data-mishap-causes-critics-cry-foul/182PpUvUX9XEF8v
O11NVGO/.

149 *try to weaken the law*: Kartikay Mehrotra, Laura Mahoney, and Daniel
Stoller, "Google and Other Tech Firms Seek to Weaken Landmark California Data-Privacy Law," *Los Angeles Times*, September 4, 2019, https://www
.latimes.com/business/story/2019-09-04/google-and-other-tech-companies
-attempt-to-water-down-privacy-law; amendments tracked in the text of
the California Privacy Rights and Enforcement Act here: https://uploads-ssl
.webflow.com/5aa18a452485b60001c301de/5d8bc3342a72fc8145920a32
_CPREA_2020_092519_Annotated_.pdf.

150 *"Newsrooms"*: Gaelle Faure, "Maria Ressa on the Battle for Truth, the Role of America's Social Media Platforms, and What Comes Next," Global Investigative Journalism Conference, September 29, 2019, https://gijc2019 .org/2019/09/29/maria-ressa-on-the-battle-for-truth-the-role-of-americas -social-media-platforms-and-what-comes-next/.

Six: Monopolies Destroy Our Planet and Control Your Food

154 *by warming it by one degree Celsius*: Umair Irfan, "A Major New Climate Report Slams the Door on Wishful Thinking," *Vox*, Oct. 7, 2018, https://www.vox .com/2018/10/5/17934174/climate-change-global-warming-un-ipcc-report -1-5-degrees.

154 *catastrophe*: "Special Report: Global Warming of 1.5 degrees C," IPCC, https:// www.ipcc.ch/sr15/.

154 *Young Thunberg spelled it out*: 2020 World Economic Forum, "Greta Thunberg: Our house is still on fire and you're fueling the flames," https://www.weforum .org/agenda/2020/01/greta-speech-our-house-is-still-on-fire-davos-2020/.

155 *"One day we'll know"*: Rachel Adams-Heard and Akshat Rathi, "Tillerson Questions Human Role in Halting Climate Change," Bloomberg, Feb. 04, 2020, https://www.bloomberg.com/news/articles/2020-02-04/rex-tillerson -questions-human-role-in-battling-climate-change; "Rex Tillerson to Oil Industry: Not Sure Humans Can Do Anything to Battle Climate Change," *Dallas Morning News*, Feb. 4, 2020, https://www.dallasnews.com/business /energy/2020/02/04/rex-tillerson-to-oil-industry-not-sure-humans-can-do -anything-to-battle-climate-change/.

156 *"If you are part"*: Naomi Klein, *On Fire: The (Burning) Case for a Green New Deal* (New York: Simon & Schuster, 2019), 289.

156 *"The great"*: Matthew Taylor and Jonathan Watts, "Revealed: The 20 Firms Behind a Third of All Carbon Emission," *Guardian*, October 9, 2019, https:// www.theguardian.com/environment/2019/oct/09/revealed-20-firms-third -carbon-emissions.

156 *cost more than $460 billion*: NOAA National Centers for Environmental Information, "U.S. Billion-Dollar Weather and Climate Disasters," 2020, https:// www.ncdc.noaa.gov/billions/time-series.

156 *on the current path*: Citi GPS: Global Perspectives & Solutions, "Energy Darwinism II: Why a Low Carbon Future Doesn't Have to Cost the Earth," August 2015, https://ir.citi.com/hsq32Jl1m4aIzicMqH8sBkPnbsqfnwy4Jgb1J2kI PYWIw5eM8yD3FY9VbGpK%2Baax.

156 *could bring in more than $2 trillion*: Sara Harrison, "Companies Expect Climate Change to Cost Them $1 Trillion in 5 Years," *Wired*, June 4, 2019, https://

www.wired.com/story/companies-expect-climate-change-to-cost-them-one
-trillion-dollars-in-5-years/.

156 *120 percent more*: Report by UN et al., "The Production Gap: The discrepancy
between countries' planned fossil fuel production and global production levels
consistent with limiting warming to 1.5 or 2 degrees Celsius," 2019, http://
productiongap.org/2019report/.

157 *"We will not get the job"*: Klein, *On Fire*, 33

158 *"Like its 1930s"*: Sandeep Vaheesan, "A Charter for a Clean, Democratic Future,"
The Trouble, May 12, 2019, https://www.the-trouble.com/content/2019/5/12/a
-charter-for-a-clean-democratic-future.

158 *"we have demonstrated"*: United States Climate Alliance, "U.S. Climate Alliance
Governors Oppose Administration's Withdrawal from the Paris Agreement,"
November 4, 2019, https://www.usclimatealliance.org/publications/pariswith
drawal.

159 *more than 10 percent of global carbon emissions*: Matthew Taylor and Jonathan
Watts, "Revealed: The 20 Firms Behind a Third of All Carbon Emission,"
Guardian, October 9, 2019, https://www.theguardian.com/environment/2019
/oct/09/revealed-20-firms-third-carbon-emissions.

159 *invested over $1 billion*: InfluenceMap Report, "Big Oil's Real Agenda on Cli-
mate Change," 2019, https://influencemap.org/report/How-Big-Oil-Contin
ues-to-Oppose-the-Paris-Agreement-38212275958aa21196dae3b76220bddc.

159 *Five out of the top ten largest global companies*: "Global 500," *Fortune*, 2019, http://
fortune.com/global500/list/.

159 *$20 billion in direct fossil fuel subsidies annually*: Klein, *On Fire*, 283.

159 *actively suppressed research*: Christopher Leonard, *Kochland: The Secret History of
Koch Industries and Corporate Power in America* (New York: Simon & Schuster,
2019), 400.

159 *own members of Congress*: Public Citizen, "Corporations United," January 15,
2020, https://www.citizen.org/article/corporations-united-citizens-united-10
-years-report/.

159 *sixteen of the top twenty recipients*: OpenSecrets.org, Center for Responsive
Politics, "Oil & Gas: Top Recipients," 2020, https://www.opensecrets.org
/industries/recips.php?ind=E01&recipdetail=A&sortorder=U&mem=Y&cy
cle=2020, visited March 22, 2020.

160 *the "Kochtopus"*: Leonard, *Kochland*, 395.

160 *"The 'big three'"*: Graham Steele, "A Regulatory Green Light: How Dodd-
Frank Can Address Wall Street's Role in the Climate Crisis," Great Democracy Initiative, January 2020, https://greatdemocracyinitiative.org/document/
dodd-frank-and-the-climate-crisis/.

160 *"veritable innovation arm of the fossil fuel extraction industry"*: Brian Merchant, "How Google, Microsoft, and Big Tech Are Automating the Climate Crisis," Gizmodo, February 21, 2019, https://gizmodo.com/how-google-microsoft -and-big-tech-are-automating-the-1832790799.

160 *threatened to fire them*: Jay Greene, "Amazon Threatens to Fire Critics Who Are Outspoken on Its Environmental Policies," *Washington Post*, January 2, 2020, https://www.washingtonpost.com/technology/2020/01/02/amazon-threatens -fire-outspoken-employee-critics-its-environmental-policies/.

160 *"Empowering Oil and Gas with AI"*: Microsoft: "Microsoft Demonstrates the Power of AI and Cloud to Oil and Gas Players, at ADIPEC 2018," November 12, 2018, https://news.microsoft.com/en-xm/2018/11/12/micro soft-demonstrates-the-power-of-ai-and-cloud-to-oil-and-gas-players-at -adipec-2018/.

161 *spent $17 million*: InfluenceMap Report, "Big Oil's Real Agenda on Climate Change," 2019, https://influencemap.org/report/How-Big-Oil-Continues-to -Oppose-the-Paris-Agreement-38212275958aa21196dae3b76220bddc.

162 *"green growth"*: John Cassidy, "Can We Have Prosperity Without Growth?" *New Yorker*, February 3, 2020.

162 *quite literally, opioids*: Trevor Haynes, "Dopamine, Smartphones, & You: A Battle For Your Time," *Harvard*, May 1, 2018, http://sitn.hms.harvard.edu /flash/2018/dopamine-smartphones-battle-time/; Susan Weinschenk, "Why We're All Addicted to Texts, Twitter and Google," *Psychology Today*, Sept. 11, 2012, https://www.psychologytoday.com/us/blog/brain-wise/201209/why -were-all-addicted-texts-twitter-and-google.

163 *crops die when Dicamba blows over*: Boyce Uphold, "A Killing Season" *The New Republic*, December 10, 2018, https://newrepublic.com/article/152304 /murder-monsanto-chemical-herbicide-arkansas, and also see Dan Mitchell, "Why Monsanto Always Wins," *Fortune*, June 26, 2014, https://fortune .com/2014/06/26/monsanto-gmo-crops/.

163 *Monsanto has sued farmers*: "Farmers vs Monsanto," Food Democracy Now, https://www.fooddemocracynow.org/farmers-vs-monsanto.

164 *antitrust enforcers let it happen!*: "Justice Department Secures Largest Negoti- ated Merger Divestiture Ever to Preserve Competition Threatened by Bayer's Acquisition of Monsanto," justice.gov, May 29, 2018, https://www.justice.gov /opa/pr/justice-department-secures-largest-merger-divestiture-ever-preserve -competition-threatened.

164 *the National Family Farm coalition wrote*: "NFFC Requests DOJ Consider Monsanto-Bayer Approval," National Family Farm Coalition, August 15, 2018, https://nffc.net/nffc-requests-doj-reconsider-monsanto-bayer-approval/.

164 *algorithms to manipulate their farming*: Jason Davidson, "Bayer, Monsanto and

Big Data: Who Will Control Our Food System in the Era of Digital Agriculture and Mega-mergers?" Medium, March 20, 2018, https://medium.com/@foe_us/bayer-monsanto-and-big-data-who-will-control-our-food-system-in -the-era-of-digital-agriculture-aae80d991e4d.

164 *RoundUp,/has ended up*: Mike Barrett, "3 Studies Proving Toxic Glyphosate Found in Urine, Blood, and Even Breast Milk," Natural Society, May 4, 2014, https://naturalsociety.com/3-studies-proving-toxic-glyphosate-found-urine -blood-even-breast-milk/.

164 *Bayer-Monsanto agreed to pay*: Patricia Cohen, "Roundup Maker to Pay $10 Billion to Settle Cancer Suits," *New York Times*, June 24, 2020, https://www .nytimes.com/2020/06/24/business/roundup-settlement-lawsuits.html.

165 *every aspect of food supply has concentrated*: Claire Kelloway and Sarah Miller, "Food and Power: Addressing Monopolization in America's Food System," Open Markets Institute, https://openmarketsinstitute.org/wp-content/uploads /2019/05/190322_MonopolyFoodReport-v7.pdf.

165 *"Beginning in the 1980s"*: Claire Kelloway "Why Are Farmers Destroying Food While Grocery Stores Are Empty?" *Washington Monthly*, April 28, 2020, https://washingtonmonthly.com/2020/04/28/why-are-farmers-destroying -food-while-grocery-stores-are-empty/.

165 *"If you pull"*: Ibid.

165 *euthanizing their animals*: Tom Polansek and P. J. Huffstutter, "Piglets Aborted, Chickens Gassed as Pandemic Slams Meat Sector," Reuters, April 27, 2020, https://www.reuters.com/article/us-health-coronavirus-livestock-insight /piglets-aborted-chickens-gassed-as-pandemic-slams-meat-sector-idUSKC N2292YS.

166 *Union representatives told the BBC*: Jessica Lussenhop, "Coronavirus at Smith-field Pork Plant: The Untold Story of America's Biggest Outbreak," BBC News, April 17, 2020, https://www.bbc.com/news/world-us-canada-52311877.

166 *550 farms*: Ibid.

166 *nearly 17,000 cattle ranchers*: Claire Kelloway and Sarah Miller, "Food and Power: Addressing Monopolization in America's Food System," Open Markets Institute, https://openmarketsinstitute.org/wp-content/uploads/2019/05/190322 _MonopolyFoodReport-v7.pdf.

166 *As of June 2020*: Leah Nylen and Liz Crampton, "'Something Isn't Right': U.S. Probes Soaring Beef Prices," *Politico*, May 25, 2020, https://www.politico .com/news/2020/05/25/meatpackers-prices-coronavirus-antitrust-275093, and Brent Kendall and Jacob Bunge, "Chicken Industry Executives, Including Pilgrim's Pride CEO, Indicted on Price-Fixing Charges," *Wall Street Journal*, June 3, 2020, https://www.wsj.com/articles/chicken-industry-executives-in cluding-pilgrim-s-pride-ceo-indicted-for-price-fixing-11591202113.

166 *exporting rotten meat*: Kelloway and Miller, "Food and Power," and Drovers, "Billionaire Co-owner of JBS Gives Himself Up to Police in Brazil," September 11, 2017, https://www.drovers.com/article/billionaire-co-owner-jbs-gives -himself-police-brazil, and Tom Polsanek, "U.S. Bans Fresh Brazil Beef Imports Over Safety Concerns," *Reuters*, June 22, 2017, https://www.reuters.com /article/us-usa-brazil-beef-idUSKBN19D2VE.

166 *"Food markets"*: Joe Maxwell, panel, "Populism and Political Economy: Science and Regulations," *Capitol Forum*, Feb. 5, 2020, https://youtu.be/cclDU4SnPV4.

167 *out of every four poultry farmers*: Tom Philpott, "The Government's Own Watchdog Says Massive Poultry Companies Are Exploiting Small Business Loans," *Mother Jones*, March 16, 2018, https://www.motherjones.com /food/2018/03/government-watchdog-audit-poultry-small-business-loans -booker-trump-inspector-general-contract-chicken-farmer/.

167 *One point eight billion dollars*: James M. MacDonald, "Technology, Organization, and Financial Performance in U.S. Broiler Production," USDA, June 2014, https://www.ers.usda.gov/webdocs/publications/43869/48159_eib126.pdf ?v=41809.

167 *"confirm that farmers"*: "Farm Aid Statement on CDC Retraction of Farmer Suicide Statistics," Farm Aid, June 28, 2018, https://www.farmaid.org/press -release/farm-aid-statement-cdc-retracton-farmer-suicide-statistics/.

167 *ousted him from office*: Kaitlyn Riley, "Wisconsin State Senate Votes against Pfaff," *WIZM News*, November 5, 2019, https://www.wizmnews.com/2019/11/05 /wisconsin-state-senate-votes-against-pfaff/; Associated Press, "Senate Majority Leader Derides Wisconsin Agricultural Head," *U.S. News & World Report*, July 24, 2019, https://www.usnews.com/news/best-states/wisconsin/ar ticles/2019-07-24/senate-majority-leader-derides-wisconsin-agriculture-head.

168 *"The folks I"*: Patty Lovera, panel, "Populism and Political Economy: Science and Regulations," *Capitol Forum*, February 5, 2020, https://youtu.be/cclDU4SnPV4.

168 *Walmart has more than a 70 percent share*: Stacy Mitchell, "Report: Walmart's Monopolization of Local Grocery Markets," ILSR, June 26, 2019, https://ilsr .org/walmarts-monopolization-of-local-grocery-markets/.

169 *$113.9 billion from 1995 to 2019*: "Corn Subsidies," EWG, https://farm.ewg .org/progdetail.php?fips=00000&progcode=corn.

169 *bigger doesn't always mean better*: "K-State Ag Economists Rank State's Farms Based on 10 Years of KFMA Data," K-State, Oct. 10, 2019, https://www .ksre.k-state.edu/news/stories/2019/10/successful-kansas-farm-rankings.html.

170 *"exercise and"*: Avivia Shen, "How Big Food Corporations Watered Down Michelle Obama's 'Let's Move' Campaign," ThinkProgress, Feb. 28, 2013, https://thinkprogress.org/how-big-food-corporations-watered-down-michelle -obamas-let-s-move-campaign-85d09b60607b/.

170 *lobbied to a tune of $175 million*: Duff Wilson and Janet Robert, "Special Report: How Washington Went Soft on Childhood Obesity," Reuters, April 27, 2012, www.reuters.com/article/2012/04/27/us-usa-foodlobby-idUSBRE83Q0E D20120427.

170 *"a political force in Washington"*: Michael Pollen, "Big Food Strikes Back," *New York Times*, Oct, 5, 2016, https://www.nytimes.com/interactive/2016/10/09 /magazine/obama-administration-big-food-policy.html.

171 *"With the adoption"*: "The Green New Deal's Key to Success—FTC Commissioner Warns of Monopolists' Harm to Democracy, Civil Rights," *Corner Newsletter*, Open Markets Institute, Feb. 21, 2019, https://openmarketsinstitute .org/newsletters/corner-newsletter-february-21-2019-green-new-deals-key -success-ftc-commissioner-warns-monopolists-harm-democracy-civil-rights/.

172 *"Farmers"*: Joe Maxwell, panel, "Populism and Political Economy: Science and Regulations," *Capitol Forum*, Feb. 5, 2020, https://youtu.be/cclDU4SnPV4.

172 *"have a meaningful"*: Timothy A. Wise, "Big Ag Is Sabotaging Progress on Climate Change," *Wired*, Aug. 28, 2019, https://www.wired.com/story/big-ag-is -sabotaging-progress-on-climate-change/.

172 *"Agriculture"*: Nick Boisvert, "How Canadian Farmers Can Go from Climate Change Polluters to a Key Part of the Solution," CBC, Feb. 11, 2020, https://www.cbc.ca/news/canada/toronto/farmers-for-climate-solutions -launch-1.5458676.

172 *emissions for the next 100 years*: "Greenhouse Gasses and Agriculture," Government of Canada, http://www.agr.gc.ca/eng/agriculture-and-climate/agricul tural-practices/climate-change-and-agriculture/greenhouse-gases-and -agriculture/?id=1329321969842.

172 *"Because we're reducing"*: Boisvert, "How Canadian Farmers Can Go from Climate Change Polluters to a Key Part of the Solution."

173 *"The climate crisis"*: "Issues: The Green New Deal," https://berniesanders.com /en/issues/green-new-deal/.

Seven: Monopolies Ramp Up Inequality

174 *more than 4.7 million likes*: Erica Gonzales, "Kylie Jenner Shares a Video of One-Year-Old Stormi Carrying a Mini Hermès Bag with Travis Scott," *Harper's Bazaar*, April 1, 2019, https://www.harpersbazaar.com/celebrity/latest /a27007208/kylie-jenner-stormi-webster-hermes-purse/.

175 *can't pay an unexpected $400 expense*: "Report on the Economic Well-Being of Households in 2018," Federal Reserve, May 2019, https://www.federalre serve.gov/publications/files/2018-report-economic-well-being-us-households -201905.pdf.

176 *more wealth than 41 percent of all Americans*: "Inequality, Exhibit A: Walmart and

the Wealth of American Families," Economic Policy Institute, July 17, 2012, https://www.epi.org/blog/inequality-exhibit-wal-mart-wealth-american/; see also Barry Lynn, America's Monopoly Problem," Open Markets Institute, June 29, 2016, https://www.youtube.com/watch?time_continue=25&v=cabTM kyTDDU&feature=emb_logo.

176 *which were often below cost*: Stacy Mitchell, "Wal-Mart Charged with Predatory Pricing," ILSR, Nov. 1, 2000, https://ilsr.org/walmart-charged-predatory-pricing/.

176 *bringing in a cool $514 billion*: "Global 500," *Fortune*, 2018, https://fortune.com/global500/.

176 *$4 million richer every hour, $100 million richer every day*: Tom Metcalf, Andrew Heathcote, Pei Yi Mak, Sophie Alexander, Tom Maloney, Devon Pendleton, Venus Feng, Yoojung Lee, Blake Schmidt, Jack Witzig, and Steven Crabill, "The World's Richest Families Get $4 Million Richer Every Hour," Bloomberg, August 10, 2019, https://www.bloomberg.com/features/richest-families-in-the-world/.

177 *annual salary of his lowest-paid employee in 11.5 seconds*: Simone Stolzoff, "Jeff Bezos Will Still Make the Annual Salary of His Lowest-Paid Employees Every 11.5 Seconds," Quartz, Oct. 2, 2018, https://qz.com/work/1410621/jeff-bezos-makes-more-than-his-least-amazon-paid-worker-in-11-5-seconds/.

177 *2,327,131 times the median U.S. household income*:"#1 – Jeff Bezos," Bloomberg, https://www.bloomberg.com/billionaires/profiles/jeffrey-p-bezos/.

177 *billions of dollars in wealth transfer*: Lina Kahn and Sandeep Vaheesan, "Market Power and Inequality: The Antitrust Counterrevolution and Its Discontents," *Harvard Law & Policy Review* 235 (2017), SSRN, April 22, 2016 (revised Feb. 22, 2017), papers.ssrn.com/sol3/papers.cfm?abstract_id=2769132.

178 *C-suite executives and major corporate shareholders*: Ibid.

178 *400 Americans have more wealth than 150 million Americans do*: Christopher Ingraham, "Wealth Concentration Returning to Levels Last Seen During the Roaring Twenties According to New Research," *Washington Post*, Feb. 12, 2019, https://www.washingtonpost.com/us-policy/2019/02/08/wealth-concentration-returning-levels-last-seen-during-roaring-twenties-according-new-research/.

178 *the gap between the top 1 percent and top .1 percent is enormous*: Emmanuel Saez and Gabriel Zucman, "Wealth Inequality in the United States Since 1913: Evidence from Capitalized Income Tax Data," *Quarterly Journal of Economics* 131, no. 2 (May 2016): 519–78, http://gabriel-zucman.eu/files/SaezZucman2016QJE.pdf.

178 *from owning 7 percent of the country's total wealth to owning 22 percent*: Ibid.

179   *"focuses particularly on equality"*: Eleanor M. Fox, "Antitrust: Tracing Inequality—from the United States to South Africa," Competition Policy International, October 14, 2017, https://www.competitionpolicyinternational.com/antitrust -tracing-inequality-from-the-united-states-to-south-africa/.

180   *rise of antidemocratic leaders worldwide*: Staffan Lindberg, "Are Increasing Inequalities Threatening Democracy in Europe?" Carnegie Europe, Feb. 4, 2019, https://carnegieeurope.eu/2019/02/04/are-increasing-inequalities-threatening -democracy-in-europe-pub-78270.

180   *"The rapid retreat of dynamism"*: Economic Innovation Group, "Dynamism in Retreat: Consequences for Regions, Markets, and Workers," EIG, February 2017, https://eig.org/wp-content/uploads/2017/07/Dynamism-in-Retreat-A.pdf.

180   *almost 80 percent of start-up investment*: Ross Baird, *The Innovation Blind Spot: Why We Back the Wrong Ideas—and What to Do About It* (Dallas: BenBella Books, 2017), 10.

180   *only 15 percent of all venture capital*: Ibid., p. 15.

181   *"These platform monopolies"*: Aral Balkan, "We Didn't Lose Control—It Was Stolen," ar.al, March 12, 2017, https://ar.al/notes/we-didnt-lose-control-it -was-stolen/.

181   *"extreme asymmetries of knowledge"*: Shoshana Zuboff, "You Are Now Remotely Controlled," *New York Times*, Jan. 24, 2020, https://www.nytimes .com/2020/01/24/opinion/sunday/surveillance-capitalism.html.

183   *The American Dream is*: "The American Dream," *Wikipedia*, https://en.wiki pedia.org/wiki/American_Dream.

183   *amount to anticompetitive regulations*: Chris Pike, "What's Gender Got to Do with Competition Policy?" SSRN, Dec. 1, 2019, https://papers.ssrn.com/sol3 /papers.cfm?abstract_id=3487588.

183   *"Competition policy"*: Estefania Santacreu-Vasut and Chris Pike, "Competition Policy and Gender," OECD, Nov. 29, 2018, https://one.oecd.org/document /DAF/COMP/GF(2018)4/en/pdf.

184   *reducing the income of the poorest 20 percent*: Sean Ennis, Pedro Gonzaga, and Chris Pike, "Inequality: A Hidden Cost of Market Power," OECD, 2017, https://www .oecd.org/daf/competition/ Inequality-hidden-cost-market-power-2017.pdf.

184   *35 percent more likely*: "Women and Poverty in America," Legal Momentum, https://www.legalmomentum.org/women-and-poverty-america.

184   *twice that of white, non-Hispanic individuals*: "Unemployment and Poverty Disproportionately Affect African Americans—Making Combatting Hunger Even Harder," Feeding America, https://www.feedingamerica.org/hunger-in -america/african-american.

184   *"If the consumer economy had a sex, it would be female"*: Top 10 Things Everyone

Should Know about Women Consumers," Bloomberg, Jan. 11, 2018, https://
www.bloomberg.com/company/stories/top-10-things-everyone-know
-women-consumers/.

185 *78 cents to a white man's dollar*: Carmen Rios, "Here's What That '78 Cents to a
Man's Dollar' Wage Gap Statistic Really Means," Everyday Feminism, July 12,
2015, https://everydayfeminism.com/2015/07/what-78-cents-wage-gap-means.

185 *Black men*: Eileen Patten, "Racial, Gender Wage Gaps Persist in U.S. Despite
Some Progress," Pew Research Center, July 1, 2016, https://www.pewresearch
.org/fact-tank/2016/07/01/racial-gender-wage-gaps-persist-in-u-s-despite
-some-progress/.

185 *C-suite executives whose pay has skyrocketed*: Lina Kahn and Sandeep Vaheesan,
"Market Power and Inequality: The Antitrust Counterrevolution and Its Discontents," *Harvard Law & Policy Review* 235 (2017), SSRN, April 22, 2016
(revised Feb. 22, 2017), https://papers.ssrn.com/sol3/papers.cfm?abstract_id
=2769132.

185 *"Unless the causes"*: Francesca Rhodes, "Women and the 1%," Oxfam, April 11,
2016, https://www.oxfam.org/en/research/women-and-1.

185 *"Many spoke of"*: Marie Tae McDermott, "'I Was Blacklisted from Employment': Speaking Up in the Workplace," *New York Times*, https://www.nytimes
.com/2017/10/11/business/i-was-blacklisted-from-employment-speaking-up
-in-the-workplace.html.

185 *women who are harassed are 6.5 times*: Heather McLoughlin, Christopher
Uggen, and Amy Blackstone, "The Economic and Career Effects of Sexual
Harassment on Working Women," Sage Journals, May 10, 2007, https://jour
nals.sagepub.com/doi/abs/10.1177/0891243217704631?journalCode=gasa.

186 *in hostile work environments*: Sally Hubbard and Sandeep Vaheesan, "Noncompete Clauses Trap #MeToo Victims in Abusive Workplaces. The FTC Should
Ban Them," *USA Today*, May 14, 2018, https://www.usatoday.com/story/opinion
/2019/05/14/sexually-harassed-women-trapped-noncompetes-abusive-work
places-column/1184622001/.

186 *"We're now empowered to create our own damn tables"*: Sally Hubbard, "Felecia
Hatcher, Co-Founder of Code Fever and BlackTech Week, Works to Make
Startup Communities More Inclusive," Women Killing It, Feb 28, 2017, https://
womenkillingit.libsyn.com/ep-46-felicia-hatcher-co-founder-of-code-fever
-and-blacktech-week-works-to-make-startup-communities-more-inclusive.

187 *"She is able to have more control"*: Stephanie Sarkis, "Gender Inequality Led to
the Rise of Women Entrepreneurs," *Forbes*, March 5, 2019, https://www.forbes
.com/sites/stephaniesarkis/2019/03/05/gender-inequality-led-to-the-rise-of
-women-entrepreneurs.

187 *less than 1 percent*: Ross Baird, "Concrete Steps You Can Take Today to

Respond to Charlottesville," Medium, August 14, 2017, https://medium.com /village-capital/concrete-steps-you-can-take-today-to-respond-to-charlottes ville-ff6f74545598.

187 *have raised .0006 percent*: "The State of Black Women Founders," Project Diane, https://projectdiane.digitalundivided.com; Larry Jacob, "3 Trends That Prevent Entrepreneurs from Accessing Capital," Kauffman, July 25, 2018, https://www .kauffman.org/currents/2018/07/3-trends-that-prevent-entrepreneurs-from -accessing-capital.

187 *"That is the incredibly limited"*: Panel, "Innovation and Entrepreneurship in an Age of Concentrated Power," Open Markets Institute, Dec. 6, 2017, https:// www.youtube.com/watch?list=PL17VSnPfVKIjDjjK9yw6bQK49641bJ _Go&time_continue=8&v=bmYBv4Zbn2Y&feature=emb_logohttps://www .youtube.com/watch?list=PL17VSnPfVKIjDjjK9yw6bQK49641bJ_Go&time _continue=8&v=bmYBv4Zbn2Y&feature=emb_logo.

188 *decreased by about 70 percent*: Raphael Bostic and Michael Johnson, "How to Keep Community Banks Thriving," *American Banker*, January 15, 2020, https:// www.americanbanker.com/opinion/how-to-keep-community-banks-thriving.

188 *"you open up* Inc.*"*: Hubbard, "Felecia Hatcher, Co-Founder of Code Fever and BlackTech Week, Works To Make Startup Communities More Inclusive," Women Killing It, Feb. 28, 2017, https://womenkillingit.libsyn.com/ep-46 -felecia-hatcher-co-founder-of-code-fever-and-blacktech-week-works-to -make-startup-communities-more-inclusive.

189 *"want to solve my world problems"*: Ross Baird, *The Innovation Blind Spot: Why We Back the Wrong Ideas—and What to Do About It* (Dallas: BenBella Books, 2017), 8.

189 *sea of white men*: Janice Gassam, "Google's 2019 Diversity Report Reveals More Progress Must Be Made," *Forbes*, April 7, 2019, https://www.forbes.com/sites /janicegassam/2019/04/07/googles-2019-diversity-report-reveals-more-prog ress-must-be-made/#4d28e4c83bef.

190 *so the techno-libertarian thinking goes*: see Adam Theirer, "Does 'Permissionless Innovation' Even Mean Anything?" tech liberation, May 18, 2017, https://tech liberation.com/2017/05/18/does-permissionless-innovation-even-mean-any thing/.

190 *lead to women being raped and murdered*: Kate Conger, "Uber Says 3,045 Sexual Assaults Were Reported in U.S. Rides Last Year," *New York Times*, Dec. 5, 2019, https://www.nytimes.com/2019/12/05/technology/uber-sexual-assaults-mur ders-deaths-safety.html.

190 *begin sending a push notification*: Cathy Bussewitz, "Uber Rolls Out Feature Urging Riders to 'Check Your Ride,'" *Boston*, April 21, 2019, https://www.bos ton.com/cars/car-news/2019/04/21/uber-rolls-out-feature-urging-riders-to -check-your-ride.

190 *88.7 percent men*: Julia Carrie Wong, "Uber Diversity Report Paints Over-whelmingly White, Male Picture," *Guardian*, March 28, 2017, https://www.theguardian.com/technology/2017/mar/28/uber-diversity-report-white-male-women-minorities.

190 *a viral blog post*: Susan Fowler, "Reflecting on One Very Strange Year at Uber," Susan Fowler, Feb 19, 2017, https://www.susanjfowler.com/blog/2017/2/19/reflecting-on-one-very-strange-year-at-uber.

191 *Uber is fighting it*: Catherine Shu, "Judge Rejects Uber and Postmates' Request for an Injunction Against California's Gig Worker Law," tech-crunch, Feb 10, 2020, https://techcrunch.com/2020/02/10/judge-rejects-uber-and-postmates-request-for-an-injunction-against-californias-gig-worker-law/.

191 *"tech fixes"*: Ibid., p. 160.

191 *"The New Jim Code"*: Ruha Benjamin, *Race After Technology: Abolitionist Tools for the New Jim Code* (Cambridge: Polity Press, 2019), 8.

191 *"people like to think of algorithms as outside"*: The Open Mind, "Death By Algorithm," PBS, September 10, 2016, https://www.pbs.org/video/open-mind-death-algorithm/, and see Cathy O'Neil, *Weapons of Math Destruction: How Big Data Increases Inequality and Threatens Democracy* (New York: Broadway Books, 2017).

191 *Each of the four tech giants*: Jamie Condliffe, "This Week In Tech: Algorithmic Bias Is Bad. Uncovering It Is Good," *New York Times*, November 15, 2019, https://www.nytimes.com/2019/11/15/technology/algorithmic-ai-bias.html, and Joy Buolamwini, "Artificial Intelligence Has a Problem With Gender and Racial Bias. Here's How to Solve It," *TIME*, Feb. 7, 2019, https://time.com/5520558/artificial-intelligence-racial-gender-bias/.

192 *discriminatory by age and gender*: Marie C. Baca, "Housing Companies Used Facebooks Ad System to Discriminate Against Older People, According to New Human Right Charges," *Washington Post*, Sept. 18, 2019, https://www.washingtonpost.com/technology/2019/09/18/housing-companies-used-facebooks-ad-system-discriminate-against-older-people-according-new-human-rights-charges/; Ava Kofman and Ariana Tobin, "Facebook Ads Can Still Discriminate Against Women and Older Workers, Despite a Civil Rights Settlement," ProPublica, Dec. 13, 2019, https://www.propublica.org/article/facebook-ads-can-still-discriminate-against-women-and-older-workers-despite-a-civil-rights-settlement.

192 *"from policing"*: Benjamin, *Race After Technology*, p. 81.

192 *"the allure of accuracy"*: Ibid., pp. 82–83.

192 *"and the potential"*: About Queer in AI," Queer in AI, https://sites.google.com/view/queer-in-ai/about.

HOW TO STOP MONOPOLIES

Eight: How to Take Back Control

198   *the solution isn't antitrust, it's blockchain*: Don Tapscott, "We're Living in an Era of
       Digital Feudalism. Here's How to Take Your Data and Identity Back," Quartz,
       Sept. 11, 2019, https://qz.com/1706221/don-tapscott-on-using-blockchain-to
       -take-back-your-digital-identity/.

198   *cutting off competitors under the guise of protecting privacy*: House of Commons
       Digital, Culture, Media and Sport Committee, UK Parliament, "Disinforma-
       tion and 'Fake News': Final Report," Feb. 14, 2019, https://publications.parlia
       ment.uk/pa/cm201719/cmselect/cmcumeds/1791/1791.pdf.

199   *The gutting of anti-monopoly policy*: Sam Peltzman, "Industrial Concentration
       under the Rule of Reason," *Journal of Law & Economics* 57 (2014), S101–S120
       (increase in concentration in manufacturing); "Corporation Concentration: The
       Creep of Consolidation Across America's Corporate Landscape," https://www
       .economist.com/blogs/graphicdetail/2016/03/daily-chart-13, March 24, 2016.

199   *cartoon shows Standard Oil as an octopus*: Keppler, Udo, J. *Puck* (N.Y. J. Ottmann
       Lith. Co., Puck Bldg, September 7, 1904), Library of Congress, https://www.loc
       .gov/pictures/item/2001695241

200   *The 1889 Bosses of the Senate cartoon*: Keppler, Udo, J. *Puck* (N.Y. J. Ottmann
       Lith. Co., Puck Bldg, 1889), Library of Congress, https://www.loc.gov/pictures/re
       source/cph.3b52004/.

201   "*The little boy [Common People] and the big boys [Trusts] prepare for the baseball sea-
       son*": Opper, Frederick, 1901, Library of Congress, https://www.loc.gov/pictures
       /item/2005685051/.

202   "*The tournament of today—a set-to between labor and monopoly*": Graetz, F. (N.Y. J.
       Ottmann Lith. Co., Puck Bldg, August, 1883), Library of Congress, https://www
       .loc.gov/pictures/item/2012645501/.

202   "*Our Uncrowned Kings*": Ehrhard, Samuel D. (N.Y. J. Ottmann Lith. Co., Puck
       Bldg, September 7, 1904), Library of Congress, https://www.loc.gov/pictures
       /item/2011645513/.

205   "*politically-engaged trade associations*": "Trade Associations and Membership
       Organizations," Google, https://services.google.com/fh/files/misc/trade_as
       sociation_and_third_party_groups.pdf; "Transparency," Google, https://www
       .google.com/publicpolicy/transparency/.

205   "*employed a Republican opposition-research firm*": Sheera Frenkel, Nicholas Con-
       fessore, Cecilia Kang, Matthew Rosenberg, and Jack Nicas, "Delay, Deny and
       Deflect: How Facebook's Leaders Fought Through Crisis," *New York Times*,
       November 14, 2018, https://www.nytimes.com/2018/11/14/technology/face
       book-data-russia-election-racism.html.

206 *current understandings of corporate law*: See, e.g., Andrea M. Matwyshyn, "Imagining the Intangible," *Delaware Journal of Corporate Law* 34, no. 3 (2009), available at https://ssrn.com/abstract=1503091.

207 *"I haven't heard from either"*: Nicholas Thompson, "Tim Wu Explains Why He Thinks Facebook Should Be Broken Up," *Wired,* July 4, 2019, https://www.wired.com/story/tim-wu-explains-why-facebook-broken-up/.

207 *"About 30%"*: Robert Reich, "American Firms Aren't Beholden to America—but That's News to Trump," *Guardian,* Jan. 11, 2020, https://www.theguardian.com/commentisfree/2020/jan/11/us-china-trump-agreement-tesla-investment.

208 *more than $9 billion*: Charles Riley and Ivana Kottasová, "Europe Hits Google with a Third, $1.7 Billion Antitrust Fine," CNN, March 3, 2019, https://www.cnn.com/2019/03/20/tech/google-eu-antitrust/index.html.

210 *filed sixty-two Sherman*: U.S. Department of Justice, "Antitrust Division Workload Statistics, FY 2008–2017," justice.gov, https://www.justice.gov/atr/file/788426/download; U.S. Department of Justice, "Antitrust Division Workload Statistics, FY 1970–1979," justice.gov, 2015, https://www.justice.gov/atr/antitrust-division-workload-statistics-fy-1970-1979.

211 *"that contravene the spirit of the antitrust laws"*: Federal Trade Commission, "Statement of Enforcement Principles Regarding 'Unfair Methods of Competition' Under Section 5 of the FTC Act," August 13, 2015, https://www.ftc.gov/system/files/documents/public_statements/735201/150813section5enforcement.pdf.

211 *fix bad court decisions*: see, e.g., *Brooke Group Ltd. v. Brown & Williamson Tobacco Corp.*, 509 U.S. 209 (1993); *Matsushita Electric Industrial Co. v. Zenith Radio Corp.*, 475 U.S. 574 (1986); *Weyerhaeuser Co. v. Ross-Simmons Hardwood Lumber Co.*, 549 U.S. 312 (2007); *Verizon Communications Inc. v. Law Offices of Curtis V. Trinko, LLP,* 540 U.S. 398 (2004); *Pacific Bell Telephone Co. v. LinkLine Communications, Inc.*, 555 U.S. 438 (2009); *Ohio v. American Express Co.*, 138 S. Ct. 2274 (2018); *Spectrum Sports, Inc. v. McQuillan*, 506 U.S. 447, 459 (1993); *Associated Gen. Contractors v. California State Council of Carpenters*, 459 U.S. 519 (1983); *Comcast v. Behrend*, 569 U.S. 27 (2013); *Bell Atlantic Corp. v. Twombly*, 550 U.S. 544 (2007).

212 *the FTC spent nearly $16 million*: "Oversight of the Enforcement of the Antitrust Laws: Before the Subcomm. on Antitrust, Competition Policy and Consumer Rights of the S. Comm. on the Judiciary, 116th Cong.," FTC, 2019, https://www.ftc.gov/system/files/documents/public_statements/1544480/senate_september_competition_oversight_testimony.pdf. See also Bureau of Economics, "Fed. Trade Comm'n," FTC, last visited April 14, 2020, https://www.ftc.gov/about-ftc/bureaus-offices/bureau-economics. Note, the FTC does also enforce consumer protection law so some of these fees may not have been antitrust-related.

213 *prohibit platforms*: Elizabeth Warren, "It's Time to Break Up Amazon, Google,

and Facebook," Medium, March 8, 2019, https://medium.com/@teamwarren
/heres-how-we-can-break-up-big-tech-9ad9e0da324c; Lina Khan, "The Separation of Platforms and Commerce," *Columbia Law Review* 119, no. 973 (May
28, 2019), SSRN, https://ssrn.com/abstract=3180174.

213 *this structural solution has been done before*: Ibid.

214 *"it was the right decision to make"*: Sally Hubbard, "Serial Entrepreneur Jillian
Wright Lifts Up Other Women Entrepreneurs with the Indie Beauty Expo,"
Women Killing It, December 20, 2017, https://womenkillingit.libsyn.com
/ep-84-serial-entrepreneur-jillian-wright-lifts-up-other-women-entrepre
neurs-with-the-indie-beauty-expo.

214 *Facebook had identified WhatsApp*: "Note by Damian Collins, MP," UK Parliament, https://www.parliament.uk/documents/commons-committees/culture
-media-and-sport/Note-by-Chair-and-selected-documents-ordered-from
-Six4Three.pdf.

215 *drive up prices anywhere from 15 to 50 percent*: Bruce A. Blonigen and Justin R.
Pierce, "Mergers May Be Profitable, but Are They Good for the Economy?"
Harvard Business Review, Nov. 15, 2016, https://hbr.org/2016/11/mergers
-may-be-profitable-but-are-they-good-for-the-economy.

215 *that vertical mergers invariably promote*: Steven C. Salop, "Invigorating Vertical
Merger Enforcement," *Yale Law Journal 1962-1994* 127 (2018), https://schol
arship.law.georgetown.edu/facpub/2002

215 *"is likely to result in reduced"*: U.S. v. Google and ITA, Case 1:11-cv-00688, justice
.gov, https://www.justice.gov/atr/case-document/file/497686/download.

216 *Senator Amy Klobuchar has proposed a bill*: News release, "In Effort to Lower
Costs for Consumers, Help Even Playing Field for Business, and Encourage
Innovation—Klobuchar, Senators Introduce Legislation to Promote Competition," September 14, 2017, https://www.klobuchar.senate.gov/public/index
.cfm/2017/9/in-effort-to-lower-costs-for-consumers-help-even-playing-field
-for-business-and-encourage-innovation-klobuchar-senators-introduce-legis
lation-to-promote-competition.

216 *a major course correction is needed*: Robert H. Lande and Sandeep Vaheesan,
"Preventing the Curse of Bigness Through Conglomerate Merger Legislation," SSRN, Oct. 4, 2019, https://papers.ssrn.com/sol3/papers.cfm?abstract
_id=3463878; Sandeep Vaheesan, "Two-and-a-Half Cheers for 1960s Merger
Policy," *Harvard Law*, Dec. 12, 2019, https://orgs.law.harvard.edu/antitrust
/2019/12/12/two-and-a-half-cheers-for-1960s-merger-policy/; "1968 Merger
Guidelines." Justice.gov, https://www.justice.gov/archives/atr/1968-merger
-guidelines.

217 *"attention shares"*: Media Subcommittee, Digital Platforms Project, "How to
Protect the News Media in the Age of Digital Platforms," Pro Market, May

10, 2019, https://promarket.org/how-to-protect-the-news-media-in-the-age -of-digital-platforms/.

217 *$330 million on federal lobbying since 2008*: Frank Bass, "As U.S. Regulators Step Up Antitrust Scrutiny, Big Tech Has Increased Lobbying Bandwidth," MapLight, Sept. 5, 2019, https://maplight.org/story/as-u-s-regulators-step -up-antitrust-scrutiny-big-tech-has-increased-lobbying-bandwidth/.

218 *99 percent of the global market*: Kate Sprague, "Why the Airbus-Boeing Duopoly Dominate 99% of the Large Plane Market," CNBC, Jan. 26, 2019, https:// www.cnbc.com/2019/01/25/why-the-airbus-boeing-companies-dominate -99percent-of-the-large-plane-market.html.

218 *$285 million in lobbying since 1998*: "Top Spenders," OpenSecrets, https://www .opensecrets.org/federal-lobbying/top-spenders?cycle=a.

218 *Boeing used its political*: Kathryn A. Wolfe and Brianna Gurciullo, "How the FAA Delegated Oversight to Boeing," *Politico*, March 21, 2019, https://www .politico.com/story/2019/03/21/congress-faa-boeing-oversight-1287902.

218 *Boeing spent more than*: Philip van Doorn, "Opinion: Airlines and Boeing Want a Bailout—but Look How Much They've Spent on Stock Buybacks," *Market Watch*, March 22, 2020, https://www.marketwatch.com/story/airlines -and-boeing-want-a-bailout-but-look-how-much-theyve-spent-on-stock -buybacks-2020-03-18; Aaron Gregg, Jeff Stein, and Josh Dawsey, "Senate Aid Package Quietly Carves Out Billions Intended for Boeing, Officials Say," *Washington Post*, March 25, 2020, https://www.washingtonpost.com/business /2020/03/25/boeing-bailout-coronavirus/.

219 *"technological tools"*: News release, "A Letter from Alastair Mactaggart, Board Chair and Founder of Californians for Consumer Privacy," Californians for Consumer Privacy, September 25, 2019, https://www.caprivacy.org/a-letter-from-alastair -mactaggart-board-chair-and-founder-of-californians-for-consumer-privacy/.

219 *opting out takes seventeen clicks*: "Privolta Consent Study: Google," August 16, 2019, https://www.youtube.com/watch?v=y3xibDW-pVw.

219 *Forty percent of people abandon*: Neil Patel, "How Loading Time Affects Your Bottom Line," https://neilpatel.com/blog/loading-time/.

220 *"Data protection"*: Chris Wylie, "Written Statement to the United States Senate Committee on the Judiciary In the Matter of Cambridge Analytica and Other Related Issues," para. 67, https://www.judiciary.senate.gov/imo/media/doc/05 -16-18%20Wylie%20Testimony.pdf.

220 *"the U.S. can"*: David Dayen, "Ban Targeted Advertising," *New Republic*, April 10, 2018, https://newrepublic.com/article/147887/ban-targeted-advertising -facebook-google; see also Gilad Edelman, "Why Don't We Just Ban Targeted Advertising?" *Wired*, March 22, 2018, https://www.wired.com/story/why -dont-we-just-ban-targeted-advertising/; Ellen L. Weintraub, "Don't Abolish

Political Ads on Social Media. Stop Microtargeting," *Washington Post*, Nov. 1, 2019, https://www.washingtonpost.com/opinions/2019/11/01/dont-abolish -political-ads-social-media-stop-microtargeting/.

220 *"Yes, I give permission":* Written Testimony of David Heinemeier Hansson CTO & Cofounder, Basecamp," justice.gov, Jan. 17, 2020, https://docs.house.gov /meetings/JU/JU05/20200117/110386/HHRG-116-JU05-Wstate-Hansson D-20200117.pdf.

221 *"Anything made":* Shoshana Zuboff, "You Are Now Remotely Controlled," *New York Times*, Jan. 24, 2020, https://www.nytimes.com/2020/01/24/opinion/sun day/surveillance-capitalism.html.

222 *required nondiscrimination policies:* Open Markets Institute Discussion Paper, "America's Free Press and Monopoly: The Historical Role of Competition Policy in Protecting Independent Journalism in America," June 2018, https:// openmarketsinstitute.org/reports/americas-free-press-monopoly/.

223 *tech companies:* Oral testimony of Tristan Harris, House Committee on Energy and Commerce, Hearing on "Americans At Risk: Manipulation and Decep- tion in the Digital Age," January 8, 2020, https://energycommerce.house.gov /committee-activity/hearings/hearing-on-americans-at-risk-manipulation -and-deception-in-the-digital.

223 *for a wide range of illegal behavior:* "Artist Rights Alliance Opposes Export- ing Safe Harbors in Trade Deals," Medium, Oct. 29, 2019, https://medium .com/@artistrightsnow/artist-rights-alliance-opposes-exporting-safe-harbors -in-trade-deals-befc5fa3976d.

INDEX

Page numbers beginning with 231 refer to notes. Page numbers in *italics* refer to graphs and drawings.

AB InBev, 24
ableism, 193
abolitionist movement, 193
Abu Dhabi, 160
acquisitions, *see* mergers and acquisitions
Acthar, 47, 49
Acton, Brian, 214
"Add to Cart" button, 94
Admob, 60, 91
advertising:
　digital, 78–79, 90–91, 93, 106, 107, 111,
　　121, 123–24, 145–51, 219–21
　on Facebook, 102
　false, 81
　Google's revenue from, 86
　political, 139–40
　targeted, *see* targeted advertising
AIDS, 43, 80–81
Airbus, 219
airlines, 32
　expenses of, 17–20
Alexa, 94, 105, 107, 110, 113, 132
algorithmic bias, 191–93
algorithms, 101–2, 118, 125, 135, 137,
　142
　discrimination fostered by, 191–93,
　　223
　disinformation in, 140
　in engagement, 128, 140, 142
　Facebook's modification of, 147, 151
　inferences drawn from, 129
　recommendation, 128
allergies, 37–38
Alter, Liz, 225–26
alt-right, 135–36

Amazon, 3, 23, 27, 33, 60–62, 77, 79, 83, 85,
　98, 103, 105, 119, 138, 146, 169, 177,
　187, 204, 217
　anti-union policy of, 72–73
　Bezos's expanding empire of, 91–96
　boycotting by, 205
　in climate change, 160
　COVID-19 response of, 72–73
　HQ2 search by, 29–31
　investigations into, 96
　laws imposed by, 224
　limited data center employment
　　opportunities of, 31
　monopoly power of, 60, 91–96
　platform privilege of, 118
　price control by, 62
　prioritizing of winners and losers by,
　　222
　private labeling by, 96–97
　products knocked off by, 95
　as profiting from food stamp program, 31
　spying by, 110, 112
　tax breaks for, 28–31
　third-party sellers in, 28–29
"AmazonBasics," 92
Amazon.com, 92–93
Amazon marketplace, 224
Amazon Prime, 62, 91, 119–20, 203, 205
Amazon Retail, 261
"Amazon's Antitrust Paradox" (Khan), 97
Amazon Web Services (AWS), 92, 95–96,
　98, 160
Amazon/Whole Foods merger, 119–20
American Airlines/US Airways merger,
　19–20, 70, 74–75

American dream, 92, 207
  defined, 84
  equal opportunity in, 182–83
  monopolies as threat to, 80–104, 224–25
American Economic Liberties Project, 204
Anderson, Gerard F., 50
Android, 60, 107
"Android Administration, The" (Dayen), 89
Angwin, Julia, 107–8
animal welfare, 165
anticommunist hysteria, 111–12
anticompetitive practices, 3–5, 9–10, 11–12, 13–14, 208, 209, 211
  by airlines, 18–20
  by Amazon, 120
  by Apple, 99–101
  by Big Tech, 55–63, 213–14
  creativity squelched by, 77
  digital, 90–91
  in drug industry, 43–49
  employee benefits limited by, 72–74
  extraction as, 177–78
  by Facebook, 101, 118–19, 142
  by Google, 86–90
  government responsibility in, 114–15
  in health care, 34–37
  in hospitals, 40–41
  illusion of choice in, 23–24
  innovation stymied by, 80–83
  in internet access, 21–23
  legislative payoffs in, 50–51
  low pricing in, 97–98
  mergers as, 18–20, 71, 214–16
  privacy compromised by, 114–16
  in salary control, 67–68, 74–76
  toward suppliers, 69
anti-corruption legislation, 217–18
anti-monopolists:
  author's credentials and commitment as, 6–7, 28, 41, 43–45, 59–60, 96, 117, 198, 210
  in betterment of society, 197
  boycotting in, 205
  historical perspective of, 3, 5–6, 198–203
  specious arguments against, 206–7
anti-monopoly laws:
  dismantling of, 4–5
  weak enforcement of, 61
anti-monopoly movement, 203–6
antitrust:
  author's credentials for and commitment to, 182–83
  gender equity and, 182–86
  mini-lesson on, 8–14
  use of term, 201

"Antitrust Case Against Facebook, The" (Srinivasan), 115–16
antitrust laws, 6, 8–11, 35, 44, 55, 59–63, 71, 84, 97, 182, 205, 219
  Chicago School interpretation of, 177, 209–10
  consumerism and, 162
  effective enforcement of, 83–84, 85, 98, 104, 114, 132–33, 178–79, 197–203, 208, 209
  enforcement strategies for, 79–80
  equality of opportunity in, 179, 183
  fixes for, 209–13
  historical perspective of, 13–14
  local enforcement of, 114–15, 119
  monopoly power in, 95
  pricing and, 12–13
  procedural barriers to, 212
  state enforcement of, 10, 212–13
  weak enforcement of, 11–14, 47, 59, 75–76, 81, 97, 116, 164–65, 178–79, 209–11
AOL, 56
Apple, 24–25, 60, 63, 74, 75, 83, 85, 87, 103, 105, 146, 217
  monopoly power of, 99–101
  prioritizing of winners and losers in, 222
  sherlocking by, 98–101
AppleInsider, 100
Apple Music, 78, 99
Apple tax, 25, 99, 101
Apple v. Pepper, 24, 100
Apple Watches, 87
Applied Semantics, 60
AppNexus, 90
apps, platform privilege in, 99
App Store, 100, 222
artificial intelligence (AI), 160–61, 192, 221
Artist Rights Alliance, 204
"astro-turfing," 205
AT&T, 22, 221
  breakup of monopoly of, 25, 102–4, 198, 202, 207, 211
Athena, 204
Atlanta Journal-Constitution (AJC), 149
Atlantic, 128
"attention shares," 217
Au Bon Pain, 23
Australian, The, 137–38
Auvi-Q, 48
Aventis Pharmaceuticals, 47
AWS cloud computing business, 98

Baer, Bill, 19–20
Baird, Ross, 187
bait and switch, 102

Balkan, Aral, 181
bankers, wealth of, 178
Bannon, Steve, 135
Barnett, David, 93
Basecamp, 88–89, 220
BASF, 163
batteries, 92
Bayer/Monsanto merger, 163–64, 171–72
Becton, Dickinson and Co., lawsuits against, 80–82
Beef Trust, 208
Ben & Jerry's, 24
Benjamin, Ruha, 191, 192
Berkeley Business Law Journal, 116
Berlin Wall, fall of, 108
beverage brands, 24
Bezos, Jeff, 29–30
    Amazon empire of, 91–96
    salary of, 177
    wealth of, 73
Big Ag, 161, 169, 173
    in environmental destruction, 170–72
    growth of, 164–65
Big Finance, in climate change, 160–61
Big Food:
    health, quality, and safety issues in, 166–67, 170–71
    monopoly power in, 163–69
"Big Food Strikes Back" (Pollan), 170
Big News, 130–32
Big Oil, 154–55, 159–62, 173
    Facebook involvement with, 161
    government subsidies for, 159, 173
Big Pharma:
    anticompetitive practices in, 43–49, 212
    and drug shortages, 44, 48–49, 165
Big Tech, 3, 11, 18, 24–26, 103, 132–33, 155, 160, 182, 198, 209, 213, 218
    acquisitions by, 60–61
    algorithmic bias in, 191–93
    anticompetitive practices of, 213–14
    in climate change, 160–61
    consumers as free labor for, 26
    dynamism squelched by, 83
    entrepreneurship and innovation controlled and limited by, 85–86, 187–88
    fixes for monopolies in, 208–9
    illegal violations of, 223–24
    interoperability in, 221
    mergers in, 215
    monopoly power of, 176–77, 180–81
    nonrecruitment collusion in, 74–76
    people vs., 55–63
    privacy-protecting start-ups locked out by, 117–18

privacy violations of, 117–18
proposed breakup of, 139, 211
spying and manipulation by, 105–33
start-ups in, 190
see also specific tech companies
blacklisting, 111–12, 186
Black Lives Matter movement, 5, 111–12
BlackRock, 160
Black Tech Week, 186
Bloomberg, 177, 184
Bloomberg, 90
Blumenthal, Richard, 62
Bodnar, Andrew, prosecution of, 45–46
body-shaming, 128
Boeing, 218
Bolsonaro, Jair, 142
border wall, 179
Bork, Robert, 12
Bosses of the Senate (cartoon), 200, *200*
boycotting, 205
BP, 159, 161
Brandeis, Louis, 140, 262
brand partnerships, 77
Brave browser, 117, 133
Brazil, 142
Brexit vote, 138
Bristol-Meyers Squibb (BMS), prosecution of, 44–46
Bristol-Meyers Squibb (BMS)/Celgene merger, 44–46
broadband providers, 21–22
bundling, 212
Bureau of Labor, 72
Burt's Bees, 24
Bush (G.W.) administration, 51, 170
"buy box," 94
buyer power (monopsony), 67–68, 100–101

Cadwalladr, Carole, 136
California, privacy laws in, 121–22, 149–50, 219
California, University of, Berkeley's Petris Center on Health Care Markets and Consumer Welfare, 40
Californians for Consumer Privacy Act (CCPA), 219
Cambridge Analytica, 116, 220
    Facebook scandal of, 135–38
campaign finance reform, 32, 218
Campaign for Family Farms, 168
cancer, Roundup as cause of, 164
Candle, 118
Capitol Forum, 167, 168
carbon emissions, 159
    in farming, 172
Cargill, 166

car safety, 218, 220
"category captain," 168
CBC News, 172
Celgene, 44–46
Center for Humane Technology, 126, 223
Center for Public Integrity, 48
Center for Responsive Politics, 50–51, 218
Centers for Disease Control (CDC), 31–32
CEOs, wealth of, 66, 178
Cerberus, 39
charitable donations, self-interest in, 27, 28
Chevron, 159, 161
Chicago, University of, 12
Chicago School of Economics, 12–13, 18,
        35, 37, 44, 70–71, 81, 85, 89, 97, 177,
        178, 184, 212, 215
    ideology of, 209–10
children:
    Big Food vs., 170–71
    online addiction of, 223
    social media as threat to, 127–28
China, 109
    in Smithfield ownership, 166
    U.S. competition with, 206
    Walmart's fake joint venture with, 31
Chisholm, Shirley, 186
Chopra, Rohit, 44, 46, 74, 123
Chop Suey Books, 29
Cicilline, David, 211
Citibank, 156
citizenry:
    in accomplishing the impossible, 224–26
    activism by, 14, 30, 32–33, 36, 51, 52–54,
        59, 103–4, 107, 110, 112, 115, 123, 130,
        132–33, 143, 150–52, 162–63, 169–70,
        173, 182, 193–94, 197–226
    anti-monopoly mobilization power of,
        203–6
    bipartisan participation of, 224
    political involvement of, 218
    power of, 5–6
    spying as threat to, 108–13
    youthful activists in, 153–56
Citizens United case, 27
"citizen welfare," consumer welfare vs., 217
civil rights law, 192
class-action lawsuits, 10, 75
Clayton Act (1914), 9, 11, 19, 41, 199, 211,
        214
    Section 7 of, 60, 91, 120
climate change, 112–13, 154–57, 160–61
    challenge and opportunity of, 172–73
    disasters of, 156
    and economic growth, 158–59
    profit-maximizing in, 156–59
Clinton, Hillary, 43, 131, 156

Clorox, 24
cloud storage, 92, 95–96, 110
Coca-Cola, 169
Code Fever, 186–87
Colgate-Palmolive, 24
college debts, 175
collusion:
    in employment, 74–76
    mergers and, 19–20
Comcast, 21, 131, 222
commission, 100
Communications Decency Act, Section 230
        of, 145–46, 223–24
community banks, decline of, 188
competition, constraints on, see
        anticompetitive practices
complication paralysis, 206
concentrated funding, 188–89
concentrated power, 161, 212, 217
    in climate change, 157–58
    crises of, 197–98
Congress, U.S., 220
    in limiting monopoly power, 211–12, 216
"consideration data," 97
consumerism, 162
    community action in, 163
    cult of, 162–63
    in environmental destruction, 162–63
    expenses of, 18
    two economic models in, 162
consumers:
    class action lawsuits by, 10
    effect of mergers on, 71–72
    women as, 184
consumer welfare, 12, 71, 162, 216–17
"consumer welfare standard," 184
copyright laws, 78–79, 223
Corner Newsletter, 171
corn subsidies, 169
Coronavirus Aid, Relief, and Economic
        Security (CARES) Act, 32, 39
corporate accounting frauds, 6
corporate bribery, 30
corporate efficiency, 12–13, 37, 41
    job loss and, 70–71
corporate giants, power concentrated in,
        3–5, 9–10, 11–12, 13–14
corporate incentives, 29–30
"corporate inversion," 37
corporate law, profiteering from, 38
corporate profit margin, 65
corporate tax breaks, 26–28, 29–32
corporations, stock buy-backs by, 32
corruption, political and corporate, 217–18
Corteva, 163
counterfeiting, 261

counterfeits, 93
counterspeech doctrine, 140–41
COVID-19 pandemic, 5, 21, 27, 31, 49, 91, 179–80
    bailout funds for, 115, 218
    corporate profits from, 32
    disinformation about, 137
    economic damage of, 1–2, 69, 104, 158, 175
    food supply chain crisis in, 165–66, 169
    government bailouts for, 69
    health care and medical shortages in, 34–37, 39, 53
    health care workers in, 53
    health care workers salaries in, 68
    in layoffs, 145
    political and media involvement in, 131–32
    reopening in, 149
    workforce risks of, 72–73
Covidien mergers, 36–37
Craigslist, advertising on, 145
creative sector, 76–80
criminal justice system, racism and discrimination in, 192
cryptocurrency, 198
culture war, 140
    online, 135

Daily Show, The (TV show), 115
Daraprim, 43, 49
"dark patterns," 79
Darrow, Charles, 193
data control, by Amazon, 96–97
data extraction, 181
data inferences, 129
data mining, 96
data portability, 222
data tracking, 25–26, 63, 78, 148, 219, 274
    in advertising, 93
    covert, 61
    by government, 110–11
    discriminatory bias in, 110
    economic inequality and, 180–82
    monopoly power supported by, 118–20
    online quizzes in, 136
    opting out of, 219–20
    for political manipulation, 135–38
    profits from, 116–17, 122
    spying through, 106–23
    US government use of, 111–13
DaVita, 42
Dayen, David, 89, 220
D.C. Circuit Court of Appeals, 6–7
decentralization of power, 198
deconcentration, 199

deductibles, in health insurance, 39
default bias, 99, 117
    defined, 87
"default morals," 192
Defense Advanced Research Projects Agency (DARPA), 136
Delrahim, Makan, 22
Del Rey, Jason, 110
Delta Air Lines, 27
Demand Progress, 204
democracy:
    Big Tech as threat to, 190–93
    economic threat to, 175
    global monopolies as threat to, 180
    monopoly power as threat to, 134–52
    surveillance threats to, 221, 224–25
    value of press in, 144
Democratic Party, 131
Demos, 204
depression, 127
detergent brands, 23
dialysis, 42
Diapers.com, 98
Dicamba, 163
digital advertising, 78–79, 90–91, 93, 106, 107, 121, 123–24, 145–51, 219–21
Digital Content Next, 145
digital expenses, 18, 21–23, 25–26
"digital labor," 26
digital media, privacy-protecting options for, 133
disabled people, 193
discrimination, 191, 192
    in Big Tech algorithms, 191–93, 223
"discriminatory refusal to deal," 119
Dish, 22
disinformation, 135–36, 139–41, 150–51
doctors' groups, bought by hospitals, 41
Dominion Voting Systems, 143
DoubleClick, 60, 90–91
Douglass, Frederick, 5
Dow-Dupont, 163
Dragnet Nation (Angwin), 107–8
drug industry, see Big Pharma
DuckDuckGo, 117–18, 133, 206
Duke University, Fuqua School of Business at, 42
duopolies, 14, 18, 42, 67, 177
dynamism, 83–85, 84, 180

Earthjustice, 163
East Germany, 108
Easton, 39–40
Eating Tomorrow (Wise), 172
echo chambers, 140
Echo Show, 95

economic dynamism, decline of, 83–85, *84*
economic expansion, 180
economic gap, 177–78
economic inequality, 1–3, 174–94
    author's opposition to, 7
    geographic factors in, 180
    historical perspective on, 8–9
    political instability and, 179–80
    scapegoats as victims of, 2–3
Economic Innovation Group, 180
Economic Policy Institute, 65
efficiency principle, 37, 41, 169, 215, 233
elections, British, of 2019, 134–35
elections, influence of monopoly power on, 134–52
elections, U.S., of 2016, 63, 131, 134–38, 180
    Facebook's influence on, 116
    monopoly power as threat to, 143–44
elections, U.S., of 2020, 142–43, 219
    Democratic primary in, 134–35
Election Systems & Software (ES&S), 143
Electoral College, 180
emotional targeting, 137–38
employee bargaining power, 72–73
employee compensation, fair, 201
employment:
    monopoly role in remuneration of, 64–80, *66*
    overachievement in, 64–65
employment mobility, 68, 185–87, 217
"Empowering Oil & Gas with AI" (Microsoft exhibition), 160–61
engagement:
    algorithms, 140, 142
    in extremism, 128–30
    maximizing algorithms in, 128–30
    on social media, 123–25
Enron scandal, 6
entrepreneurs, 209, 213
    appropriation of innovation by, 100, 101–2
    undercutting prices of, 97
entrepreneurship:
    discriminatory limitations on, 186–89
    innovation in, 209
    monopolies as threat to, 80–104
environment:
    monopoly power in destruction of, 153–73
    weak oversight of, 153–54
Environmental Protection Agency, 153, 211
EPIC, 110
EpiPens, 3, 37–38, 47–49, 53
"epistemic inequality," 181

European Commission, 86, 90, 96, 208, 214, 219
    antitrust enforcement by, 10–11
    Google's noncompliance investigation by, 88–89
Everything Store, The (Stone), 98
"exclusionary conduct," 58
exercise, in Obama fitness campaign, 170
extraction, 4, 177–78, 180, 191
extractive business model, 159
extremism, in social media, 128–30
Exxon, 159, 161
ExxonMobil, 155

Facebook, 3, 25–26, 83, 85, 98, 103, 106, 114, 125, 126–27, 129–30, 139, 150, 151, 187, 198, 206, 208, 214, 216, 217, 219, 221–22, 223
    acquisitions by, 60–61
    algorithmic bias in, 192
    in climate change, 161
    data tracking by, 106–7, 118–19, 274
    discrimination fostered by, 192
    election interference in, 142
    fear and anger promoted by, 123–26
    FTC fine of, 122
    GDPR opposed by, 121
    interoperability within, 221–22
    IRS lawsuit against, 27
    "like" button on, 107
    as manipulation tool, 137–39
    monopoly power of, 62–63
    MySpace vs., 115–16
    news sources threatened by, 147–51
    online dominance of, 130, 145–51
    platform privilege of, 101–2, 118–19
    political involvement of, 134–38, 139–41
    prioritizing of winners and losers in, 221–22
    privacy violations by, 116–17
    propaganda on, 145
    spying architecture of, 106, 112, 148–49
    time spent on, 124
    young people targeted by, 137–38
Facebook Audience Network, 107
Facebook-Cambridge Analytica scandal, 135–38
facial recognition technology, 107, 110
"fake news," 144
    proliferation of, 150–51
Family Farm Action, 167, 171
Farm Aid, 167
farmers, farming:
    activism in, 204
    large corporate, *see* Big Ag
    monopoly exploitation of, 163–69

FBI, 111
fear-mongering, 128–29
Federal Communications Commission
    (FCC), 25, 130–31, 211, 217
    weak enforcement by, 130–31
federalism, 10
Federal Trade Commission (FTC), 9–11,
    36–37, 43, 47, 50, 62, 74, 80, 82, 102,
    122, 199, 212–14, 220
    antitrust investigation of, 101–2
    in attempts to block hospital mergers,
        40–41
    Economics Bureau of, 89, 212
    Facebook's settlement with, 208
    Google investigation dropped by,
        89–90
    in pharmaceutical mergers, 44–46
    weak enforcement by, 90–91, 119–20,
        122–23, 213, 215
Fight for the Future, 110
filter bubbles, 140
financial security, 175
FindMy, 99
First Amendment, 140, 152
"first-party" products, 92–93
First Question, The (Bodnar), 46
FitBit, Google's merger with, 120
Food and Drug Administration (FDA), 49
food industry:
    anticompetitive practices in, 23–24
    monopoly control of sources of, 163–73
    see also Big Food
"Food and Power: Addressing
    Monopolization in America's Food
    System" (Kelloway and Miller), 165
food lobby, 170
food stamp recipients, 31
food supply, monopoly power over, 165
Ford motor company, 218
fossil fuels, 173
    Big Finance involvement in, 160–61
    extractive business model in, 159
Foundem, 88
Fountain Books, 29
Foursquare, 101
Fourth Amendment, 113
Fowler, Susan, 190
Fox, Eleanor, 179
Fox News:
    on auto-play, 128–29
    media power of, 131–32
Freedom from Facebook and Google
    Coalition, 204
free-enterprise system, 84
free expression, digital threats to, 139–40
"free market" ideology, 14

free press, limited by monopoly power,
    144–46, 148–51
Fresenius Medical Care, 42
friction strategy, 205
fuel tax, French protests against, 157–58
Future of Music Coalition, 79–80

Gadek, Emily, 128–29
gag orders, 110
Galloway, Scott, 124
Gates, Bill, 98
GDPR, 221
Geitmann, Anja, 172
gender inequity, 182–86
General Data Protection Regulation
    (GDPR; 2016), 121, 219–21
generic drugs, 43, 45, 212
Gen-X, employment competition for, 68–69
geo-fencing, 143
Gilded Age, 8, 177
Gillette, 70
Gizmodo, 160
Global Competition Review, 76
global corporations, 10–11
global economy, U.S. in, 207
globalization, 67
global mergers, 214
glysophate, 164
Gmail, 107, 112
Goldman Sachs, 87
golf, 92–93
Google, 3, 6, 25–26, 58–59, 63, 74, 75, 76,
    78, 83, 85, 86–98, 101, 103, 105, 120,
    126, 129–30, 139, 142, 150, 151, 160,
    169, 187–88, 208, 215, 217, 219, 223
    acquisitions by, 60
    Alphabet, 188, 217
    anti-union policy of, 73
    in climate change, 160
    data tracking by, 106–7, 111, 219
    digital advertising dominance of, 90–91
    EC lawsuits against, 10–11
    fear and anger promoted by, 123–26
    GDPR opposed by, 121
    location data of, 113
    monopoly search engine of, 77
    multiple monopolies in monopoly power
        of, 86–90
    online dominance of, 130, 145–51
    platform privilege of, 118
    prioritizing of winners and losers in, 222
    privacy violations by, 116–17
    propaganda on, 145
    Sonos lawsuit against, 95
    spying architecture of, 106, 112–13,
        148–49

Google (*cont.*)
  substitutes for, 206
  U.S. Government Affairs and Public
    Policy team of, 205
Google Android phones, 86–87, 117
Google Books, 78
Google Chrome, 86–87, 107
Google Docs, 112
Google/FitBit merger, 120
Google Home, 107, 112
Google Maps, 26, 86
Google News, 78
Google Play, 100, 107
Google Search, 78, 86–89
government, U.S.:
  corporate influence on, 27–28
  lenient antitrust enforcement by, 10–11
  monopolies' involvement in, 5
  see also politics
Graph API, 118–19
grass fed, 172
Great Democracy Initiative, 160
Great Recession, 46, 68–69
  anticompetitive practices in housing
    market during, 21
  stimulus package in, 21
Great Reversal, The (Philippon), 103–4
greenhouse gas emissions, 172
green innovations, 161, 173
Green New Deal, 162–63
  provisions of, 157–58
Greenpeace, 163
grocery stores, 173
  shelf space control in, 168–69
gross domestic product (GDP), decline of,
  65–66
group purchasing organizations (GPOs),
  35–36
Guardian, 72, 136, 138, 156, 159, 207

Halliburton, 27
Hammond, Scott D., 46
Handmaid's Tale, The (Atwood), 132
Hansson, David Heinemeier, 220
Harris, Tristan, 126–27, 223
Hatcher, Derek, 186–87
Hatcher, Felicia, 186, 189
hate-mongering, 139–40
HB 129, 21–22
Health and Human Services Department,
  U.S., 36, 223
health care, 175
  data tracking in, 120
  exorbitant pricing in, 42, 52–53
  Google's data gathering on, 106
  ideal scenario for, 52–54

limited innovation in, 80–83
monopolies in, 34–54
news industry influence on, 131–32
salary control in, 68
spying and, 113
U.S. vs. global, 49–50
health insurance, 40, 120
  career opportunities limited by, 52
  increasing cost of, 37–43
  lack of coverage for, 53
  mergers in, 42
heart attack mortality rate, 40
helipad, 30
Hendrickson, Mary, 165
herbicides, food contamination by, 163–64
Hertz, 23
History of the Standard Oil Company, The
  (Tarbell), 6, 199
HIV, 80–81
Homeland Security Department, U.S., 111
homophobia, 129
Hoover, J. Edgar, 111–12
hormones, in meat industry, 168
Hornig, Cynthia, 124–25
hospital bills:
  increasing cost of, 39–41
  price comparisons of, 49–50
hospital mergers, 39–41, 50
household expenses, 20–21
House Judiciary Antitrust Subcommittee,
  90, 96
House of Representatives, U.S., Judiciary
  Subcommittee hearing of, 87
housing market, 20–21
  anticompetitive practices by, 20–21
"How Big Food Corporations Watered
  Down Michelle Obama's 'Let's Move'
  Campaign" (ThinkProgress article),
  170
"How Google, Microsoft, and Big Tech
  are Automating the Climate Crisis"
  (Merchant), 160
human futures market, 221

IBM, 207
IHS Markit, 50
immigrants, as scapegoats, 179
immigration, sentiment against, 128–29,
  179
Immigration and Custom Enforcement,
  deportation operations of, 110
independent farmers, 171
  financial pressures of, 167–68
Indie Beauty Expo, 213–14
"Inequality: A Hidden Cost of Market
  Power" (OECD study), 184

infant seizures, 47
inferences, 112–13
inflation, 66
InfluenceMap, 159, 161
information, lack of common basis of, 140–41
information dominance, 136
information-poor viewers, 131
innovation, 202
  exploitation in, 177, 198
  fostering of, 104
  health and safety dismissed in, 190–91
  limitations on, 261
  monopoly power limitations on, 130, 186–89
  in news media, 144
  pro-democracy, 141, 209, 219
Innovation Blind Spot, The (Baird), 187, 189
In Order to Live (Park), 109
Instacart, 120
Instagram, 60, 63, 101, 107, 116, 124, 127, 138, 174, 206, 214
  disinformation on, 141
  Facebook ownership of, 63
Institute for Local Self-Reliance, 92, 168, 203, 204
Institute on Taxation and Economic Policy, 27
insurance companies, 48
Intel, 75
Intercept, 89
internet, centralization of news sources on, 146–51
internet access, 21
internet browser market, 55–63, 86
Internet Explorer, 55–59, 98, 151
"internet of things," 182
Internet Research Agency (IRA), 141
internet search engines, 205–6, 222
interoperability, 103, 208
  competition promoted by, 221–22
iOS, 60, 99
iPads, 87, 99–100
iPhone apps, commission charges in, 24–25
iPhones, 87, 99–100
  data tracking by, 110
Ireland, 37
IRS, 25
  corporations paid by, 27–28
ITA, 215
Ivors Academy, 76

JAB Holding Company, 23, 32, 33
Japan, U.S. competition with, 207
JBS, 166, 168, 171
Jenner, Kylie, 174

job loss, mergers as source of, 70–71
Jobs, Steve, 74
Johns Hopkins University, 50
Johnson, Christyl, 225
Jones, Jen, 124–25
Jones Harbour, Pamela, 90–91
Justice, Kelly, 29
Justice Department, U.S. (DOJ), 9–11, 48, 55, 59, 75–76, 79, 90, 96, 166, 213, 215
  Antitrust Division of, 22–23, 46
  Microsoft lawsuit of, 97–98
  weak antitrust enforcement by, 19–20, 22–23, 41, 82, 209–10, 213, 215–16, 249
"just in time" production, 35

Karelia Software, 99
Kauffman-RAND Institute for Entrepreneurship Public Policy Studies, 52
Keating, Edward, 7
Kelloway, Claire, 165–66, 168–69, 170–71
Kemp, Brian, 149
Khan, Lina, 97, 213
kickbacks, 35, 48
"killer acquisition," 36
"kill zones," 187
Kindle, 112
Kindle Unlimited, 79
King, Martin Luther, Jr., 111–12
Kint, Jason, 145–46
Kirby, Scott, 19
Klein, Naomi, 156, 157
Klobuchar, Amy, 216
knockoffs, 95, 101, 261
knowledge inequality, 181–82
Knox, Ron, 76
Koch Industries, 159–60
Kochland (Leonard), 159–60
"Kochtopus," 160
Kogan, Aleksandr, 136
Kraft Heinz, 70, 168, 171
Kroger, 168
Kushner, Jared, 202

labor share, *66, 84*
labor unions, declining membership and power of, 71–73
Land of the Giants (podcast), 110
lawlessness, online, 223–24
"legacy" airlines, 19–20
legal precedent, 12
legislation:
  anti-corruption, 217–18
  to limit monopolies, 211–13
  see also antitrust laws; *specific cases*

Lengsfeld, Vera ("Virus"), 108–9
Leonard, Christopher, 159–60
LGBTQ+ community, 129, 175, 192
Libra, 198
life expectancy, 50
Lindvall, Helienne, 76–77
LinkedIn, 63
LiSAF laser oscillator, 225
"Little Boy and the Big Boys, The"
    (cartoon), 200–201, 201
lobbying, lobbyists:
    by Big Food, 170–71
    by Big Oil, 159–60
    in health care, 51
    political influence of, 4, 20, 21, 31, 36, 51,
        116, 121, 132, 144, 171, 217, 218
Longman, Phillip, 51, 83–84
Lovera, Patty, 168
low pricing strategy, 97–98
Luna Display, 99–100
Lynn, Barry, 83–84, 240

McCarthy, Joseph, 111
McCarthyism, 111–12
McClure's Magazine, 6
McConnell, Mitch, 143, 159
Macron, Emmanuel, 157–58
Macs, 57, 87
Mactaggart, Alastair, 219
Magie, Lizzie, 193, 197
male white privilege, 189–91
Mann, Michael, 156
manufacturing sector, 85
Maps, 107
marginalized groups:
    economic inequality in, 175, 181, 184,
        186–89
    health and safety issues of, 190–91
    as targets of spying, 192
Maritz, Paul, 97
market, definition of, 57–58
"marketplace sellers," 92
market share, 61
Markup, The, 137
Marshall, Thurgood, 84
Maxwell, Joe, 166–67, 171–72
meat industry, 165–68, 169, 171–72, 208
media:
    concentrated control of, 130–32, 217
    polarization in, 130–32
median household income, 38–39
Medicaid fraud, 48
medical expenses, 37
medical supply chain, 240
Medicare, 52
    rates, 42

Medicare Part D, 51
Medicare Prices for All, 51, 53
Medtronic, Covidien acquisition by, 37
Mercer, Robert, 135
Merchant, Brian, 160–61
Merck, 48
mergers and acquisitions, 13, 13, 119–20
    of airlines, 18–20
    as cause of job loss, 70–71
    data tracking in, 119–20
    fixes for, 214–16
    in health care, 34, 36
    in health insurance, 42
    high prices and, 17–33, 45–49
    of hospitals, 39–41
    in housing market, 20–21
    pharmaceutical, 43–49
    vertical, 215
    of wireless providers, 22–23
Messenger, 61, 124
#MeToo movement, 185, 190
Microsoft, 25, 61, 85, 100, 151, 160–61, 221
    breakup of monopoly of, 198
    DOJ lawsuit against, 97–98
    government lawsuit against, 249
    PC monopoly of, 86–87
    US government lawsuit against, 55–61,
        202, 211
Microsoft Azure, 161
Microsoft Windows, 55
micro-targeted advertising, proposed
    banning of, 143
Millennials, 144
    employment competition for, 68–69
Miller, Sarah, 165
Mitchell, Stacy, 203
mobile messaging apps, 61
Molina, Jorge, 113
Molson Coors, 24, 27
monopolies:
    addiction and, 126–28
    anti-labor policies in, 71–73
    business dynamism squelched by, 83–85
    citizen rule as replacement for, 203–4
    economic impact of, 1–14
    economic inequality fostered by, 174–94
    in environmental destruction, 153
    extremism fostered by, 128–30
    fair and competitive, 59
    gender inequality fostered by, 182–86
    giant technologies in, see Big Tech
    global, 180
    in health care, 34–54
    high prices and, 17–33
    historical perspective on, 3, 5–6
    lack of oversight of, 149–50

manipulation by, 126–28
news sources limited by, 144–51
opposition to, *see* anti-monopolists
as pervasive, 3–5, 11
polarization fostered by, 130–32
privacy and, 129–30
reciprocal influence of politics and, 20,
     21–22, 27–28, 30–31, 51, 89, 101, 103,
     107–8, 110–14, 121–23, 125, 134–52,
     155–56, 159, 165, 192, 199–200, 203,
     208–9, 217–18
in rising prices, 67
salary control by, 64–80
self-regulation of, 206
short history of, 14
as source of economic inequality, 1–3
as sources of stress and anxiety, 123–26
taking control back from, 197–206
use of term, 14
MonopoliesSuck.com, 171, 204
Monopolists, The (Pilon), 193
monopolization, mini lesson on, 55
Monopoly (board game), 193, 197
monopoly leveraging, 85, 211
monopoly power, 56–60, 104
     as anticompetitive, 85
     in antitrust laws, 95
     of Apple, 99–101
     Congress in limitation of, 211–12, 216
     covert, 61–63
     in customer relations, 115
     data tracking and, 118–20
     as exclusionary, 58
     of Facebook, 142
     fixes for, 208–9
     privacy issues and, 113–15
     as threat to democracy, 134–52
monopoly rents, 20
monopsony (buyer power), 67–68, 100–101
     of YouTube, 76–80
Monsanto, 167, 181
     monopoly exploitation by, 163–64, 169
     see also Bayer/Monsanto merger
monthly expenses, 17–18
     monopoly control of, 20–23
Mother Jones, 147
Mozilla Foundation, 129
Mueller, Robert, 143
Mukuria, Megan, 225
Murdoch, Rupert, 131
music industry, economic exploitation of
     creators and artists in, 76–80, 253
Muslims, bias against, 109, 131
Mylan, Sanofi lawsuit against, 47–49
MySpace, Facebook's competition with,
     115–16

NASA, 225
National Beef, 166
"national champions" strategy, 206–7
National Family Farm Coalition, 164
National Institutes of Health (NIH), 80
National Labor Relations Board (NLRB),
     73
negative tax rates, 27
Nemorin, Jerry, 189
Netflix, 83
net neutrality, nondiscrimination and,
     222–23
Netscape, 86, 97–98, 100, 151
Netscape Navigator, 55–59
network effects, 102–3
     barrier, 221
New Deal, 158
New Gilded Age, 2, 40, 193, 202
New Knowledge, 141
Newport, 36–37
New Republic, 220
news, concentrated control of, 130–32
News Corporation, 131
newspapers, declining numbers and
     influence of, 144–46, 149–51
news publishers, online dominance of
     Facebook and Google over, 146–51
"The New Jim Code," 191
New York, N.Y., Amazon HQ2 deal
     rejected by, 30
New York Attorney General's Office, 41, 43
     antitrust enforcement by, 7, 210
New York City public schools, 28
New York Times, 22, 35, 36, 95, 98, 113, 138,
     142, 185, 220–21
New York Times Magazine, 170
1984 (Orwell), 132
Nix, Alexander, 135
Nixon, Richard, 12
Noah, Trevor, 115
noncompete clauses, 73–74, 186
nondiscrimination, 211
     net neutrality and, 222–23
     rules, 208
North Carolina, broadband monopoly in,
     21–22
North Korea, 109
NPR, 25
nurses, 68, 75, 80–81

Obama, Barack, 226
     Democratic National Convention speech
     of, 5
Obama, Michelle, 140, 226
     healthy food and exercise campaign of,
     170

Obama administration, 75, 89
Big Food's defeat of goals of, 170
offshore manufacturing, 34–35
O'Kelley, Brian, 90
oligopolies, 18, 20, 22, 27, 32, 42, 67, 68, 69, 72, 103–4, 132, 177
on climate crisis, 159–62
use of term, 14
Onavo app, 60–61, 214
"one-click" purchases, 205
O'Neil, Cathy, 191
On Fire: The (Burning) Case for a Green New Deal (Klein), 156
online advertising, 78–79, 106, 107, 111, 121, 123–24, 148
fraud in, 223
online media services, 3
online news company, 144
Open Markets America's Monopoly Moment conference, 187
Open Markets Institute, 69, 74, 84, 158, 165, 171, 204, 240
Open Secrets, 51, 159
opioids, 162
organic food, 168–69, 171
Organisation for Economic Co-operation and Development (OECD), 183–84
Otellini, Paul, 75
"Our Uncrowned Kings" (cartoon), 202, 203
Oxfam, 185

Pai, Ajit, 131
PAIN, 208–9
Palihapitiya, Chamath, 92, 126–27
Pandora, 77
Panera, 23
parenting, 127–28
The Parent Maze, 102
Paris Climate Accord, 153, 159
Park, Yeonmi, 109
Parker, Sean, 126, 127
Parliament, British, 61
patents, as legal monopolies, 45
patient advocacy, 41
patriarchy, 184
Paxton, Ken, 91
pay-for-delay, 248
"pay-for-delay" deals, 45, 51, 212
penal process, discrimination in, 192
people of color, 3, 75, 191–92
economic inequality of, 184–86
entrepreneurial discrimination against, 186–89
noncompete clauses for, 74
Pepsi, 169, 215

Perdue, 167
Perkins, Lynn, 188
Persuasive Technology Lab, 126
Pfaff, Brad, 167
pharmaceutical mergers, 43–49
pharmacy benefit managers, 48
Phelps, Michael, 226
Philippon, Thomas, 103–4
Philips, 36
Pichai, Sundar, 188
Pike, Chris, 183–84
Pilon, Mary, 193
platform privilege, 90, 92, 118, 236–37
Alexa in, 94
Apple, 99–100
defined, 85
of Facebook, 101–2, 118
fixes for, 213–14
of Google, 88–89
Plavix, 45–46
polarization, media in, 130–32
police departments, spying technology used by, 113
policing, 192
political ads, false, 139–40
political cartoons, 199–203, 201, 202
politics:
global, 134–35
instability in, 179–80
in partisan news sources, 131–32
reciprocal influence of monopolies and, 20, 21–22, 27–28, 30–31, 51, 89, 101, 103, 107–8, 110–14, 121–23, 125, 134–52, 155–56, 159, 165, 192, 199–200, 203, 208–9, 217–18
Pollan, Michael, 170
pollution, 63, 171
by Big Ag, 169
PopGrips, 261
PopSockets, 93
pork processing, 166
pornography sites, 107
poultry industry, 23
financial pressures in, 167
processing in, 166–68
poverty:
dismissal of, 17
rates of, 184
"precautionary principle," Uber's dismissal of, 190–91
predatory loans, 189
predatory pricing, 97, 176, 211–12, 262
preferred provider organization (PPO) plan, 38
"preferred" vendors, 35
Pret a Manger, 23

price control, 62, 70, 82, 167–68
  monopolies in, 166
price-cutting, 97
price-fixing, 9, 115, 210
price fixing, of prescriptions, 242
privacy:
  abuses of, 161
  Big Tech infringements on, 105–33
  covert violations of, 116–18, 130
  failures to protect, 114–16, 122
  monopolies and, 129–30
  threats to, 274
privacy issues, fixes for, 218–21
privacy laws, 108, 111, 132, 197–98
  in California, 121–22
  effective enforcement of, 150
  fines for violation of, 122–23
  monopoly power as obstacle to, 120–23
  weak enforcement of, 121–23, 149–50
privacy protection, 119
privacy regulation, 218–21
privacy rules, 211
private equity firms, in hospital buy outs, 39
private labels, 96–97
Procter & Gamble, companies owned by, 23
Procter & Gamble/Gillette merger, 70
productivity, 66–67
Project Voldemort, 101–2
pro-monopoly talking points, 206–7
propaganda, 63, 135
  incendiary, 150–51
  online, 145
ProPublica, 223
Protonmail, 133
psychological profiling, 136–38
psyops (psychological operations), 136
Public Citizen, 204
public opinion, manipulation of, 131–32
Puck, 203
Puck Building, 203

Quartz, 177
Queer in AI, 192
Questcor (now called Mallinckrodt), 47

Race After Technology (Benjamin), 191
racism, 1, 7, 131, 137, 184, 186, 191, 192
Raff, Adam and Shivaun, 88
railroad monopolies, 202
rape, 190
Rappler, 150–51
Rausch, Daniel, 110
recommendation algorithms, 128–30
Red Scare, Second, 111–12
Reich, Robert, 207

renewable energy, 173
  transition to, 157
Republican Party, 167
  Big Oil supported by, 159–60
Research app, 214
Ressa, Maria, 150–51
retail market, 61–62
  monopoly power in, 176
retail sector, 85
  Amazon in, 92
Retractable Technologies Inc. (RTI), 80–81
Richmond Times-Dispatch, 29
Riley, Kevin, 149
Ring smart doorbells, spying by, 113
Rinz, Kevin, 69
robber barons, 3, 5, 97
Roberts, John, 6–7
Rolnick, Guy, 217
Ronge, Matt, 99–100
Roosevelt, Franklin Delano, 158
Roosevelt, Theodore, 6
Roosevelt Institute, 68, 204
Roundup, 164
Rural Electrification Administration, 158
Russia, 138
  in data gathering, 136
  U.S. political discourse influenced by, 141, 143
Russian propaganda, 63

Sainato, Michael, 72
salaries, 201
  monopolies in decline of, 64–80
  stagnation of, 65–66
salary gap, 184–85
  gender and racial inequality in, 185
Salerno, Lillian, 80–82
sales tax:
  breaks for, 28
  in third-party sellers, 28–29
San Bernardino shootings, 110
Sanders, Bernie, 173
Sanofi, 47–49
Santacreu-Vasut, Estefania, 184
Sarkis, Stephanie, 187
Schmidt, Eric, 74–75
school funding, 28–29
school lunches, 173
  health issues in, 169–71
school taxes, 26
SCL, 135–36
Search, 107
search engine optimization, 77
search engines:
  prioritizing in, 222
  privacy-protecting alternatives in, 205–6

seeds, 163–64, 168
self-care, 69–70
self-employment, health care limitations on, 52
Senate Intelligence Committee, 141
Separation of Platforms and Commerce (Khan), 213
sexism, 183
sexual harassment, 185–87, 191
"shadow profiles," 107
shareholder profits, 67
shareholders, non-American, 207
Shaw, Thomas, 80–82
Shell, 159, 161
sherlocking, by Apple, 98–101
Sherman, John, 8, 29, 71
Sherman Act (1890), 71, 81, 200, 211
    provisions of, 8–9
    Section 1 of, 75, 166, 210
    Section 2 of, 56, 58, 59, 85, 119, 210
    underenforcement of, 11–13
Shkreli, Martin, 43
Sidecar, 100
Signal, 133
Sinclair Broadcast Group, 131
6pm.com, 23
skin care, 92
Slate, 147
Slaughter, Rebecca, 44
Slomp, Paul, 172
Small Business Administration, 167
small businesses, unfair practices against, 29
Smalls, Christian, 72–73
Smart Home, 110
smartphones, 86–87
smart speakers, *see* voice assistants
Smith, Brad, 25–26
Smithfield pork processing plant, 168
    COVID-19 in, 165–66, 168
Snapchat, 101–2
Social Capital, 92
social media:
    addiction and manipulation fostered by, 126–28
    anxiety, fear, and anger promoted by, 123–26
    taking a break from, 206
Sohn Investment Conference (May 2016), 92
Solé, Roger, 22
sole-supply contracts, 81
Songwriter Committee, 76
songwriters, 76–77
Sonos, 95
Spotify, 77
    Apple sued by, 99
Sprint/T-Mobile merger, 22–23, 131

spying:
    by Big Tech, 105–23
    discrimination and, 192
    fixes for, 218–21
    freedom from, 132
    legality of, 223
    social control through, 108–9
    U.S. government use of, 111–13
Srinivasan, Dina, 115–16
Standard Oil, breakup of, 232
Standard Oil company, breakup of, 6, 9, 199
start-ups, 180, 183, 209
    in Big Tech, 190
    exit buyout strategies for, 187–88
    funding for, 187–88
    privacy-protecting, 117–18
Stasi, 108
status quo, protection of, 156, 171, 225
Steele, Graham, 160
stimulus packages, 21
stock market, in mergers and acquisitions, 13–14, *13*
Stone, Brad, 98
"Stop the Concentration of Wealth" (Brandeis), 7
"strip-mining," 95–96
structural racism, 184
suicides:
    by farmers, 167
    social media use and, 127
Sunrise Movement, 163
suppliers, effect of monopoly for, 69
supply and demand, labor as, 67
Supreme Court, U.S., 7, 24, 27, 84, 100, 131, 140
surveillance capitalism, 181, 220–21
Surveillance Capitalism (Zuboff), 181
survival instinct, 125
sustainability, 173
sustainable farming, 168
Synachten, 47
Syngenta Group, 163
syringes, innovation in, 80–83
systemic racism, 1

Tarbell, Ida, 6, 232
Target.com, 62
targeted advertising, 25–26, 111, 121, 148, 219–21
    profits from, 123–24
    proposed ban on, 220–21
    traditional vs., 132
taxation, 92
    by government, 26
    by private companies, 24–25, 88, 92, 99, 101

tax breaks, corporate, 26–28
tax reform, 32
technological change, 67
technology, giants of, *see* Big Tech
"technology transfer," 207
tech platforms, 219
Tefft, Ward, 29
Telecom, 22
Teleogramma obamarum, 225–26
"Texans for Natural Gas," 161
textbook publishers, 11
ThinkProgress, 170
think tanks, 204
third-party sellers, 28–29, 62
Thompson, Nicholas, 207
Thrifty, 23
Thunberg, Greta, 154–55
"tiger chair," 109
TikTok, 134
Tile, 99
Tillerson, Rex, 155
Time Warner, 131
T-Mobile/Sprint merger, 22–23, 131
Tom's of Maine, 24
"too big to fail," 69
torture, 109
Toscano, Joe, 26
Total, 159
"Tournament of Today, The" (cartoon), *202*
travel expenses, 17–20
Trump, Donald, 155, 159, 180
    media coverage of, 132
    propaganda in support of, 135
    rallies of, 143
    rally videos of, 128
    Zuckerberg and, 139
Trump administration, 142
    corporate tax cuts by, 32
    food reforms rescinded by, 170
    monopoly deregulation by, 131
Tufekci, Zeynep, 128, 140
TV cable boxes, limited innovation in, 82–83
Twitter, 63, 119, 134
Tyson, 168

Uber, 190–91
Uighur Muslim minority, 109
ultrarich, 174, 177–78
unemployment, mergers as source of, 70–71
Unilever, 24
United States Climate Alliance, 158
United States v. Microsoft Corp., 211
UrbanSitter app, 188
US Airways, 19–20, 70, 74–75
user interfaces, 78

U.S. v. Microsoft, 55–61, 249
utilities, government regulation of, 103
utility bills, 33
utility costs, corporate, 30–31

Vaheesan, Sandeep, 69, 158
ventilator shortage, 36
venture capitalists (VCs), 188–89
Verizon, 22
vertical mergers, 215
"vertical search" markets, 88–89, 93–95
Vestager, Margrethe, 118
Viacom/CBS merger, 70
VICE News, 73
Vine, 119
violence, gender-based, 125
Virginia, Amazon data center in, 30–31
voice assistants, 113
    live feed of, 112
    privacy-protecting, 118
    spying by, 105–6, 112
voter fraud, 143–44
voter manipulation, 223
voting by mail, 144
voting machines, 143–44
Vox, 147
Vyera (now Phoenixus), 43

Wakabayashi, Daisuke, 95
Wall Street Journal, 21, 43, 89, 101
Walmart, 33, 62, 167–68, 171
    cost and salary control by, 69
    grocery market share of, 168
    profiting from food stamp program, 31
    tax breaks for, 31
    wholesale and retail monopoly power of, 176–77
Walton family, wealth of, 176
"Want to Work for Google? You Already Do" (Toscano), 26
Warren, Elizabeth, 139, 211, 213
Washington Monthly, 51, 165
Watergate scandal, 12
Watson, 99
wealth:
    excesses of, 73, 174, 176–77
    market power and, 184
wealth distribution, 178–80, *179*
    equitable, 193–94
    monopolies in, 174–94
Weapons of Math Destruction (O'Neil), 191
WeChat, 109
Weintraub, Ellen L., 143
"We're Building a Dystopia Just to Get People to Click on Ads" (Tufekci), 128, 140

WhatsApp, 60–61, 107, 138, 214
Whirlpool, 27
Whistle Blower (Fowler), 190
whistle-blower laws, 73
white male privilege, 46
white privilege, 182–86
white supremacy movement, 128
Whitney v. California, 141
Whole Foods, 169
   Amazon's merger with, 119–20
wholesale market, monopoly power in, 176
Wired, 172, 207
wireless providers, 22–23, 33
Wise, Timothy, 172
women:
   economic inequality of, 183–86
   empowerment of, 124–25
   entrepreneurial discrimination against,
      187–89
   noncompete clauses for, 74
   poverty rates for, 184
   rape and murder of, 190
"Women and the 1%: How Extreme
   Economic Inequality and Gender
   Inequality Must Be Tackled Together"
   (2016 study), 185
Women Killing It! (podcast), 182, 188, 213,
   225, 226
women's equity, author's commitment to,
   6–7
women's rights movement, 193

"women's welfare standard," 184
Women You Should Know, 124–25, 147
working conditions, mergers in decline of,
   71–73
workplace, globalization of, 180
workplace discrimination, gender and
   racially based, 185–86
World Economic Forum (Davos; 2020),
   154
Wright, Jillian, 213–14
Wu, Tim, 207
Wylie, Christopher, 135–38, 142, 220

xenophobia, 179

Yale Law Journal, 97
YouTube, 60, 86, 107, 112, 125, 134, 142,
   148, 150, 223
   algorithms and, 128–29
   auto-play feature of, 128–29
   fear and anger promoted by, 123–26
   monopoly power of, 90–91
   songwriters and musicians exploited by,
      76–80

ZanaAfrica, 225
Zappos, 23
Zuboff, Shoshana, 181, 220–21
Zuckerberg, Mark, 27, 101, 114, 118–19,
   124, 221
   Georgetown University speech of, 139–40

ABOUT THE AUTHOR

SALLY HUBBARD is an antitrust expert and director of enforcement strategy at the Open Markets Institute, an organization developing solutions to America's monopoly crisis. She has served as an assistant attorney general in the Antitrust Bureau of the Office of the New York State Attorney General, and was previously an investigative journalist covering mergers, monopolies, and privacy. She has testified as a competition expert before the U.S. Senate, House of Representatives, and Federal Trade Commission. She appears and is cited regularly in a wide range of media, including the *New York Times*, CNN, BBC *World News*, *Vanity Fair*, *Washington Post*, *The Atlantic*, and *Wired*, and hosts the podcast *Women Killing It!* Hubbard lives in Brooklyn with her husband and two children.